Cyber Security in Business Analytics

There is a growing need for insights and practical experiences in the evolving field of cyber security for business analytics, a need addressed by *Cyber Security in Business Analytics*. Divided into sections covering cyber security basics, artificial intelligence (AI) methods for threat detection, and practical applications in e-commerce and e-banking, the book's team of experts provides valuable insights into securing business data and improving decision-making processes. It covers topics such as data privacy, threat detection, risk assessment, and ethical considerations, catering to both technical and managerial audiences.

- Presents real-case scenarios for enhancing understanding of how cyber security principles are applied in diverse organizational settings
- Offers advanced technologies such as AI methods for cyber threat detection
- Provides a detailed exploration of how AI can make cyber security better by helping detect threats, unusual activities, and potential risks
- Focuses on the convergence of cyber security and data-driven decision-making and explores how businesses can leverage analytics while safeguarding sensitive information
- Includes insights into cutting-edge techniques in the field, such as detailed explorations of various cyber security tools within the context of business analytics

Cyber Security in Business Analytics will be useful for scholars, researchers, and professionals of computer science and analytics.

Artificial Intelligence, Machine Learning, Data Analytics and Automation for Business Management

This series of books illustrates the widespread adoption of emerging technologies to address business challenges and drive innovation. It serves as an indispensable resource for professionals and scholars seeking to harness the power of technology to drive organisational growth in this highly competitive world.

Predictive Analytics and Generative AI for Data-Driven Marketing Strategies
By Hemachandran K, Debdutta Choudhury, Raul Villamarin Rodriguez, Jorge A. Wise, Revathi T

Digital HR
Technologies for HR Transformation and Performance Improvement
By Deepa Gupta, Mukul Gupta, Balamurugan Balusamy, Rajesh Kumar Dhanaraj, Parth M. Gupta

Green Engineering for Optimizing Firm Performance
AI and Automation for Sustainable Technologies
By Sonal Trivedi, Balamurugan Balusamy, Liza Macasukit Gernal, Mahmoud Ahmad Al-Khasawneh

Organizational Excellence
Data, Technology and Leadership
Shyama Prasad Mukherjee

Artificial Intelligence, Machine Learning and IoT for Smart Business Management
By Garima Jain, Ankush Jain, Veena Grover, Balamurugan Balusamy, Praveen Tomar

Cyber Security in Business Analytics
By Gururaj H L, B Ramesh, Chandrika J and Hong Lin

For more information about this series, please visit: www.routledge.com/Artificial-Intelligence-Machine-Learning-Data-Analytics-and-Automation/book-series/AIBM

Cyber Security in Business Analytics

Edited by Gururaj H L, B Ramesh,
Chandrika J and Hong Lin

CRC Press
Taylor & Francis Group
Boca Raton London New York

CRC Press is an imprint of the
Taylor & Francis Group, an **informa** business
A CHAPMAN & HALL BOOK

Front cover image: FGC/Shutterstock

First edition published 2026
by CRC Press
2385 NW Executive Center Drive, Suite 320, Boca Raton FL 33431

and by CRC Press
4 Park Square, Milton Park, Abingdon, Oxon, OX14 4RN

CRC Press is an imprint of Taylor & Francis Group, LLC

ISBN: 978-1-032-85941-5 (hbk)
ISBN: 978-1-032-88867-5 (pbk)
ISBN: 978-1-003-54004-5 (ebk)

DOI: 10.1201/9781003540045

Typeset in Times
by Apex CoVantage, LLC

Contents

About the Editors

Dr. Gururaj H L is currently working as Associate Professor, Department of Computer Science and Engineering, Manipal Institute of Technology, Bengaluru, India. He holds a PhD in computer science and engineering from Visweswaraya Technological University, Belagavi, India. He is a professional member of the Association of Computing Machinery (ACM) and works as ACM Distinguished Speaker. He is the founder of the Wireless Internetworking Group (WiNG). He is a senior member of IEEE and a lifetime member of ISTE and CSI. Dr. Gururaj received the Young Scientist International Travel Grant from the Government of India in 2016. He has eight years of teaching experience at both the undergraduate (UG) and the postgraduate (PG) levels. His research interests include blockchain technology, cyber security, wireless sensor networks, ad hoc networks, the Internet of Things, data mining, cloud computing, and machine learning. He has guided 30 UG students and 10 PG students. He is an editorial board member of the *International Journal of Blockchains and Cryptocurrencies* (IJBC) and Editor of EAI publishers. He has published more than 75 research papers, including two ESCI publications, in various international journals such as the *Science Citation Index*, *IEEE Access*, *Scopus*, and UGC-referred journals. He has presented 20 papers at various international conferences and authored one book on network simulators. He also works as a reviewer for various journals and conferences.

Dr. B Ramesh completed his Bachelor of Engineering (BE) degree in computer science and engineering from Mysore University, Karnataka, India, in 1991; Master of Technology (MTech) degree in computer science from DAVV, Indore, Madhya Pradesh, India, in 1995; and his PhD from Anna University, Chennai, India, in 2009. Currently, he is working as a professor and the head of the Department of Computer Science and Engineering at Malnad College of Engineering, Hassan, India. His current research interests lie in the areas of congestion control and QoS-aware routing algorithms in ad hoc networks and multimedia networks.

Dr. Chandrika J completed her BE degree in computer science and engineering from Mysore University, Karnataka, India, in 1991; MTech degree in computer science and engineering from Mysore University, Karnataka, India, in 1997; and PhD from VTU, Belgaum, India, in 2014. Currently, she is working as an associate professor in the Department of Computer Science and Engineering at Malnad College of Engineering, Hassan, India. Her current research interests lie in the areas of data mining algorithms and streaming and multimedia databases. She has published papers in the *International Journal of Computer Theory and Engineering*.

Dr. Hong Lin holds a PhD in computer science. His graduate work includes theoretical and empirical studies of parallel programming models and implementations. Dr. Lin has worked on large-scale computational biology at Purdue University, active networks at the National Research Council Canada, and network security at

Nokia, Inc. Dr. Lin joined Universal Hi-Tech Development (UHD) in 2001, and he is currently a professor in computer science. He has worked on parallel computing, multi-agent systems, and affective computing since he joined UHD. He established the Grid Computing Lab at UHD through an NSF MRI grant. He has been a Scholars Academy mentor, an REU faculty mentor, and a CAHSI faculty mentor. He is a senior member of ACM and a faculty member at the University of Houston-Downtown since 2001.

List of Contributors

Rose Oluwaseun Adetunji
Research Group on Data, Artificial Intelligence, and Innovations for Digital Transformation
JBS Innovation Lab, Johannesburg Business School
University of Johannesburg
South Africa

Gurushankar H B
Department of Information Technology
Manipal Institute of Technology Bengaluru
MAHE, India

Praise Aanuoluwa Bobola
Bachelor of Laws
Redeemer's University
Nigeria

Nalini H C
Department of Information Science and Engineering
Rajeev Institute of Technology
Hassan, India

Divya C D
Department of Computer Science and Engineering
Vidyavardhaka College of Engineering
Mysuru, India

Francesco Flammini
Department of Computer Science, Mälardalen University
Sweden

Jaroslav Frnda
Department of Quantitative Methods and Economic Informatics
Faculty of Operation and Economics of Transport and Communication, University of Zilina
Slovakia

Shaheen H
Department of Computing and Engineering
University of West London—RAK Branch Campus
United Arab Emirates

Yu-Chen Hu
Department of Computer Science
Distinguished Professor at Tunghai University
Taiwan

Shivani T J
Department of Information Science and Engineering
Vidyavardhaka College of Engineering
Mysuru, India

Shreyas J
Department of Information Technology, Manipal Institute of Technology Bengaluru, MAHE
India

Anupama K
Department of Computer Science and Engineering
AJ Institute of Engineering and Technology
Mangalore, India

Lolakshi P K
Department of Artificial Intelligence and Machine Learning
Nagarjuna College of Engineering and Technology
India

Udayaprasad P K
Department of Computer Science
BMS Institute of Technology
Bengaluru, India

Gururaj H L
Department of Information Technology
Manipal Institute of Technology Bengaluru, MAHE
India

Hong Lin
Department of Computer Science and Engineering
University of Houston-Downtown
United States

Spoorthi M
Department of Information Science and Engineering
Vidyavardhaka College of Engineering
Mysuru, India

Thejaswini K M
Department of Information Science and Engineering
Nagarjuna College of Engineering and Technology
India

Priyanka Mohan
Department of Information Science and Engineering
Vidyavardhaka College of Engineering
Mysuru, India

Chaithra K N
Department of Electronics and Communication Engineering
Nitte Meenakshi Institute of Technology
Bengaluru, India

Ashitha V Naik
Department of Electronics and Communication Engineering
Nitte Meenakshi Institute of Technology Bengaluru
India

Pradyumna V N
Department of Computer Science and Engineering
Vidyavardhaka College of Engineering Mysuru
India

Subramanya V Odeyar
Department of Information Science and Engineering
Nagarjuna College of Engineering and Technology
India

Olaniyi Felix Olayinka
Department of Private and Property Law
Redeemer's University
Nigeria

Bhuvaneshwari P
Department of Computer Science and Engineering, Manipal Institute of Technology Bengaluru
Manipal Academy of Higher Education
India

Pallavi T P
Department of Computer Science and Engineering (Cyber Security)
MS Ramaiah Institute of Technology
Bengaluru, India

Vidyashree K P
Department of Information Science and Engineering
Vidyavardhaka College of Engineering, Mysuru
India

Smitha G Prabhu
Department of Electronics and Communication Engineering
Nitte Meenakshi Institute of Technology
Bengaluru, India

Pranav Koushik R
Department of Computer Science and Engineering
Vidyavardhaka College of Engineering
Mysuru, India

Asha R
Department of ECE
Vidya Vikas Institute of Engineering and Technology
Mysuru, India

Vinayakumar Ravi
Center for Artificial Intelligence
Prince Mohammad Bin Fahd University
Saudi Arabia

Anusha K S
Department of Computer Science and Engineering
Vidyavardhaka College of Engineering
Mysuru, India

Shilpa K S
Department of Information Science and Engineering
Vidyavardhaka College of Engineering
Mysuru, India

Ayesha Siddiqua
Department of Electronics and Communication Engineering
Nitte Meenakshi Institute of Technology
Bengaluru, India

Megha V
Department of Information Science and Engineering
Vidyavardhaka College of Engineering, Mysuru, India

Jhanjhi N Z
School of Computer Science
Taylor's University
Subang Jaya, Malaysia

Preface

The book, *Cyber Security in Business Analytics*, aims to explore the intersection of cyber security and business analytics, highlighting the various challenges, strategies, and innovations that are essential to thriving in a data-centric business environment. Our goal is to provide a comprehensive understanding of how cyber security practices can be embedded within the framework of business analytics, offering practical and theoretical insights to both novice and expert readers.

The book begins with an overview of learning methods for business analytics, discussing their potential and limitations, followed by Chapter 2, which dives into the emerging cyber security challenges that are prevalent in today's business world. As e-commerce continues to grow, Chapter 3 on cyber security issues and challenges in e-shopping/e-commerce provides essential insights into the specific threats that online businesses face and how they can mitigate these risks.

Chapter 4 provides the knowledge representation of various business models, which offers a perspective on how businesses can align their operational strategies with robust cyber security frameworks. The distinction between reactive and proactive cyber security strategies is explored in Chapter 5, along with the importance of real-time threat protection, providing a guide for organizations to balance prevention with response.

In Chapters 6 and 7, the book also emphasizes the critical role of incident management in modern organizations, showing how proper preparation and response can minimize damage from cyber incidents. Through a case study on e-banking, the book examines specific vulnerabilities and protective measures tailored for the financial sector.

With the rise of machine learning systems in business data analysis, securing these systems becomes crucial. Chapters 8 and 9 address the cyber security of machine learning systems and explore privacy-preserving deep learning techniques for business big data, offering innovative solutions to maintain privacy without compromising analytical power.

Additionally, Chapter 10 gives a detailed analysis of cyber security tools, taking readers from the basics to more intermediate strategies while highlighting the importance of tailored solutions for various business needs. To conclude, Chapter 11 delves into cyber security measures for e-commerce platforms in Africa, focusing on the unique challenges faced by businesses in this region, and offers solutions shaped by local contexts. Chapter 12 discusses Optimizing User Engagement with Personalized Recommendations and Targeted Advertising for e-commerce profit.

This book will serve as a valuable resource for business leaders, analysts, information technology professionals, and researchers, providing theoretical knowledge, case studies, and practical solutions to navigate the complexities of cyber security in business analytics.

1 Introduction to Learning Methods for Business Analytics

Divya C D, Anupama K, Yu-Chen Hu, Ayesha Siddiqua, and Jhanjhi N Z

1.1 INTRODUCTION TO BUSINESS ANALYTICS AND THE IMPORTANCE OF EFFECTIVE LEARNING METHODS

Business analytics promises high value for organizations in an environment that is increasingly characterized by complexity, volatility, threat, and opportunities. However, many organizations have yet to see the anticipated benefits from their analytics efforts. Academic programs aiming to prepare students for the practice of business analytics have become popular. The challenge of preparing students for business analytics–related careers is compounded by the fact that, in most cases, the business analytics student is not familiar with the discipline. This chapter reports on an exploratory study to investigate the effectiveness of popular teaching methods that business analytics instructors can use. To this end, we identify three effective learning methods: team-based, practice-focused, and outcome-driven approaches.

Business analytics serves as a critical pillar for gaining and maintaining a competitive edge in today's dynamic organizational landscape. Ranging from basic reporting to complex advanced analytics, it offers substantial value in an environment marked by increasing complexity, uncertainty, risks, and emerging opportunities [1]. Despite its potential, many organizations have yet to fully capitalize on the benefits of their analytics initiatives. In response, academic programs focused on equipping students with practical business analytics skills have seen a surge in popularity [2]. The growing demand for business analytics talent has led to the creation of new programs that are mostly offered by business schools as specialized masters or certificate programs [3]. The demand for business analytics professionals is expected to remain strong due to a dynamic market with different employment opportunities for people with a combined business and technical background [4]. A brief analysis of the field of business analytics and the importance of effective learning methods are presented in Figure 1.1.

DOI: 10.1201/9781003540045-1

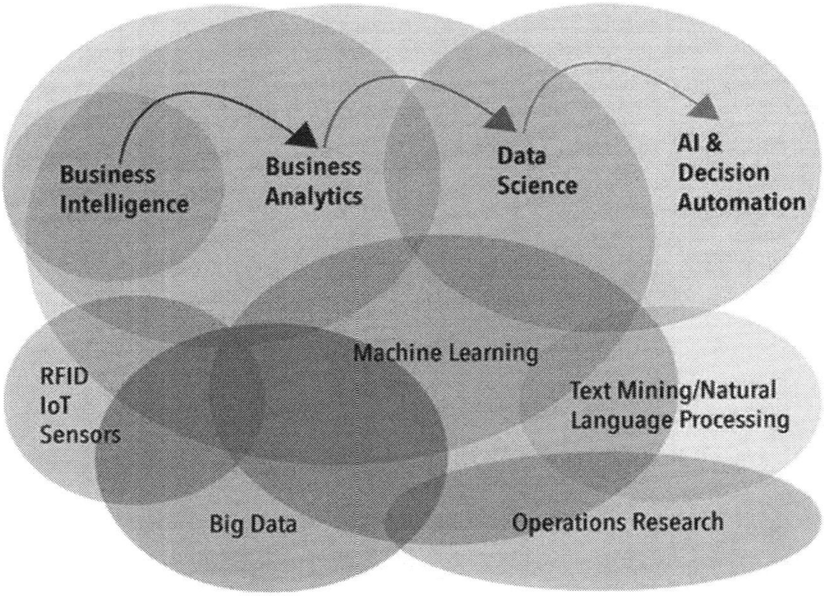

FIGURE 1.1 Business Analytics and the Importance of Effective Learning Methods.

1.2 TRADITIONAL LEARNING METHODS IN BUSINESS ANALYTICS

Traditional classroom-based learning may be ineffective for students without the technical prerequisites to engage with sophisticated data analysis tools [5]. In addition, university access policies generally limit the number of students allowed to enroll in specific business analytics subjects. This deprives many business students of the opportunity to develop core business analytics skills [6]. As many of these future managers are more likely to engage with less technically demanding business analytics tasks, the lack of opportunity for them to become analytics literate engenders an undesirable career path [7]. How to effectively teach business analytics in an environment where few students have a technical background is a concern for many business schools.

Traditional methods of teaching business analytics have included approaches to increasing student engagement to address the lack of technical prerequisites [8]. Applied business analytics courses often incorporate hands-on use of data and associated analytics tools into teaching methods [9]. Such teaching approaches can add relevance and engagement and manage the diverse abilities and experiences of large class sizes. However, engaging students and customizing learning activities for diverse abilities can require many teaching hours, including significant hours for support staff such as teaching assistants [10]. With issues such as class size constraints and what can realistically be taught with available staff, it is desirable to explore methods that can also extend the access to learning within and support for

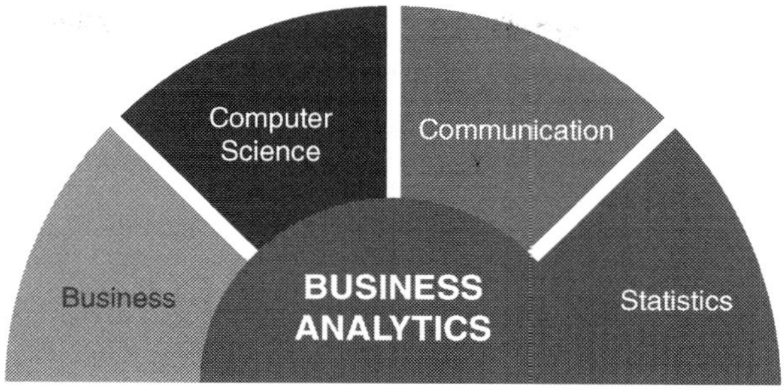

FIGURE 1.2 Business Analytics.

the development of analytics skills within the broader business curriculum [11]. The process involved in business analytics is presented in Figure 1.2.

1.2.1 Classroom-Based Learning

Besides the generally recognized advantages of joining a college, such as interactive learning and exposure, a business analytics classroom has its own unique value proposition. Core academic modules contain all relevant concepts of business analytics [12]. These concepts are initially learned by students in a classroom environment and then transformed to job functions later. One core property of a learning environment is that students not only learn from faculty members but also learn from each other, probably having different backgrounds and experiences [13]. Students have to act as both advocates and critics in class discussions. They learn from the comments and perspectives of colleagues. These relationships are formed in the classroom after the start of the course but will be maintained throughout the entire program and probably beyond [14]. In other words, a classroom is the starting point of their professional network.

Classroom-based education will continue to be an important method of learning, offering specific opportunities for developing advanced knowledge and analytic communication at the graduate level [15]. However, business analytics programs also attract attention as the center of research. For workforce development of general properties, classroom-based learning is advantageous [16]. The curriculum should be developed as an integral part of long-term business–corporate collaboration, ensuring that academic learning aligns with industry needs and evolving professional standards. Guest speakers are other ways of promoting interaction and knowledge dissemination through close interaction [17]. The sheer volume of information is a coursework disadvantage. In order to handle varying topics, students have to do their own background reading [18]. Also, in practice, simply looking for information in a short period in a public library is not easy. As another main disadvantage of classroom-based learning, educators are extremely slow to accept the use of claimed software [19]. Office software implementation is mostly the reason for this.

1.2.2 Textbook-Based Learning

Given such a knowledge gap, the most reasonable learning approach to a student-centered business analytics course in the curriculum is to use a textbook [20]. A textbook is certainly an effective instructional tool. For example, student learning is enhanced by well-structured textbooks, and students are capable of delivering more powerful solutions after reading from such books. In consequence, a high-quality textbook educates students on the importance of the concepts that business managers ought to understand [21]. Thoughtful consideration of the materials in the textbook can provide students with the necessary basic knowledge, which in turn helps them to go beyond mere knowledge and apply critical thinking in practice [22]. As an introductory subject, a textbook is an important source not only for mastering the general background but also for providing a foundation for future business analytics courses and other business-critical subjects [23].

Instructors regularly require students to read textbooks or other written materials for learning both principles and concepts. Instructors also instruct students in small groups when presenting explicit instruction to encourage dialog and reflection of business-related real-world needs and constraints [24]. This depends on the students' previous knowledge. It is therefore reasonable to assume that some textbook-reading sessions and case-study discussions should take place as part of the business analytics lessons [25]. In addition, a significant portion of business analytics concepts and implementation mimic real-world business practices. The suggestion to use the textbook as a standard learning tool in order to assist students is supported by a national agenda to design curricula that incorporate connection with organized by the system or community events to contextualize principles and outcomes and for teachers to illustrate the importance and relevance of the curriculum subject [26].

1.3 EMERGING LEARNING METHODS IN BUSINESS ANALYTICS

1.3.1 Online Courses and Massive Open Online Courses

Several of the firms we studied used online courses and/or Massive Open Online Courses (MOOCs) offered by companies ranging from Coursera to DataCamp to Udacity. In fact, the relative cost and ease of deploying engineers to these offerings was a factor in several of the companies' decisions to transform their data scientists from generalists to specialists [27]. However, as the field of business analytics evolves, one should ask the question: is everyone a data scientist? As specialization grows, would it be wiser to expose existing developers whose specialist requirements normally do not justify an offline full-time course at prestigious universities [28]? Another question related to scaling the number of specialists is: when does the need exist to train a target population distributed around many countries [29]? Finally, because of the rise of DataOps, DevOps for Data, and distributed data environments, other company roles will soon be exposed to more technical and possibly specialist requirements [30].

The explosion of data has led to an explosion of demand for an associated skill set. The management consulting firm McKinsey forecasts a shortage of analytic talent necessary for insights-driven decision-making at 250,000–290,000 in 2018 and a gap in managerial talent of 1.5 million managers necessary to utilize big data for making decisions [31]. Unlike most of the previous business failures that led to the field of business analytics, the past several years have seen spectacular failures [32]. From Elizabeth Holmes' Theranos to rising skepticism surrounding products of the Big Four advertising giants, these products involve data and analytics at their core. Within the broader field of analytics, a sector of data scientists bring the ability to invent, structure, and gain new insights while earning a salary bonus of 10–25% more than their analytics colleagues [33]. At the forefront of the business analytics battle line, the influx of a large number of more junior employees affecting the decisions made, the tools developed, and the models deployed now argues for developers embarking on a two-year training program [34].

1.3.2 Interactive Data Visualization Tools

Many companies have already introduced business intelligence (BI) solutions to help users access and analyze data and provide interactive information visualization [35]. For example, Google released Data Studio, a reporting tool that allows users to create informative visual insights using data-length reports, in 2016. The distinctive feature of Data Studio is that it integrates with other Google products such as Google Analytics, Google AdSense, and YouTube [36]. Microsoft Excel and Access are widely used as data visualization tools on the market. However, these tools are not designed to be distributed on the web [37]. Additionally, other open source BI solutions on the market, such as R Shiny, are not immediately suited for BI systems and require in-depth technical knowledge. Therefore, we need a solution that is simple and easy to use for business users.

Currently, there are some web-based visualization tools that are relatively easy to use. Especially Shiny, offered by R Studio as an open source BI solution, is widely considered a data visualization tool for data analysis and reporting. The interactive web applications with R codes for data visualization and frontend coding can be created to make simple data-based decisions, yet safeguard more security and governance than Microsoft Excel. These visualization applications are assessed from a technical or a programmer's point of view. However, there is little empirical research from business students who create a project-based data analysis task in a business course. The objective of this research is to identify the effectiveness of R Shiny learning techniques for business students through a project-based task. The main findings in our study are that R Shiny provides significant help to business students in not only learning data visualization techniques but also understanding descriptive statistical analysis.

1.4 CASE STUDIES AND PRACTICAL APPLICATIONS IN BUSINESS ANALYTICS LEARNING

Employing a theory-based teaching method for teaching business and economics at the undergraduate level improves content learning, particularly among students who can analyze and evaluate. A blended learning approach has been found effective in teaching business-related subjects at the higher education level. Combining project-based learning for learners' practical orientation and interactive learning for learning experiences improves the creation of contexts for applied learning. Teachers' experiential knowledge and course design impact students' performance, tailored to target groups. This chapter reports case studies related to classroom exercises, the effect of pre-class tasks, the application of project management theory, teaching foreign direct investment (FDI) with business theories in the background, business terminology, and problem solving in the context of business.

1.5 ASSESSMENT AND EVALUATION OF LEARNING METHODS IN BUSINESS ANALYTICS

1.5.1 Business Analytics—Formative and Summative Assessment

Education for Business Managers and Administrators (EBMA) is essentially an approach for collecting and analyzing information for decision-making in managerial and business settings. At the core of the EBMA approach is the notion of assessment in the form of formative and summative assessment that guides analytics education and its learning and teaching methods. Each learning method in business analytics will likely require to be assessed in a manner that individual students, scholars, and professional educators can evaluate. The students, scholars, and professional educators who are analyzing, interpreting, and evaluating methods of analytics may wish to utilize such methods. It is the aim of this chapter to detail how to carry out such analyses in an effort for continuous learning and improvement of business analytics methods. Relying on the methods are important data to help influence our learning at every level, from shifting and adapting our pedagogies to potentially making relevant contributions to the challenging fields of business analytics and data-driven education at the individual level, and in the fields of business analytics and pedagogy at the institutional, societal, and global levels.

The concept of formative assessment has been widely used in the educational literature, and in the field of business analytics where formative assessment has been used by analytics educators in their efforts to understand the students' process of learning, gaining skills, and following up on what these educators are doing. Formative assessment has also been used in empirical studies to enable researchers and training development teams to test the validity, reliability, and enablers of new measures, tools, and frameworks. In updating the existing concepts about formative assessment, we argue that a potential challenge toward a comprehensive perspective about this process might be associated with the common understanding that assessment processes are initiated and determined primarily by analysis of students' learning and/or performance. Our understanding is that the process of formative assessment also needs to encompass the enhancing of teaching methods, peer-to-peer learning, and the overarching goal of assessing course development.

Summative assessment, on the other hand, is primarily concerned with the end result. It measures and reports information after the instruction has been completed.

Summative assessment has developed characteristically been evaluated with regards to students' certification, for example, regarding what technical skills they possess. It can also complement a particular analytics instructional design, which is important both for the understanding of educational researchers and for information about what constitutes good performance. Given this understanding of the two dimensions of assessment, useful in a business analytics learning scenario is a commitment to the fact that while there may not be a deterministic relationship between how a student learns business analytics and how well they apply the knowledge, one would expect that an analytics course helps students to succeed in working with data analysis for business decision-making in the working environment that they are likely to face after the course. It is only natural that the course content, learning and teaching methods, and assessment content are designed in a way that supports this course–modus operandi sum objective.

1.6 TECHNOLOGIES ADAPTED

What are the potential future technologies for facilitating improvements in business analytics in this space? We provide a list of 20 technologies that may be relevant to the higher education sector in the medium term. Have you heard of them all? We encourage readers to explore background information on each of these incredibly important emerging technologies. Their lists closely resemble ours, so we feel some confidence that our list represents an important segment of emerging and horizon technologies in general. When we say "effectiveness and/or efficiency," we mean the technology may significantly increase or accelerate the helpfulness of current learning approaches. If we had written this chapter in 2011, we might have said "major technical challenges that would be required to be overcome."

Smart learning applications that increase inbuilt pedagogic effectiveness in tutoring and critical thinking aided personalized and informal learning opportunities and reflective learning approaches. Artificial intelligence (AI) in sensory interfaces and new human-to-computing paradigms allow faster learner input. Several challenges are associated with open textbooks, including increasing costs related to authoring, implementation, and value assessment; issues surrounding the commons; the often limited quality of available resources; expenses tied to sponsorship; and legal or regulatory compliance. Additionally, there is a need to evaluate the design performance and learning impact of open educational resources, as well as the effectiveness of large, existing repositories in facilitating meaningful use.

1.7 FUTURE TRENDS AND INNOVATIONS IN LEARNING METHODS FOR BUSINESS ANALYTICS

The instructors have integrated technologies including Web 2.0, analytic tools such as Microsoft Structured Query Language (SQL) Server or SAS Visual Analytics, and the Learning Management System (LMS). The apprenticeship program developed a cost-effective open source Extract, Transform, Load (ETL) tool package to help the students prepare big data in a range of topics and in an easy-to-understand way. The instructors have implemented outcome-based learning to enable students to develop professional competencies and generic skills in tandem with gaining knowledge. The use of competition among students as an active learning method has also increased student motivation and interest in competition.

Rapid changes include industry needs, the availability of digital contents, and advances in technology in the era of big data. Our results imply that instructors may need to provide students with the new knowledge, experience, and competencies, particularly in the context of deeper industrial collaboration and state-of-the-art course syllabi. In addition, this era presents a new platform in the design of learning systems as support mechanisms to enhance learning outcomes based on existing innovative methods. The training of instructors in the modern teaching methods is important. This chapter also provides advice for analytics course instructors and administrators. Educational institutions may leverage our findings to enhance and refine their existing or future programs.

1.8 RESULTS

Table 1.1 and Figure 1.3 present the emerging learning methods in business analytics considering the method category, learning method, and accuracy.

TABLE 1.1
Emerging Learning Methods in Business Analytics

Method Category	Learning Method	Description	Accuracy/Efficiency
Emerging Learning Methods	**Online Courses and MOOCs**	Flexible, self-paced courses with structured content	High (80–90%)
	Interactive Simulations	Hands-on virtual tools for real-time analytics practice	Very High (85–95%)
	Data Labs	Collaborative labs for exploring real datasets and tools	Very High (90–95%)
	Collaborative Projects	Group-based learning to solve real-world analytics problems	High (80–90%)
	Real-World Case Studies	Case analysis for application of theory in real scenarios	High (85–90%)
Traditional Learning Methods	**Classroom Lectures**	Instructor-led lectures with limited interactivity	Moderate (60–75%)
	Textbook Learning	Self-study through structured content with limited engagement	Moderate (60–70%)
	Instructor-Led Workshops	Workshops for hands-on practice, but with fixed resources	High (70–80%)
	Case Study Discussions	Instructor-led discussions on pre-selected case studies	Moderate (65–75%)
	Exams and Quizzes	Traditional testing methods for knowledge assessment	Moderate (60–70%)

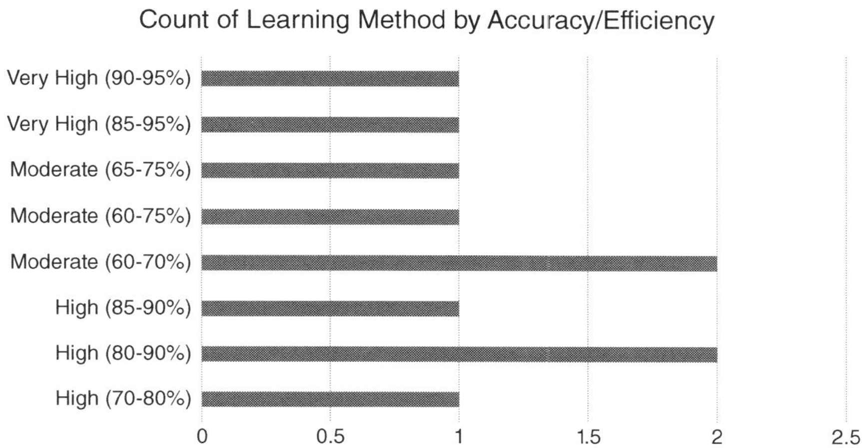

FIGURE 1.3 Emerging Learning Methods in Business Analytics.

Emerging learning methods, such as online courses, interactive simulations, and collaborative projects, offer high to very high accuracy and efficiency, enabling hands-on practice and real-world applications. Traditional methods like classroom lectures and textbook learning tend to have moderate efficiency, with limited interactivity and engagement, often relying on passive learning and structured assessments like exams. The blend of both approaches can optimize learning outcomes.

Table 1.2 and Figure 1.4 present different emerging and traditional methods involved in business analytics. Practical applications in learning, such as case studies, capstone projects, and data challenges, offer very high efficiency, providing hands-on experience and real-world problem solving. Assessment methods like quizzes and assignments gauge foundational knowledge, while adapted technologies like LMS, data visualization tools, and cloud-based labs enable efficient, real-time learning and skill application in advanced analytics.

1.9 CONCLUSION

This chapter reviews literature on learning methods and tools in analytics. It recommends incorporating active learning approaches in business analytics programs to enhance students' skills. This includes classroom discussion, group work, and case analyses. This opinion is supported by evidence from attendees, industry panels, two student business and industry survey reports, and student opinion pieces, as well as the attention paid by the academicians who were interviewed to assess the use in teaching of such tools and techniques.

The importance of good pedagogy and the teaching of different analytic components is acknowledged. Analysts should consider various approaches to business problems and stay updated with new technologies. Knowledge of specific techniques is desirable now, but in the future, employers will value a wide understanding of general concepts. Thus, the development and deployment of analytics in industry depend on teaching them effectively in higher education.

TABLE 1.2
Emerging and Traditional Methods

Learning Category	Method	Description	Accuracy/Efficiency
Practical Applications in Learning	**Case Studies**	Analysis of real-world cases to apply analytics theory in context	High (85–90%)
	Practical Projects	Real or simulated projects to build hands-on experience	Very High (90–95%)
	Capstone Projects	End-of-course projects synthesizing learned skills in real tasks	Very High (90–95%)
	Data Challenges and Hackathons	Competitive events that apply analytics in real-world situation	Very High (90–95%)
Assessment and Evaluation	**Quizzes and Tests**	Traditional assessment for understanding foundational concepts	Moderate (60–75%)
	Assignments and Projects	Evaluating skills through specific assignments or project work	High (80–90%)
	Peer Review and Group Evaluation	Feedback from peers in collaborative projects for soft skills	Moderate to High (70–85%)
	Real-World Performance Analysis	Assessing performance based on applied skills in internships	Very High (85–95%)
Adapted Technologies in Learning	**Learning Management Systems (LMS)**	Platforms to organize and track coursework and progress	High (80–90%)
	Data Visualization Tools	Tools like Tableau or Power BI for hands-on analytics practice	Very High (90–95%)
	Programming Environments	Python, R, or SQL for practical data analysis tasks	Very High (85–95%)
	Cloud-Based Data Labs	Cloud services for access to big data and real-time analytics	Very High (90–95%)
	AI and Machine Learning Platforms	Platforms for advanced analytics and predictive modeling	Very High (90–95%)

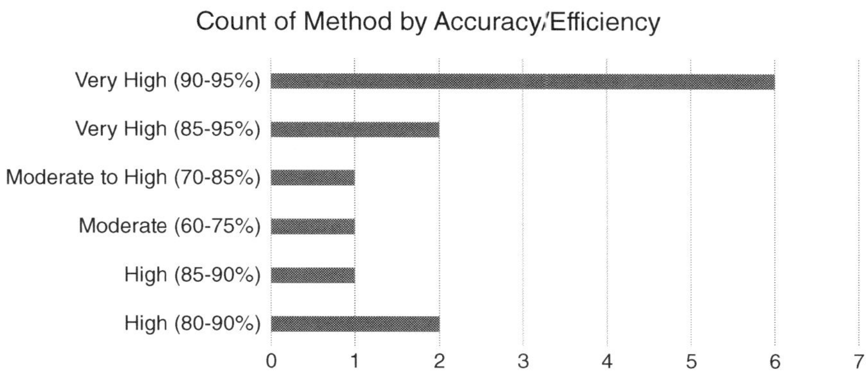

FIGURE 1.4 Emerging and Traditional Methods.

REFERENCES

1. N. Almazmomi, A. Ilmudeen, and A. A. Qaffas. "The impact of business analytics capability on data-driven culture and exploration: Achieving a competitive advantage." *Benchmarking: An International Journal*, vol. 29, no. 4, pp. 1264–1283, 2021.
2. J. Ranjan and C. Foropon. "Big data analytics in building the competitive intelligence of organizations." *International Journal of Information Management*, vol. 56, p. 102231, 2021.
3. B. B. Schlegelmilch, "Why business schools need radical innovations: Drivers and development trajectories," *Journal of Marketing Education*, 2020. sagepub.com
4. E. Kristoffersen, P. Mikalef, F. Blomsma, and J. Li, "The effects of business analytics capability on circular economy implementation, resource orchestration capability, and firm performance," *International Journal of*. . . , 2021. Elsevier. sciencedirect.com
5. V. Sukackė, A. O. P. C. Guerra, D. Ellinger, and V. Carlos, "Towards active evidence-based learning in engineering education: A systematic literature review of PBL, PjBL, and CBL," *Sustainability*, 2022. mdpi.com
6. A. H. Duin and J. Tham, "The current state of analytics: Implications for learning management system (LMS) use in writing pedagogy." *Computers and Composition*, vol. 55, p. 102544, 2020.
7. U. Gal, T. B. Jensen, and M. K. Stein, "Breaking the vicious cycle of algorithmic management: A virtue ethics approach to people analytics," *Information and Organization*, 2020. cbs.dk
8. L. M. Nkomo, B. K. Daniel, and R. J. Butson, "Synthesis of student engagement with digital technologies: A systematic review of the literature," *Technology in Higher Education*, 2021. Springer. springer.com
9. S. Jaggia, A. Kelly, K. Lertwachara, and L. Chen, "Applying the CRISP-DM framework for teaching business analytics," *Decision Sciences Journal of Innovative Education*, vol. 18, no. 4, pp. 612–634, 2020.

10. H. A. El-Sabagh, "Adaptive e-learning environment based on learning styles and its impact on development students' engagement," *Journal of Educational Technology in Higher Education*, 2021. Springer. springer.com
11. D. Ifenthaler and J. Y. K. Yau, "Utilising learning analytics to support study success in higher education: A systematic review," *Educational Technology Research and Development*, vol. 68, no. 3, pp. 1–25, 2020. springer.com
12. A. Alam and A. Mohanty, "Business models, business strategies, and innovations in EdTech companies: Integration of learning analytics and artificial intelligence in higher education," in *2022 IEEE 6th Conference on Information*, 2022. researchgate.net
13. H. R. Milner, "Start where you are, but don't stay there: Understanding diversity, opportunity gaps, and teaching in today's classrooms," 2021. tesl-ej.org
14. L. Allal, "Assessment and the co-regulation of learning in the classroom," *Assessment in Education: Principles*. academia.edu
15. B. D. Bowen and T. Shume, "Developing workforce skills in K-12 classrooms: How teacher externships increase awareness of the critical role of effective communication Bradley Bowen," 2020. vt.edu
16. X. Du, *Business Education Classroom Engagement Using Technology: Keeping Students Engaged in a Post-Pandemic Environment*. Illinois State University, 2023.
17. C. Cothren, "Selling the experience: studying the impact of real-world experiential learning on sales knowledge." PhD diss., University of Missouri-Columbia, 2022.
18. S. P. Rollins, *Teaching Vulnerable Learners: Strategies for Students Who Are Bored, Distracted, Discouraged, or Likely to Drop Out*. WW Norton & Company, 2020.
19. J. Reich, *Failure to Disrupt: Why Technology Alone Can't Transform Education*. Harvard University Press, 2020.
20. J. Caulfield, *How to Design and Teach a Hybrid Course: Achieving Student-Centered Learning Through Blended Classroom, Online and Experiential Activities*. Taylor & Francis, 2023.
21. A. Arsul and A. Johanna, "The principal's business in improving the quality of Islamic education (case study at SDIT AZ Jambi city)," *At-Tasyrih: Journal*, vol. 2021, 2021. iainbatanghari.ac.id
22. A. Ramdani, A. W. Jufri, and G. Gunawan, "Analysis of students' critical thinking skills in terms of gender using science teaching materials based on the 5E learning cycle integrated with local wisdom," *Jurnal Pendidikan*, 2021. unnes.ac.id
23. L. Zhang, F. Chen, and W. Wei, "A foundation course in business analytics: Design and implementation at two universities," *Journal of Information Systems Education*, 2020. jise.org
24. C. Rapanta and M. K. Felton, "Learning to argue through dialogue: A review of instructional approaches," *Educational Psychology Review*, 2022. springer.com
25. R. J. Morris, "The ultimate guide to compact cases: Case research, writing, and teaching," 2022. emerald.com
26. M. Kraus, S. Feuerriegel, and A. Oztekin, "Deep learning in business analytics and operations research: Models, applications and managerial implications," *European Journal of Operational Research*, 2020. Elsevier. sciencedirect.com
27. A. R. Nurutdinova and D. S. Shakirova, "The content modification within the framework of the massive open online courses (case study: International and Russian practices)," *Open Online Courses*, 2023. intechopen.com
28. D. R. Raban and A. Gordon, "The evolution of data science and big data research: A bibliometric analysis," *Scientometrics*, 2020. springer.com
29. H. M. James, C. Papoutsi, and J. Wherton, "Spread, scale-up, and sustainability of video consulting in health care: Systematic review and synthesis guided by the NASSS framework," *Journal of Medical Internet Research*, 2021. jmir.org

30. B. T. Klein, C. Tyler, and S. Fields, "DevOps and data: Faster-time-to-knowledge through SageOps, MLOps, and DataOps," 2022. osti.gov
31. A. S. George and T. Baskar, "Driving business transformation through technology innovation: Emerging priorities for IT leaders," *Partners Universal Innovative Research*, 2024. puirp.com
32. D. Zunino and G. Dushnitsky, "How do investors evaluate past entrepreneurial failure? Unpacking failure due to lack of skill versus bad luck," *Academy of Management*, 2022. cbs.dk
33. A. J. Gutman and J. Goldmeier. *Becoming a Data Head: How to Think, Speak, and Understand Data Science, Statistics, and Machine Learning*. John Wiley & Sons, 2021.
34. L. Li, J. Lin, Y. Ouyang, and X. R. Luo, "Evaluating the impact of big data analytics usage on the decision-making quality of organizations," *Technological Forecasting and Social Change*, vol. 202, p. 123456, 2022. [HTML]
35. C. Shao, Y. Yang, S. Juneja, and T. G. Seetharam, "IoT data visualization for business intelligence in corporate finance," *Information Processing & Management*, 2022. Elsevier. e-tarjome.com
36. A. Songa, S. Edara, S. T. Raavi, and S. V. Somisetty, "The societal and transformational impacts of data science," *International Journal*, 2021. researchgate.net
37. G. D. Zion and B. K. Tripathy, "Comparative analysis of tools for big data visualization and challenges," in *Data Visualization: Trends and Challenges*, 2020. Springer. [HTML]

2 Emerging Cyber Security Challenges and Trends in the Business World

Bhuvaneshwari P, Shaheen H, Pallavi T P, and Hong Lin

2.1 INTRODUCTION

In the process of digitization, data of every kind, including sensitive data, are being stored digitally. It is anticipated that in the next ten years, information technology (IT) and digital technologies will play a more significant role in companies' overall business operations, as digital transformation has become a significant topic on leadership agendas [1]. Digital technologies are focused on externally connecting devices, providing extremely good digital services, and increasing customer experience; in contrast, IT activities are more internally focused, primarily with the purpose of combining with current business processes. They will be exposed to several additional risks as a result of these initiatives, including risks related to cyber security [2]. Security is the technique of maintaining digital data safe from harm or theft while preserving its availability and confidentiality. However, as technology improves rapidly, the frequency and sophistication of cybercrimes are also increasing. Insufficient software, outdated security technologies, programming errors, design flaws, easily accessible online hacking tools, public ignorance, huge financial returns, and so forth are all contributing factors to the extraordinary rise in cybercrime. Technical attackers create enormous potent attack tools to find the target's vulnerabilities and subsequently attack the target.

IT security incidents have evolved over the past few decades from solitary attacks on information systems to deliberate, focused, and delicate cyber threats at the institutional, individual, or even national level [3]. Information security became cyber security, primarily as the result of a paradigm shift in defense against persistent threats. While it was sufficient to undertake basic defense against "common" assaults in the information security era, organizations now need to build creative, inventive, and effective procedures to identify and prevent sophisticated and evolving cyberattacks. Cyber Security initiatives must involve the entire organization, not just IT departments or designated personnel [4]. Instead, all staff members should be involved. Digital technologies and company strategy should be strategically connected, and the same is true of cyber security. Handling and avoiding emerging threats becomes challenging due to the constantly evolving nature of cybercrime. Because advanced dangers are so prevalent in cyberspace, protecting

 DOI: 10.1201/9781003540045-2

it is the hardest and most daunting undertaking there is. Consequently, understanding the principles behind security defensive systems, various approaches, and current issues in the field of information security is essential. In this chapter, the most important concepts related to cyber security challenges and solutions, especially in the context of small and medium-sized enterprises (SMEs) and financial institutions, are analyzed.

2.2 THE EVOLVING IMPACT OF CYBER SECURITY

2.2.1 The Rise of Cybercrime and its Impact on Businesses

Cyberattacks including ransomware, data breaches, distributive denial-of-service (DDoS) attacks, and phishing threaten businesses in a number of industries with severe financial losses, operational interruptions, penalties from regulators, and destroyed customer trust. Apart from the direct financial consequences, customers' increased awareness of cyber security threats has increased the analysis of companies' security protocols. Consumers today expect that companies would protect their digital assets and personal information; otherwise, they risk losing their trust, damaging their brand, and losing market share. In order to keep customers trusting them, businesses need to emphasize cyber security as an essential part of their operations and make investments to secure their digital assets.

2.2.2 The Need for a Proactive Approach to Cyber Security

It is essential for organizations to adopt a proactive approach toward cyber security, beyond conventional reactive measures such as firewalls and antivirus software. This involves discovering vulnerabilities, regularly monitoring and evaluating security their posture, and quickly responding to threats utilizing cutting-edge technologies. To reduce the risk of human attacks, including phishing and social engineering, employee training is important. "Security by design," which integrates security into the development life cycle, helps to detect vulnerabilities early [5]. Building stronger defenses requires collaboration and information sharing among businesses. Executive leadership is required to establish definite goals and guarantee continuous improvement while incorporating cyber security into the overall risk management plan. Organizations can protect trust, maintain digital assets, and remain resilient against evolving cyber threats.

2.3 REGULATORY AND COMPLIANCE ISSUES

Technology is heavily reliant on cyber security, and securing data is one of the most significant problems confronting modern civilization. Given the steadily increasing incidence of cybercrimes, several organizations and the government are implementing various measures to deter these kinds of offenses from happening. Cybercrime is any form of illegal action where the main tool used to commit crime is a laptop or a computer. Along with computer-enabled crimes like bullying and stalking and other frauds that constitute a serious threat to the public and the government, a growing number of these crimes also entail computer-enabled crimes like network espionage and the transmission of laptop viruses [6]. Figure 2.1 shows the simple technological solutions for the most prevalent cybercrimes.

2.3.1 Difficulty in Complying with the Regulations by Financial Institutions

The continuous evolving nature of cyber threats and the consequent requirement for maintaining cyber security solutions make achieving cyber security compliance one of the primary obstacles. For their cyber security protocols to remain up to date with evolving rules and emerging threats, financial institutions need to periodically monitor and evaluate them [7]. There are some similar trends and differences in cyber security laws for financial institutions, in addition to the convergence of global cyber security standards and the differences in data protection and breach reporting regulations. Financial institutions must approach compliance in a risk-based manner in order to address these issues. Resources and efforts need to be deployed in accordance with the cyber security risks that are most important to their firm. They should also make use of technology and automation to expedite compliance procedures and lessen the amount of paperwork and administrative load related to regulatory reporting and documentation.

FIGURE 2.1 Technological Solutions for the Cybercrime.

Allegations are made by a number of individuals indicating that financial institutions are at risk due to more sophisticated and persistent hostile attacks. Emerging technologies further complicate the cyber security environment, providing new attack methods and vulnerabilities. In order to keep ahead of constantly changing threats, financial institutions need to adopt a continuous improvement culture by regularly reviewing their cyber security policies, processes, and strategies. To disseminate threat intelligence and best practices, this involves working together with cyber security professionals and industry peers, investing in threat intelligence capabilities, and carrying out frequent penetration tests and security assessments.

2.4 CYBER SECURITY FOR SMALL AND MEDIUM-SIZED ENTERPRISES

The contribution of SMEs to the global economy accounts for between 50% and 60% of the total value added [8]. While SMEs are very adaptable and innovative, they also barely follow rules and regulations. Every organization has been impacted by cybercrime, but SMEs and small and medium-sized businesses (SMBs) are particularly at risk. Their competitive attitude makes them more vulnerable to hackers, which contributes to their wide embrace of digital technologies. Perhaps they simply believe the targets aren't worth attacking, or maybe they are too preoccupied with running their company to see the threats that arise. Attacks on SMEs/SMBs may be on the rise as a result of weak corporate cyber security. Due to a lack of knowledge, expertise, and funding, small businesses usually struggle to put security measures into place. For instance, a 2017 survey conducted in the UK revealed that over 60% of SMEs had experienced ransomware attacks. Unfortunately, after six months of the attack, more than half of the hacked SMEs declared bankruptcy. This is especially true when it comes to new regulations like the European Union (EU) General Data Protection Regulation (GDPR).

SMEs in developing nations are already aware of the necessity of increasing their cyber security abilities. In order to fulfill the responsibilities in accordance with relevant agreements, laws, and procedures, it is recommended that organizations give their partners and staff cyber security awareness training. Also suggests that all employees of the organization, including those in charge of operations and physical security, external stakeholders, and senior management, should receive training. Figure 2.2 and Table 2.1 outline the cost-effective cyber security solutions for SMEs.

As discussed previously, we can say that the following points are the main points we need to focus on when trying to develop cyber security awareness in SMEs:

- Significance of a strong security culture;
- Program interoperability with SMEs' resources;
- Significance of asset- and harm-based strategy;
- The involvement of government agencies through programs to support SMEs; and
- Improved commitment from SMEs.

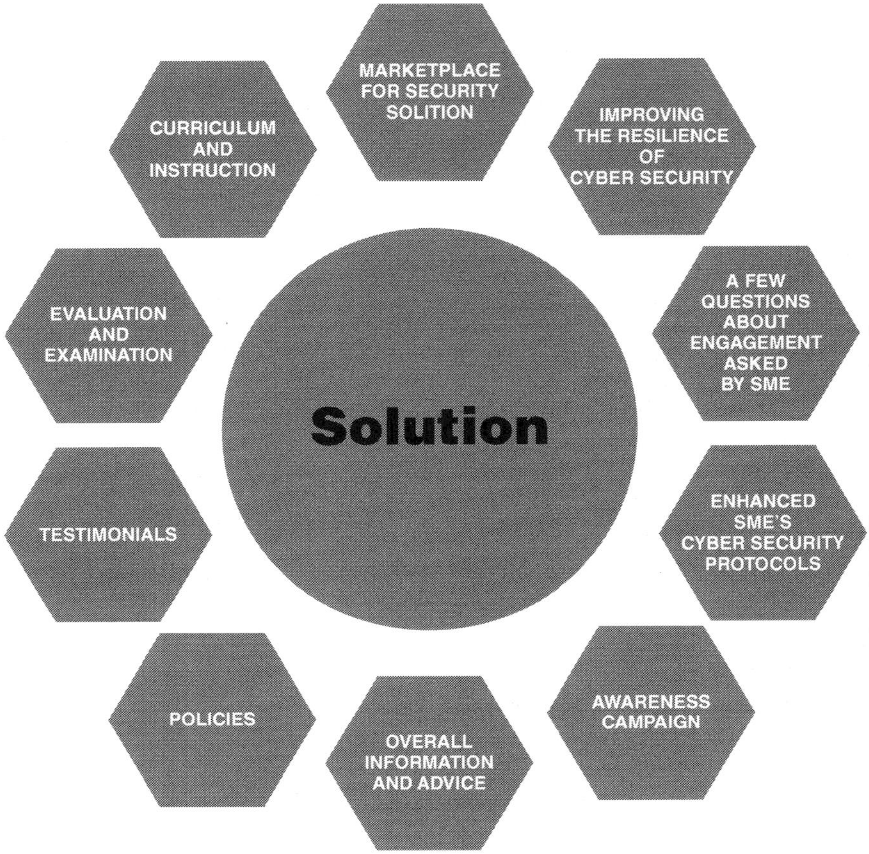

FIGURE 2.2 Solutions for SMEs' Cyber Security Challenges.

2.5 THE FUTURE OF CYBER SECURITY

When considering the future of cyber security, it's crucial to keep in mind that anything can happen at any time. Every year, the industry evolves. In order to effectively secure ever-more-complex networks, countermeasures against cyber threats also constantly evolve. It's hard to forecast the future of cyber security. Everything is continually changing: new attacks and strategies, defenses, and technology. However, in spite of these strong defenses, hackers still take advantage of vulnerabilities in security frameworks, particularly since the pandemic caused a shift in work environments from in-office to remote, which added additional cyber security concerns. Among these dangers include the advanced persistent threats (APTs) [9], malware [10], ransomware [11], phishing [10], insider threats, DDoS attacks [12], and man-in-the-middle attacks [13].

TABLE 2.1
Outlining Cost-effective Cyber Security Solutions for SMEs

S. No.	Solution	Description	Benefits	Cost Considerations
1	**Antivirus Software**	Protects against malware and viruses.	Essential protection; often has low cost	Typically subscription based; $30–$60/year/device
2	**Firewall**	Keeps track of and manages the incoming and outgoing traffic in the network	Prevents inappropriate access; improves network security	Hardware based or software based; $50–$500 one-time or annual fees
3	**Email Security**	Filters and scans emails to prevent phishing and malware	Reduces risk of phishing and malware attacks	$2–$5/user/month for cloud-based services
4	**Multifactor Authentication (MFA)**	Strengthens with an additional layer of security beyond just a password	Enhances account security; easy to implement	Free or low cost; some services are $1–$3/user/month.
5	**Regular Software Updates**	Keeps software and systems up to date with security patches	Fixes vulnerabilities; prevents exploits	Usually free, but may require some administrative effort
6	**Backup Solutions**	Regularly backs up data to protect against loss or ransomware	Ensures data recovery; reduces downtime	$50–$200/year for cloud services or hardware
7	**Security Awareness Training**	Educates employees about security best practices and recognizing threats	Reduces human error; improves overall security	$10–$50/employee/year for online training programs
8	**Virtual Private Network (VPN)**	Conceals Internet protocol (IP) address and encrypts internet traffic	Secures remote connections; protects sensitive data	$5–$15/user/month for reputable services
9	**Secure Password Management**	Tools to generate and store complex passwords	Simplifies password management; enhances security	$2–$5/user/month for subscription services
10	**Intrusion Detection System (IDS)**	Analyzes the network for any unusual behavior	Detects potential threats in real-time	Basic versions may be free; advanced solutions can cost $500–$2,000/year

2.5.1 Predictions and Trends in Cyber Security

In cyber security, predictive analysis can enhance a company's ability to allocate defense resources efficiently. Although anticipating attacks is not new, automating this method has gained popularity recently. By reducing biases and the amount of time specialists spend making predictions, automation helps reduce the first-mover advantage held by attackers. Organizations can better anticipate and respond to future threats by tracking attacker activity and creating attack profiles.

The field of cyber security is changing due to emerging technology, which provides creative methods and tools for continually fending off evolving threats.

A few emerging trends and technological developments are anticipated to have significance on cyber security in the future. Future safety may be impacted by the following changes.

2.5.1.1 Future of Cyber Security in Internet of Things

Future prospects for Internet of Things (IoT) security against cyberattacks are promising. Future IoT security will focus on comprehensive protection of the entire ecosystem, employing zero-trust models and leveraging real-time threat detection [14].

2.5.1.2 Future of Cyber Security in Artificial Intelligence

Artificial intelligence (AI) has the caliber to gradually increase cyber security by improving the detection, response, and prevention of attacks [15]. A combination of innovative technologies, robust security frameworks, and collaboration between industry, government, and academia will be needed for effective cyber security in AI. An example of how AI can identify and react to cyber threats by picking up on and adjusting to novel attack patterns is provided by a case study of Darktrace's AI solution.

2.5.1.3 Aviation Cyber Security Future

Several trends will impact aircraft cyber security going ahead [16].

1. Increasing the use of connected systems: As airplanes have more connected systems, the potential of cyberattacks increases, requiring strong security measures.
2. Emphasis on data security: Ensuring data security will become increasingly important as more data are gathered and shared.
3. Complex attacks: As attacks become more sophisticated, money will need to be spent on innovative cyber security measures like AI and machine learning.
4. Regulatory requirements: Governments' increased attention to aviation cyber security will result in more stringent rules that companies must abide by in order to avoid penalties.
5. Greater collaboration: To effectively combat cyber threats and exchange best practices, there will need to be greater collaboration between aviation companies, cyber security specialists, and governmental organizations.

2.6 CONCLUSION

One of the biggest concerns of business systems is cyber security. A successful cyberattack on a system may reduce the company's competitiveness and productivity, potentially compromising its strategic goals. The first step in addressing cyber security challenges is evaluating cyber risks, which involves identifying the crucial resources that need to be safeguarded from cyberattacks and the associated business impacts. Continuously more research and development are required to solve the issues and meet the needs of the present and the future, particularly in the areas of integrated information security management within organizations and information security issues related to both individuals and entire communities. In order to do this, evaluating the financial effects of cyberattacks on SME and financial systems could be the main focus. Our comprehensive research has been helpful in offering a broad understanding of the topic and demonstrating the connections between the various entities involved.

REFERENCES

1. Soldatova, A.V., Budrin, A.G., Budrina, E.V., Presnova, A.A., and Girsh, L.V. 2021. September. Customer loyalty management in the context of digital transformation of business. In *2021 International Conference on Quality Management, Transport and Information Security, Information Technologies (IT&QM&IS)* (pp. 907–910). IEEE.
2. Huang, K., Zhou, C., Tian, Y.C., Yang, S. and Qin, Y. 2018. Assessing the physical impact of cyberattacks on industrial cyber-physical systems. *IEEE Transactions on Industrial Electronics*, *65*(10), pp. 8153–8162.
3. Alassaf, M. and Alkhalifah, A. 2021. Exploring the influence of direct and indirect factors on information security policy compliance: A systematic literature review. *IEEE Access*, *9*, pp. 162687–162705.
4. Mahesh, P., Tiwari, A., Jin, C., Kumar, P.R., Reddy, A.N., Bukkapatanam, S.T., Gupta, N. and Karri, R. 2020. A survey of cybersecurity of digital manufacturing. *Proceedings of the IEEE*, *109*(4), pp. 495–516.
5. Yu, Z., Kaplan, Z., Yan, Q. and Zhang, N. 2021. Security and privacy in the emerging cyber-physical world: A survey. *IEEE Communications Surveys & Tutorials*, *23*(3), pp. 1879–1919.
6. Ali, Md L., Thakur, K. and Atobatele, B. 2019. Challenges of cyber security and the emerging trends. In *Proceedings of the 2019 ACM International Symposium on Blockchain and Secure Critical Infrastructure* (pp. 107–112).
7. Uzougbo, N.S., Ikegwu, C.G. and Adewusi, A.O. 2024. Cybersecurity compliance in financial institutions: A comparative analysis of global standards and regulations. *International Journal of Science and Research Archive*, *12*(1), pp. 533–548. https://doi.org/10.30574/ijsra.2024.12.1.0802.
8. Christophe, P., Grandclaudon, J. and Bal, S. 2019. Survey and lessons learned on raising SME awareness about cybersecurity. *ICISSP* (pp. 558–563).
9. Ren, Y., Xiao, Y., Zhou, Y., Zhang, Z. and Tian, Z. 2022. Cskg4apt: A cybersecurity knowledge graph for advanced persistent threat organization attribution. *IEEE Transactions on Knowledge and Data Engineering*, *35*(6), pp. 5695–5709.
10. Parthy, P.P. and Rajendran, G. 2019, October. Identification and prevention of social engineering attacks on an enterprise. In *2019 International Carnahan Conference on Security Technology (ICCST)* (pp. 1–5). IEEE.

11. Aldauiji, F., Batarfi, O. and Bayousef, M. 2022. Utilizing cyber threat hunting techniques to find ransomware attacks: A survey of the state of the art. *IEEE Access*, *10*, pp. 61695–61706.
12. Rios, V.D.M., Inácio, P.R., Magoni, D. and Freire, M.M. 2022. Detection and mitigation of low-rate denial-of-service attacks: A survey. *IEEE Access*, *10*, pp. 76648–76668.
13. Nam, S.Y., Kim, D. and Kim, J. 2010. Enhanced ARP: Preventing ARP poisoning-based man-in-the-middle attacks. *IEEE Communications Letters*, *14*(2), pp. 187–189.
14. Cook, J., Rehman, S.U. and Khan, M.A. 2023. Security and privacy for low power iot devices on 5g and beyond networks: Challenges and future directions. *IEEE Access*, *11*, pp. 39295–39317.
15. Chaudhry, Y.S., Sharma, U. and Rana, A. 2020, June. Enhancing security measures of AI applications. In *2020 8th International Conference on Reliability, Infocom Technologies and Optimization (Trends and Future Directions)(ICRITO)* (pp. 713–716). IEEE.
16. Elmarady, A.A. and Rahouma, K. 2021. Studying cybersecurity in civil aviation, including developing and applying aviation cybersecurity risk assessment. *IEEE Access*, *9*, pp. 143997–144016.

3 Cyber Security Issues, Challenges in E-Shopping/E-Commerce

Udayaprasad P K, Shreyas J, Francesco Flammini, and Hong Lin

3.1 INTRODUCTION

3.1.1 Background and Motivation

The world economy has changed due to the quick development of information and communication technology (ICT) and the widespread use of the internet, which has fueled the expansion of e-commerce. Cyberspace is now a prime target for cybercriminals due to this transformation, which has also increased cyber security threats. The rise in cyber security threats can be attributed to various factors, including financial gain, political objectives, and the theft of personal data [1, 2]. These dangers are not limited to specific individuals or companies; they also endanger the stability of the economy and national security. As trade and communication become more dependent on digital platforms, it is imperative to protect e-commerce environments from cyber security threats [3, 4] and it is shown in Tables 3.1 and 3.2.

The growing number of cyberattacks that target e-commerce platforms, which have an effect on both consumers and businesses as shown in Figure 3.1, is what inspired this study [5, 6]. Cyber security risks that jeopardize e-commerce's integrity and dependability include data breaches, identity theft, and financial fraud. The dynamic nature of cyber threats presents ongoing challenges to the secure operation of online platforms, even with advancements in security protocols. The purpose of this research is to pinpoint the cyber security gaps that currently exist in e-commerce and to suggest methods for improving security frameworks [7, 8] as from Figure 3.2.

3.1.2 Problem Statement

E-commerce platforms are susceptible to various cyber security risks that may lead to notable financial losses, compromised data, and harm to their reputations. To combat sophisticated cyber threats, the cyber security policies and procedures currently in place frequently fall short. A thorough grasp of the numerous elements causing these vulnerabilities is required, as is the creation of strong cyber security frameworks that deal with both present and new risks to e-commerce.

DOI: 10.1201/9781003540045-3

TABLE 3.1
Overview of Common Cyber Security Threats and Their Impact on E-commerce

Cyber Security Threat	Description	Impact on E-Commerce
Phishing [1]	Fraudulent attempts to obtain sensitive information (e.g., passwords, credit card details) by disguising as a trustworthy entity in electronic communication	Loss of customer trust, financial losses, potential regulatory fines, and damage to brand reputation
Malware [1]	Malicious software (such as viruses, worms, Trojans) designed to damage, disrupt, or gain unauthorized access to systems, networks, or devices	Data breaches, unauthorized access to sensitive data, operational disruption, and financial losses
Distributed Denial-of-Service (DDoS) Attacks [1, 2]	Overwhelming a website or network with excessive traffic to render it unavailable to users	Website downtime, loss of sales, damage to customer relationships, and increased costs for mitigation and recovery
Data Breaches [3]	Unauthorized access to and disclosure of confidential data, such as customer information, financial details, or intellectual property	Legal liabilities, financial losses, erosion of customer trust, and potential regulatory sanctions
Ransomware [1]	Malware that encrypts files on a victim's system, demanding a ransom to restore access	Data loss, potential financial losses due to ransom payment, downtime, and damage to business operations
Structured Query Language (SQL) Injection Attacks [4]	Insertion of malicious SQL queries into input fields to manipulate databases, potentially gaining unauthorized access to sensitive data	Exposure of sensitive information, data theft, financial damage, and loss of customer trust
Cross-Site Scripting (XSS) [4]	Attacks where malicious scripts are injected into trusted websites, targeting users by running scripts in their browsers without their knowledge	Data theft, user account compromise, reputational damage, and potential regulatory fines
Man-in-the-Middle (MitM) Attacks [4]	Interception and possible manipulation of communication between two parties (e.g., customers and e-commerce websites) without their knowledge	Interception of sensitive data, unauthorized transactions, identity theft, and financial losses

TABLE 3.2
Comparison of Existing Cyber Security Measures and Policies Across Different Regions (Sourced from Google)

Region/ Country	Cyber Security Measure/Policy	Focus Area	Effectiveness
USA	Cyber Security Enhancement Act, Federal Trade Commission (FTC) Act, and Payment Card Industry Data Security Standard (PCI DSS)	Data security, consumer protection, and online payment security	High effectiveness in financial sector but limited protection in cross-sectoral applications
European Union (EU)	General Data Protection Regulation (GDPR), Network and Information Security (NIS) Directive, and E-Commerce Directive	Data privacy, secure transactions, and digital rights management	Strong legal framework for data protection and consumer rights, although cross-border enforcement is complex
Australia	Australian National Privacy Act, Cybercrime Act, and Privacy Amendment Act	Privacy protection, cybercrime prevention, and e-commerce regulation	Effective at the national level but requires continuous updates to address emerging threats
Canada	Personal Information Protection and Electronic Documents Act (PIPEDA), and Anti-Spam Legislation (CASL)	Data protection, anti-spam measures, and online payment security	Moderate effectiveness; challenges with enforcement and adaptation to evolving threats
China	Cyber Security Law, E-Commerce Law, and Data Security Law	National security, data localization, and privacy protection	Strong regulatory framework but often criticized for limited transparency and oversight
India	Information Technology (IT) Act, Personal Data Protection Bill (Draft), and E-Commerce Rules	Data protection, consumer rights, and cybercrime control	Developing regulatory environment with ongoing efforts to align with global standards
Malaysia	National Cyber Security Policy (NCSP), Personal Data Protection Act (PDPA), and Digital Signature Act	Network security, data privacy, and online transaction safety	Relatively effective but needs more focus on public awareness and cross-sectoral coordination

3.1.3 Objectives of the Study

The principal aim of this study is to examine the cyber security obstacles in e-commerce and suggest approaches to reduce these hazards. Among the specific goals are the following:

- examine the different kinds of cyber security risks that impact online shopping;
- evaluate the efficacy of current cyber security regulations and guidelines;

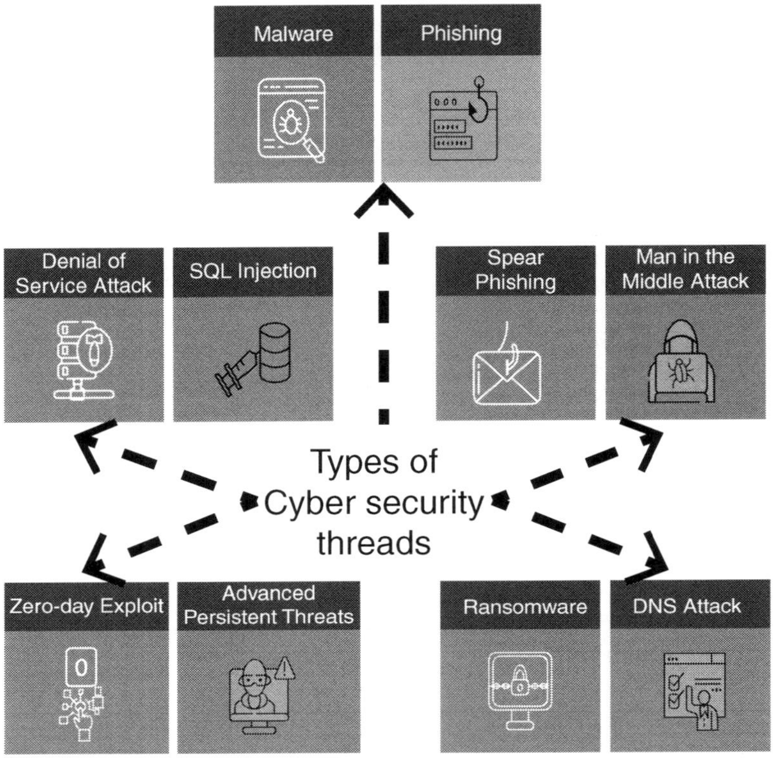

FIGURE 3.1 Diagram Illustrating the Common Types of Cyber Threats in E-Commerce (e.g., Phishing, Malware, DDoS attacks, and Data breaches).

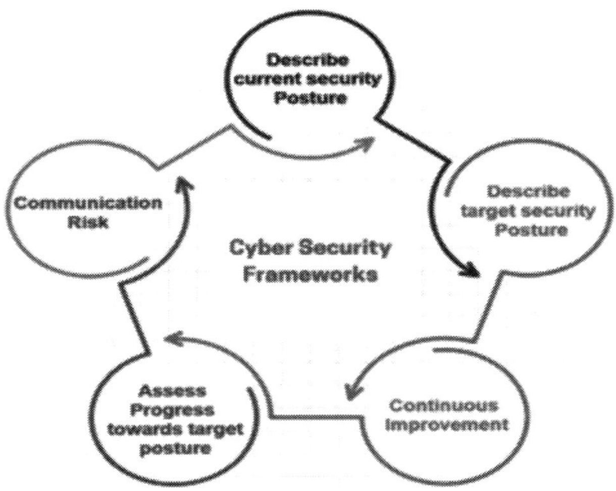

FIGURE 3.2 Framework of Cyber Security Measures and Policies for E-Commerce.

- determine new methods and technologies that can improve e-commerce cyber security; and
- make a framework recommendation for enhancing e-commerce security against existing and potential cyber threats.

3.1.4 Structure of the Chapter

The format of the chapter is as follows:

- An overview of previous studies on cyber security in e-commerce is given in Section 2, "Literature Review," which focuses on the different kinds of threats, contemporary methods, and legal frameworks.
- In Section 3, "Research Methodology," data collection and analysis techniques for cyber security issues in e-commerce are described.
- The study's findings are presented in Section 4, "Findings and Discussion," which also highlights important cyber security problems and e-commerce challenges.
- To improve cyber security in e-commerce, Section 5, "Recommendations," provides policy recommendations and strategic solutions.
- Section 6, "Conclusion," provides an overview of the main conclusions and recommendations for further study.

3.2 LITERATURE REVIEW

3.2.1 Overview of E-Commerce Growth and Cyber Security Challenges

The demand for convenience, growing internet penetration, and technological advancements have all contributed to the rapid growth of e-commerce worldwide. Due to its expansion, e-commerce is now a vital part of the digital economy, generating jobs, national growth, and import tax income. It also brings with it serious cyber security risks, such as identity theft, data breaches, and other types of cybercrime [9]. Cybercriminals' tactics are becoming more complex along with e-commerce platforms, so strong cyber security measures are required to safeguard private information and uphold customer confidence [10].

3.2.2 Cyber Threats in E-Commerce

3.2.2.1 Types of Cyber Threats

Cyber threats in e-commerce encompass a variety of malevolent actions, including the following:

- Social engineering attacks: manipulation strategies used to trick users into divulging private information, such as bank account information or passwords;
- Denial of service (DoS): these involve flooding servers with traffic, which disrupts services and causes downtime;
- Malware and ransomware: malicious software that can encrypt data or take down systems and demand a ransom to be released are known as malware or ransomware;

- Data breaches: unauthorized access to private data that could be used fraudulently, such as customer information;
- Phishing attacks: deceptive attempts to masquerade as reliable organizations in order to obtain sensitive information [10–12].

3.2.2.2 Impact of Cyber Threats on E-Commerce

Cyber security risks have a big impact on e-commerce because of the following:

- Financial loss: actual losses brought on by data theft, fraud, and fines;
- Reputational damage: the loss of brand value and customer trust as a result of a breach;
- Operational disruption: attack-induced downtime and disturbance that negatively impacts sales and customer satisfaction; and
- Regulatory penalties: amounts fined and imposed for breaking data protection laws [13, 14].

3.2.3 Emerging Technologies in E-Commerce Security

3.2.3.1 Blockchain

A decentralized ledger system made possible by blockchain technology improves transaction security, traceability, and transparency. Thanks to the detailed data logs and immutable transaction recording, fraud detection and investigation are made easier. Blockchain's adoption in high-volume e-commerce environments is limited by issues like scalability and high computational requirements, despite its advantages [15].

3.2.3.2 Artificial Intelligence and Machine Learning

In e-commerce security, artificial intelligence (AI) and machine learning are being utilized more and more for automated response systems, predictive analytics, and real-time threat detection. These tools lessen the possibility of breaches by quickly recognizing patterns in cyberattacks and taking appropriate action. However, their implementation can be expensive and technically difficult due to their high requirements for computational power and significant data inputs [16, 17].

3.2.4 Regulatory Frameworks and Policies

Cyber security in e-commerce is governed by a number of legislative frameworks and policies, including the following:

- The General Data Protection Regulation (GDPR): requires individuals in the EU to maintain their privacy and data protection;
- The Cyber security Information Sharing Act (CISA): incentivizes the US government and private sectors to exchange cyber threat intelligence;

- Payment Card Industry Data Security Standard (PCI DSS): guarantees the safe processing of credit card data during online transactions; and
- Consumer Protection Act (CPA) in different countries, such as the California Consumer Protection Act (CCPA): safeguard consumer rights and control online business practices [18, 19].

3.2.5 Gaps in Existing Research

Even though e-commerce security measures have advanced, there are still a number of research gaps.

- Inadequate attention to Small and Medium-sized Businesses: Despite their susceptibility to cyber threats, S mall and Medium-sized Businesses (SMBs) are underrepresented in research, which primarily focuses on large corporations;
- Lack of comprehensive cyber security models: Studies that already exist frequently do not have comprehensive models that incorporate organizational procedures, technology, and legal requirements;
- Limited cross-national analysis: Additional comparative research is required to determine the efficacy of various cyber security policies in various countries and areas; and
- Integration of emerging technologies: Additional study is required to determine how to incorporate blockchain, AI, and other technologies into current cyber security frameworks.

Risk Assessment Equation is as follows: Risk=Threat × Vulnerability × Impact

3.3 RESEARCH METHODOLOGY

3.3.1 Research Design

A descriptive and exploratory framework incorporating both qualitative and quantitative methods guides the research design. This method works well for comprehending complicated phenomena, especially when developing cyber security policies for various countries. The study looks into important cyber security-related factors like governmental infrastructure, legal frameworks, and technological advancements using comparative analysis and literature review.

Data are collected from a variety of sources, such as scientific journals, government reports as shown from Figure 3.3, policy documents, and cyber security databases, in order to investigate these issues. The triangulation of data is ensured by this all-encompassing approach, which improves the validity and reliability of the findings. Additionally, the study design places a strong emphasis on using secondary data analysis to extrapolate findings from earlier research on cyber security across seven different countries [20].

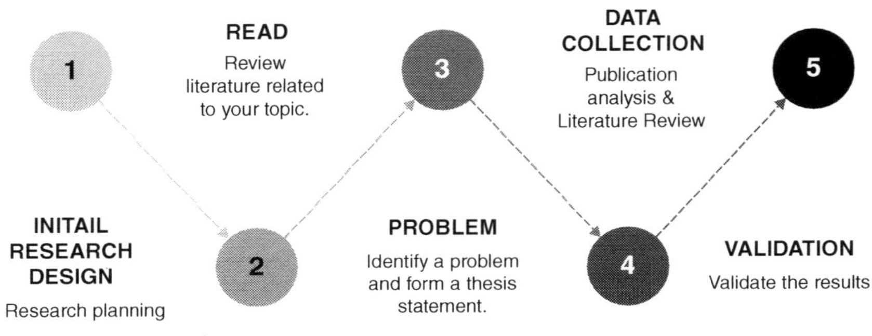

FIGURE 3.3 A Flowchart Showing the Research Design Phases, Starting with Data Collection, Data Analysis, and Comparison Between Countries.

3.3.2 Data Collection Methods

There were two stages to the data collection process, as follows:

- Primary data collection: Key informants, including cyber security specialists, legislators, and IT workers, were interviewed. Their experience implementing policies, the unique threats that their organizations face, and the metrics they use to assess the efficacy of cyber security frameworks were the main topics of discussion during these interviews.
- Secondary data collection: Information was acquired by reading through published reports, laws, and cyber security policy documents that were readily available. Countries with notable policies (USA, EU, Canada, Australia, China, India, and Malaysia) received particular attention. Websites run by governments, Elsevier, and Google Scholar were the sources of the secondary data.

The following were the tools used for gathering data:

- Surveys: To assess the efficacy of their cyber security policies, stakeholders from various countries were sent online and paper-based surveys.
- Documents review: In order to evaluate the coherence and applicability of the policies, important policy documents and cyber security frameworks were examined closely [21].

3.3.3 Data Analysis Techniques

For the Analysis of the Collected Data, the Following Techniques from Table 3.3 Were Used

- Thematic analysis: The major themes and trends found in the interviews and document analysis were categorized using thematic analysis, a qualitative technique. The themes centered on the characteristics,

TABLE 3.3
Summary of Data Collection Methods, Including the Sources of Primary and Secondary Data, Target Groups, and Instruments Used

Data Source	Method	Target Group	Instrument
Primary Data	Interviews	Cyber Security Experts	Structured Interviews
Secondary Data	Document Review	National Cyber Security Policies	Document Analysis
Surveys	Questionnaire	IT professionals, Policymakers	Online/Offline Surveys

difficulties, and implementation gaps of cyber security policies in the chosen countries.

- Comparative policy analysis: Using information from policy documents, a cross-national analysis was carried out with an emphasis on the institutional and legal frameworks. This made it possible for the study to pinpoint the variations and convergences in cyber security methodologies.
- Statistical methods: Descriptive statistics like means, frequencies, and percentages were applied to the quantitative data and as shown from Fig 3.4. This made it easier to measure the frequency of important cyber security practices and the effectiveness of various policies. Regression (2) analysis and other more intricate analyses were used to investigate the connection between cyber security risks and the efficacy of policies [22].

$$Y=\beta 0+\beta 1X1+\beta 2X2+\in \tag{3.1}$$

3.3.4 Limitations of the Study

This study faced several limitations, as shown from Table 3.4:

- Restricted national scope: Despite concentrating on seven nations, the study might not accurately reflect trends in cyber security policies worldwide. Language limitations and the lack of complete data prevented the inclusion of other important nations like South Korea and Japan.
- Data access restrictions: It was difficult to conduct a more thorough examination of the policies in those nations because some official cyber security documents were not readily available to the general public.
- Rapid evolution of cyber threats: The field of cyber security is developing quickly. Current policies might not be able to handle emerging cyber threats. As a result, the findings might only be applicable for a certain amount of time.
- Subjectivity in interviews: Depending on their roles and organizational affiliations, cyber security professionals' responses in interviews may be biased.

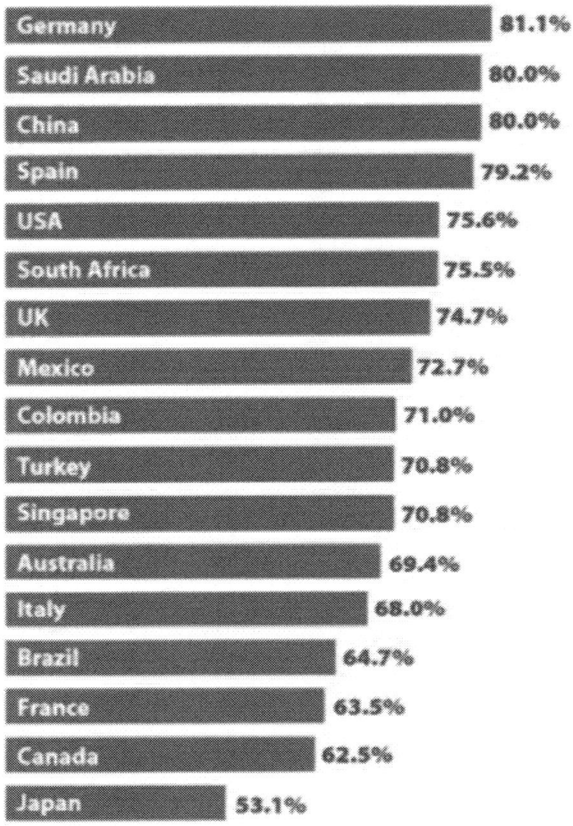

FIGURE 3.4 A Bar Graph Depicting the Frequency of Specific Cyberattacks Across the Seven Nations Studied.

TABLE 3.4
List of Study Limitations and Mitigation Strategies

Limitation	Description	Mitigation Strategy
Limited Scope of Nations	Focus on only seven nations	Expanding scope in future work
Data Access Constraints	Restricted access to government cyber security data	Use of public datasets
Evolution of Cyber Threats	Policies may become outdated	Ongoing monitoring of trends
Subjectivity in Interviews	Bias in expert opinions	Triangulation with secondary data

3.4 FINDINGS AND DISCUSSION

3.4.1 Key Cyber Security Issues in E-Commerce

Although they facilitate international trade, e-commerce platforms are vulnerable to a number of cyber security risks. These dangers have the potential to seriously harm a company's or a customer's finances and reputation.

3.4.1.1 Social Engineering and Phishing

One of the most common types of social engineering attacks that targets workers and customers in e-commerce is phishing attack. Attackers deceive people into divulging sensitive information, like credit card numbers, login credentials, or personal identification information, by sending them misleading emails, messages, or websites as from Fig. 3.5. Because e-commerce platforms handle so many financial transactions, they are frequently desirable targets [23].

Standard Equation: Return on Security Investment (ROSI)

$$\text{ROSI}=(\text{LossSaved}-\text{CostofSolution})/\text{CostofSolution} \quad (3.2)$$

This equation helps organizations quantify the effectiveness of cyber security solutions [24].

3.4.1.2 DoS Attacks

DoS attacks are intended to send an excessive volume of requests to e-commerce websites, crashing the system and rendering the platform unavailable to authorized users. DoS attacks have the potential to cause significant financial losses because they can disrupt services and cause customers to leave as shown from Fig 3.6 [25].

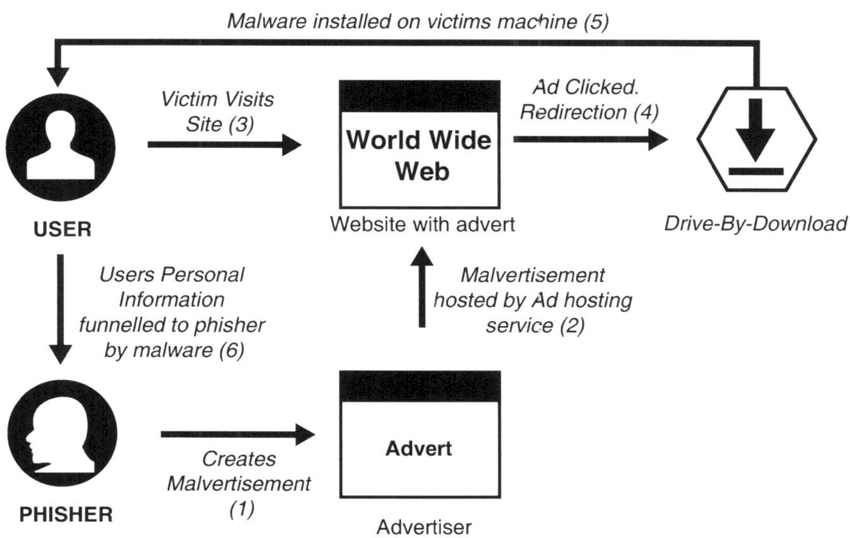

FIGURE 3.5 A Flowchart Demonstrating How Phishing Attacks Work, Highlighting Key Vulnerabilities in E-Commerce Systems.

3.4.1.3 Malware and Ransomware

E-commerce websites are susceptible to ransomware and malware attacks, which have the potential to compromise sensitive customer data, hold data hostage, or corrupt critical systems. The confidentiality, integrity, and availability of data may be impacted by these attacks as shown in Figure 3.7 [26].

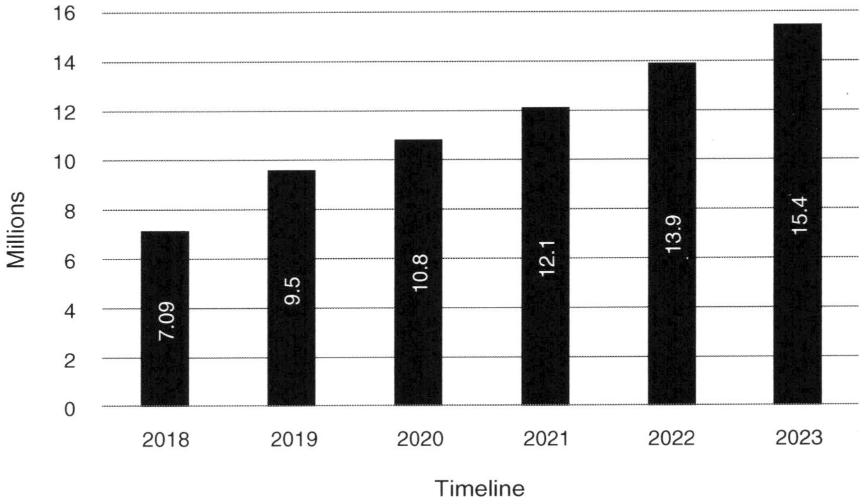

FIGURE 3.6 A Bar Graph Comparing the Frequency and Cost Impact of DoS Attacks on E-Commerce Sites Over a Period of Five Years.

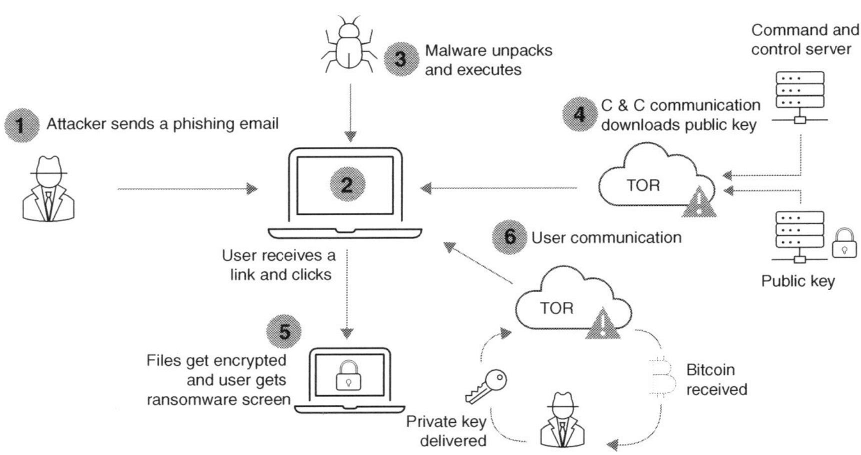

FIGURE 3.7 A Diagram Illustrating the Life Cycle of a Ransomware Attack on an E-Commerce System.

3.4.1.4 Data Breaches and Identity Theft

Sensitive consumer information may be exposed by data breaches, opening the door to fraud and identity theft. Because e-commerce platforms gather a lot of financial and personal data, hackers find them to be attractive targets. Publicized data breaches have the potential to damage consumer confidence and result in fines [27].

3.4.2 Challenges in E-Commerce Security Adoption

Even with the availability of cutting-edge cyber security technologies, implementing strong security measures is still difficult for many e-commerce businesses.

3.4.2.1 Technological Barriers

The cost and complexity of contemporary security technologies make it difficult for many small and medium-sized enterprises (SMEs) to implement cyber security measures. It's common knowledge that integrating firewalls, secure authentication procedures, and advanced encryption protocols into legacy systems is challenging as in Figure 3.8.

3.4.2.2 Organizational and Policy Challenges

Weak security adoption occurs even when cyber security solutions are available because of a lack of clear organizational policies, security awareness, and training. E-commerce platforms frequently put company expansion ahead of cyber security expenditures, which results in serious vulnerabilities going unfixed.

3.4.3 Role of Emerging Technologies

Because they offer innovative approaches to identifying, stopping, and mitigating cyberattacks, emerging technologies have the potential to significantly improve e-commerce security as shown from Table 3.5 and 3.6.

TABLE 3.5
Top Five E-Commerce Platforms That Have Suffered Major Data Breaches, With Information on The Number Of Records Compromised and The Financial Cost of The Breach

E-Commerce Platform	Year of Breach	Records Compromised	Type of Data Exposed	Financial Cost of Breach
eBay	2014	145 million	Names, Addresses, Passwords	$200 million
Alibaba	2019	1.1 billion	User IDs, Purchase History	Not disclosed
Amazon	2020	24 million	Email Addresses, Credit Card Information	$150 million
Target	2013	40 million	Credit Card Numbers	$162 million
Shopify	2020	200,000	Names, Emails, Payment Details	$50 million

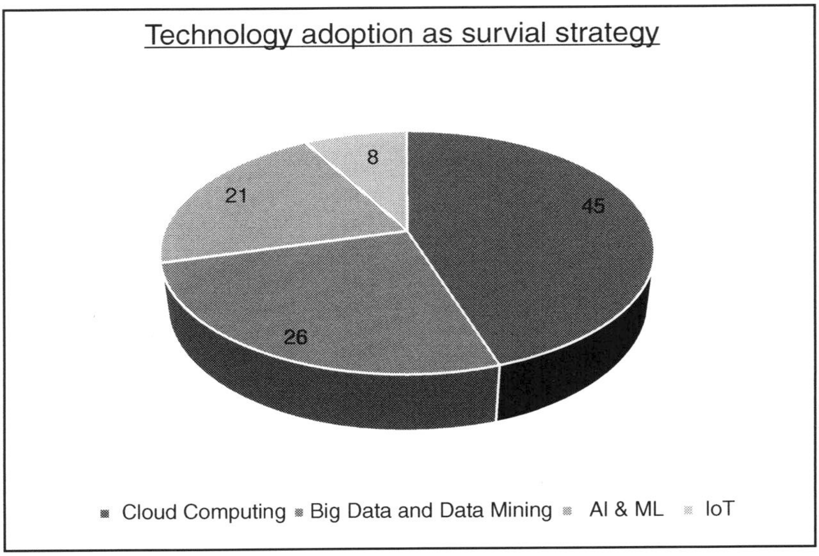

FIGURE 3.8 The Distribution of SMEs Facing Different Technological Barriers to Cyber Security Adoption.

TABLE 3.6
A Comparison of Common Cyber Security Policies in Large versus Small E-Commerce Businesses

Cyber Security Policy	Adoption Rate in Large Enterprises	Adoption Rate in Small Businesses	Challenges Faced by Small Businesses
Data Encryption Standards [Advanced Encryption Standards (AES), Rivest–Shamir–Adleman (RSA)]	95%	45%	High cost, complexity
Multifactor Authentication (MFA)	90%	35%	Integration challenges
Regular Security Audits	85%	30%	Limited budget, lack of in-house experts
Incident Response Plans	80%	25%	Low prioritization, inadequate training
Compliance with GDPR/CCPA	92%	40%	Lack of awareness, resource constraints

3.4.3.1 Blockchain for Secure Transactions

Blockchain technology offers safe, decentralized transaction records, which can improve the security of e-commerce. Because every transaction is documented in a distributed ledger, data manipulation by cybercriminals is impacted as in Figure 3.9 [3].

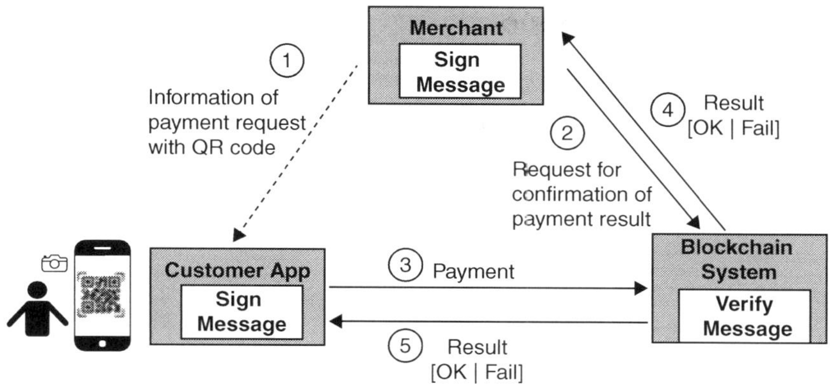

FIGURE 3.9 A Conceptual Diagram of How Blockchain Technology Ensures Secure E-Commerce Transactions.

Standard Equation: Blockchain Hash Function

$$H(x)=y$$

Here, H represents the cryptographic hash function applied to transaction data x, and y is the fixed-length output used to verify the integrity of the transaction [10].

3.4.3.2 AI-Driven Threat Detection

More intelligent threat detection systems that can recognize anomalous activity in e-commerce networks and anticipate possible security breaches are being created using AI. AI-based security systems improve their ability to detect threats in real time by learning from previous incidents.

3.4.4 Impact of Regulatory Policies

Regulations to safeguard customer data in e-commerce are being implemented by governments and international organizations more frequently. E-commerce platforms have been compelled by regulations like the GDPR to implement more stringent data protection protocols, especially with regard to the handling of customer data [14].

3.4.5 Case Studies and Practical Examples

Case Study 1: How Amazon Handles Data Breach Incidents

To defend against cyberattacks, Amazon has implemented a multilayered security strategy on its e-commerce platform. Following an attempted data breach in 2020, Amazon strengthened customer data encryption and tightened authentication procedures.

Case Study 2: Blockchain Integration with Alibaba

TABLE 3.7
The Key Regulations Affecting E-Commerce Cyber Security Across Different Regions (e.g., GDPR, CCPA)

Region	Regulation	Key Focus Areas	Compliance Requirements
EU	GDPR	Data Privacy, Consumer Rights, Data Breach Notifications	Strict encryption, user consent for data collection, breach reporting within 72 hours
United States (California)	CCPA	Consumer Data Rights, Data Security	Opt-out option for data sharing, protection against unauthorized access
China	China Cyber Security Law	Data Localization, Personal Data Security	Mandatory data storage in-country, stringent security audits
Australia	Privacy Amendment (Notifiable Data Breaches) Act	Data Breach Notifications, User Privacy	Report breaches affecting personal data, penalties for noncompliance
Canada	Personal Information Protection and Electronic Documents Act (PIPEDA)	Data Security, Data Breach Notifications	Consent for data use, mandatory breach reporting

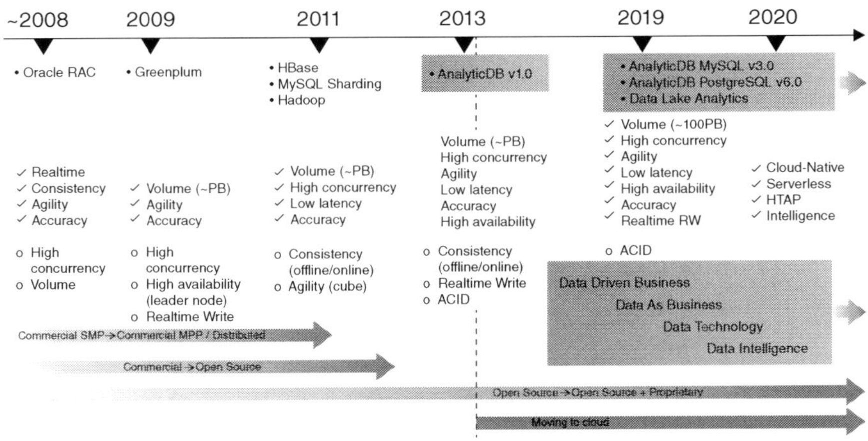

FIGURE 3.10 A Timeline of Alibaba's Integration of Blockchain Technology into its E-Commerce Platform.

In order to safeguard its supply chain and online transactions, Alibaba has incorporated blockchain technology, making sure that each stage—from order placement to delivery—is documented in an unchangeable ledger as in Figure 3.10. This has improved consumer confidence in cross-border transactions and decreased fraud as from Table 3.7.

3.5 RECOMMENDATIONS

3.5.1 Multifaceted Cyber Security Strategies

The integration of technical, operational, and policy-driven approaches is imperative in cyber security strategies to guarantee a comprehensive defense against dynamic cyber threats. Building resilience, exchanging real-time threat intelligence, and using cutting-edge technologies like AI and machine learning to identify abnormalities should be the main priorities.

The key aspects of a multifaceted strategy include the following:

- Proactive threat monitoring: Creating systems for ongoing network activity monitoring via Security Operations Centers (SOCs) is known as proactive threat monitoring. Relevant stakeholders should exchange threat intelligence.
- Defense in depth: Putting in place several levels of protection, including endpoint security, perimeter security (firewalls, intrusion detection systems), and encryption for data in transit and at rest.
- User education and awareness: To lower the risk of phishing and social engineering attacks, employees and end users must receive regular cyber security training as in Figure 3.11.

3.5.2 Policy Recommendations for Stakeholders

3.5.2.1 Governments

Governments ought to create and implement laws that deal with the digital economy as well as national security. It is essential to have clear cyber security guidelines that require data privacy protection, incident reporting, and baseline security measures.

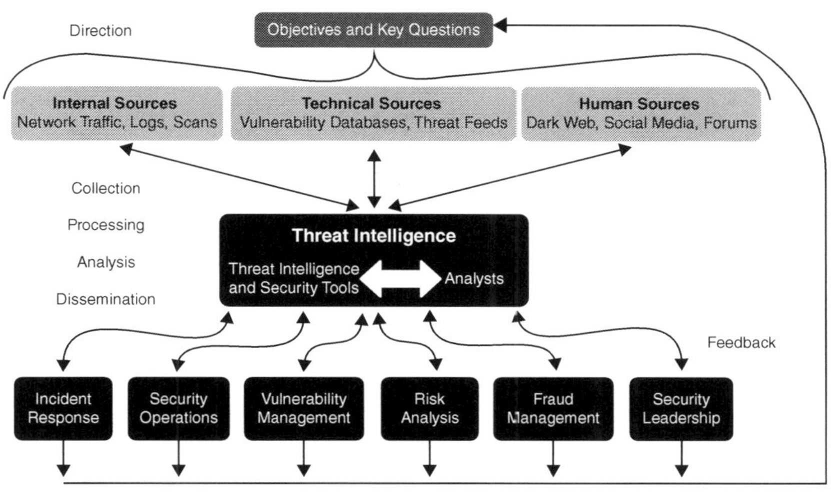

FIGURE 3.11 A Flow Diagram of Real-Time Threat Intelligence Sharing between Organizations and Government Agencies.

Important suggestions:

National cyber security frameworks: To specify roles and responsibilities in incident response, governments should create or update cyber security frameworks.

International collaboration: Information sharing and cooperative cyber security exercises should be addressed on an international level due to the cross-border nature of cyber threats.

3.5.2.2 E-Commerce Platforms

Cyberattacks frequently target e-commerce platforms due to the increased volume of transactions conducted online. It is imperative that these platforms implement best practices for security, such as the following:

- Completely encryption: It is recommended to encrypt all sensitive user data, including credit card information.
- Secure payment gateways: The PCI DSS should be followed by e-commerce platforms.

Measure	Description	Relevance to E-commerce
End-to-End Encryption	Encryption of data during transmission	Protects customer data
Secure Payment Gateways	PCI DSS compliance for transactions	Ensures secure payments
Two-Factor Authentication	Additional verification step for transactions	Reduces fraud risks

3.5.2.3 SMBs

SMBs frequently lack the funding necessary for strong cyber security defenses. Governments ought to offer discounted access to cyber security resources. SMBs should also put the following into practice:

- Cloud security: Since many SMBs depend on cloud services, multifactor authentication and strict cloud security policies should be implemented.
- Managed Security Services Providers (MSSPs): SMBs can benefit from the implementation of vital defenses like intrusion detection systems, firewalls, and real-time threat monitoring with the aid of cyber security outsourcing services.

3.5.3 Technological and Organizational Solutions

There are other ways to address cyber security issues besides technology. Organizational practices like transparent governance frameworks and cross-team cooperation are also very important. Organizational strategies must be complemented by technological solutions, as follows:

- Zero Trust architecture: This security concept highlights the idea that no actor—internal or external to the network—should be presumed trustworthy by default. Continuous verification is required, even within the network.
- Automation in threat response: By automating response processes, like incident response and automated patch management, threat mitigation times can be greatly lowered.

Technology/Framework	Key Benefit	Organizational Impact
Zero Trust Architecture	Continuous validation of network access	Improved security posture
Automated Threat Response	Faster incident mitigation	Reduced response time
Security Information and Event Management (SIEM)	Real-time analysis of security alerts	Centralized threat monitoring

3.5.4 Future Research Directions

Since the field of cyber security is constantly changing, new threats must be addressed through ongoing research. Among the crucial topics for additional study are the following:

- Quantum computing and cryptography: Current cryptographic algorithms may become outdated as a result of quantum computing. Quantum-resistant encryption techniques should be the subject of future research as from Table 3.8.
- AI and Machine Learning in Cyber Security: By instantly analyzing enormous volumes of data, AI-based solutions can completely transform threat detection. But it's also important to research adversarial AI, which is used by attackers to get around defenses.
- Internet of Things (IoT) cyber security: As IoT devices proliferate, the attack surface has grown. Research on the security of these devices is urgent, particularly in critical infrastructure.

Encryption and Decryption (AES):

$$C=EK(M)$$

where C is the ciphertext, E_K is the encryption function using key K, and M is the plaintext message.

RSA Algorithm (for public-key cryptography):

$$C=M\ e \bmod n$$

where C is the ciphertext, M is the message, e is the public exponent, and n is the modulus.

TABLE 3.8
Summary of Key Threats, Mitigation Strategies, and Their Effectiveness

Threat Type	Mitigation Strategy	Effectiveness	Example Implementations
Social Engineering	Employee Training, Awareness Programs	High	Regular phishing simulations, Security workshops
Denial of Service	AI-based Detection, Cloud-Based Mitigation	Medium	DDoS protection, Machine learning models to detect abnormal traffic patterns
Malware/ Ransomware	Multifactor Authentication (MFA), Encryption	High	Implementation of MFA in customer logins, End-to-end data encryption on platforms
Data Breaches	Blockchain for Secure Transactions	Medium to High	Blockchain-based payment gateways, Secure ledger technology for transactions

3.6 CONCLUSION

3.6.1 Summary of Key Findings

According to the study, e-commerce cyber security faces a variety of challenges, including malware, DoS attacks, social engineering attacks, and data breaches. Key findings show that although new technologies such as blockchain and AI-driven threat detection provide promising solutions, there are adoption, scalability, and implementation challenges, especially for SMBs and in developing nations. Strong data privacy laws and regulatory frameworks are necessary to reduce these risks, but their implementation will need international cooperation and coordination.

3.6.2 Contributions to Knowledge and Practice

This study adds the following to our understanding of academic research and practical applications:

- Academic contribution: It offers a thorough analysis of the cyber security environment in e-commerce, stressing important risks, countermeasures, and the function of cutting-edge technologies. By concentrating on both developing and developed markets and identifying particular opportunities and challenges in each context, the study closes a gap in the existing body of literature.
- Practical contribution: The results provide policymakers and e-commerce companies, especially SMBs, with useful insights. The study offers a road map for improving cyber security procedures in the e-commerce industry by presenting a multifaceted approach to cyber security that includes

TABLE 3.9
Cyber Security Readiness Framework for E-commerce Platforms

Readiness Level	Description	Required Actions	Compliance Standards
Basic	Minimal cyber security measures; vulnerable to common threats	Implement basic firewalls, anti-malware, regular software updates	International Organization for Standardization (ISO) 27001 (Initial), PCI DSS (Basic)
Intermediate	Moderate measures; protection against advanced threats	Deploy intrusion detection systems, establish incident response protocols	ISO 27001 (Certified), GDPR (EU), CCPA
Advanced	Comprehensive security; proactive threat hunting and monitoring	Integrate AI-based threat detection, regular penetration testing, full encryption	National Institute of Standards and Technology (NIST) Cyber Security Framework, PCI DSS (Advanced), System and Organization Controls 2 (SOC 2)
Optimal	Full-scale security; continuous monitoring and quick response	Real-time monitoring, decentralized ledger (blockchain), zero trust architecture	ISO 27032, GDPR, SOC 2, PCI DSS (Full)

technological solutions, regulatory compliance, and customer education as presented in Table 3.9.

3.6.3 Final Thoughts

The global market has undergone a revolution thanks to e-commerce, which presents countless growth prospects. But as it has grown, so too have the cyber security issues. To tackle these obstacles, a cooperative strategy incorporating technology, legislation, and instruction is necessary. Subsequent investigations ought to concentrate on numerical evaluations and international cooperation in order to create stronger security structures. With the help of cutting-edge technologies and comprehensive approaches, the e-commerce industry can reduce cyber security threats and guarantee long-term expansion.

REFERENCES

1. Alahakoon, U. M. D. B., S. M. T. N. Samarakoon, S. M. K. P. K. Sakalasooriya, Y. G. I. S. Wickramanayake, D. I. De Silva, and D. Cooray. Implementing E-"Commerce for the Future." *International Journal of Engineering and Management Research* 12, no. 5 (2022): 425–431.
2. Udayaprasad, P. K., J. Shreyas, N. N. Srinidhi, S. M. Dilip Kumar, P. Dayananda, S. S. Askar, and M. Abouhawwash. "Energy efficient optimized routing technique with distributed SDN-AI to large scale I-IoT networks." *IEEE Access* 12 (2024): 2742–2759.

3. Liu, Xiang, Sayed Fayaz Ahmad, Muhammad Khalid Anser, Jingying Ke, Muhammad Irshad, Jabbar Ul-Haq, and Shujaat Abbas. "Cyber Security Threats: A Never-Ending Challenge for E-Commerce." *Frontiers in Psychology* 13 (2022): 927398.
4. Shreyas, J., Dharamendra Chouhan, Sowmya T. Rao, P. K. Udayaprasad, N. N. Srinidhi, and S. M. Dilip Kumar. "An Energy Efficient Optimal Path Selection Technique for IoT Using Genetic Algorithm." *International Journal of Intelligent Internet of Things Computing* 1, no. 3 (2021): 230–248.
5. Jamra, Resty Kurnia, Bayu Anggorojati, Dana Indra Sensuse, and Ryan Randy Suryono. "Systematic Review of Issues and Solutions for Security in E-Commerce." In *2020 International Conference on Electrical Engineering and Informatics (ICELTICs)*, pp. 1–5. IEEE, 2020.
6. Abdelhafeez, Ahmed, J. Shreyas, and P. K. Udayaprasad. "A Fuzzy TOPSIS Method for Assessment Blockchain Technology Strategies." *Information Sciences with Applications* 1 (2024): 1–9.
7. D'Adamo, Idiano, Rocío González-Sánchez, Maria Sonia Medina-Salgado, and Davide Settembre-Blundo. "E-Commerce Calls for Cyber-Security and Sustainability: How European Citizens Look for a Trusted Online Environment." *Sustainability* 13, no. 12 (2021): 6752.
8. Reddy, Chethana S., Dharamendra Chouhan, P. K. Udayaprasad, N. N. Srinidhi, and S. M. Dilipkumar. "Geographic Routing Scheme for Resource and Communication Efficiency in the IoT Ecosystem Using Swarm-Intelligence Based BFO Algorithm." *Journal of Information Technology Management* 14, no. 1 (2022): 41–64.
9. Mishra, Alok, Yehia Ibrahim Alzoubi, Memoona Javeria Anwar, and Asif Qumer Gill. "Attributes Impacting Cybersecurity Policy Development: An Evidence from Seven Nations." *Computers & Security* 120 (2022): 102820.
10. Hendricks, Saarah, and Samwel Dick Mwapwele. "A Systematic Literature Review on the Factors Influencing E-Commerce Adoption in Developing Countries." *Data and Information Management* 8, no. 1 (2024): 100045.
11. Gupta, Srikant, Pooja S. Kushwaha, Usha Badhera, Prasenjit Chatterjee, and Ernesto D. R. Santibanez Gonzalez. "Identification of Benefits, Challenges, and Pathways in E-Commerce Industries: An Integrated Two-Phase Decision-Making Model." *Sustainable Operations and Computers* 4 (2023): 200–218.
12. Ethan, Oliver, and Hasnain Umar. "Comparative Analysis of E-Commerce Database Technologies: Blockchain, Scalable Storage, and Cyber Defense Strategies." Unpublished (2024). https://doi.org/10.13140/RG.2.2.34115.82723
13. Reddy, Vijay Mallik. "Data Privacy and Security in E-commerce: Modern Database Solutions." *International Journal of Advanced Engineering Technologies and Innovations* 1, no. 3 (2023): 248–263.
14. Khan, Abdul Wahid, Shah Zaib, Faheem Khan, Ilhan Tarimer, Jung Taek Seo, and Jiho Shin. "Analyzing and Evaluating Critical Cyber Security Challenges Faced by Vendor Organizations in Software Development: SLR Based Approach." *IEEE Access* 10 (2022): 65044–65054.
15. Kumar, Biresh, Sharmistha Roy, Kamred Udham Singh, Saroj Kumar Pandey, Ankit Kumar, Anurag Sinha, Shubham Shukla, Mohd Asif Shah, and Adil Rasool. "A Static Machine Learning Based Evaluation Method for Usability and Security Analysis in E-Commerce Website." *IEEE Access* 11 (2023): 40488–40510.
16. Kalkha, Hicham, Azeddine Khiat, Ayoub Bahnasse, and Hassan Ouajji. "The Rising Trends of Smart E-Commerce Logistics." *IEEE Access* 11 (2023): 33839–33857.
17. Chidukwani, Alladean, Sebastian Zander, and Polychronis Koutsakis. "A Survey on the Cyber Security of Small-to-Medium Businesses: Challenges, Research Focus and Recommendations." *IEEE Access* 10 (2022): 85701–85719.
18. Saeed, Saqib. "A Customer-Centric View of E-Commerce Security and Privacy." *Applied Sciences* 13, no. 2 (2023): 1020.

19. Albshaier, Latifa, Seetah Almarri, and M. M. Hafizur Rahman. "A Review of Blockchain's Role in E-Commerce Transactions: Open Challenges, and Future Research Directions." *Computers* 13, no. 1 (2024): 27.
20. Taherdoost, Hamed, and Mitra Madanchian. "Blockchain-Based E-Commerce: A Review on Applications and Challenges." *Electronics* 12, no. 8 (2023): 1889.
21. Liu, Xiang, Sayed Fayaz Ahmad, Muhammad Khalid Anser, Jingying Ke, Muhammad Irshad, Jabbar Ul-Haq, and Shujaat Abbas. "Cyber Security Threats: A Never-Ending Challenge for E-Commerce." *Frontiers in Psychology* 13 (2022): 927398.
22. Pan, Chung Lien, Ya Liu, and Yu Chun Pan. "Research on the Status of E-Commerce Development Based on Big Data and Internet Technology." *International Journal of Electronic Commerce Studies* 13, no. 2 (2022): 27–48.
23. Chawla, Neelam, and Basanta Kumar. "E-Commerce and Consumer Protection in India: The Emerging Trend." *Journal of Business Ethics* 180, no. 2 (2022): 581–604.
24. Cebeci, Sena Efsun, Kubra Nari, and Enver Ozdemir. "Secure E-Commerce Scheme." *IEEE Access* 10 (2022): 10359–10370.
25. Mishra, Alok, Yehia Ibrahim Alzoubi, Asif Qumer Gill, and Memoona Javeria Anwar. "Cybersecurity Enterprises Policies: A Comparative Study." *Sensors* 22, no. 2 (2022): 538.
26. Saeed, Saqib, Salha A. Altamimi, Norah A. Alkayyal, Ebtisam Alshehri, and Dina A. Alabbad. "Digital Transformation and Cybersecurity Challenges for Businesses Resilience: Issues and Recommendations." *Sensors* 23, no. 15 (2023): 6666.
27. Groenewald, Elma, and Osias Kit Kilag. "E-Commerce Inventory Auditing: Best Practices, Challenges, and the Role of Technology." *International Multidisciplinary Journal of Research for Innovation, Sustainability, and Excellence (IMJRISE)* 1, no. 2 (2024): 36–42.

4 Knowledge Representation of Various Business Models

Spoorthi M, Harshitha Suresh, Megha V, and Francesco Flammini

4.1 INTRODUCTION

Overview of cyber security business models: The forthcoming wireless communication era, labeled as the sixth generation (6G), is supposed to change the connectivity scenario to have the dream speeds, unbelievable latency, and a gigantic number of interconnected devices. Such groundbreaking advancement opens up multiple avenues and challenges, with one of the significant areas being cyber security. As billions of devices get connected, the scope of vulnerabilities increases, calling for innovative security solutions. In order to foster adaptive and predictive security, the cyber security business models of the 6G era will likely rely on cutting-edge technologies like artificial intelligence (AI) and machine learning. AI-based security systems will have the ability to automate most of the manual procedures and also respond to threats in real time. Therefore, the effectiveness as well as efficiency of cyber security can be increased. In addition, edge security services will become highly relevant as they offer enhanced protection at the source of data and ensure close processing that is secure to the devices. Quantum-resistant encryption techniques will also play a very important role in securing data against future threats from the increased capability of quantum computing [1, 2]. Moreover, the implementation of Zero Trust architectures, which require continuous verification of users and devices to minimize the risk of unauthorized access, will see a rise within the framework of the 6G ecosystem. Growing subscription-based security solutions that are scalable and customizable to meet the unique requirements of enterprises will be made possible by cyber security-as-a-service (CSaaS) models, which give organizations on-demand access to the newest security technology and knowledge [3]. By providing decentralized and immutable record-keeping, guaranteeing data integrity, and facilitating safe identity management, blockchain technology will significantly improve security. These developments do, however, pose a new set of challenges, including scalability to handle the vast number of connected devices, interoperability across numerous platforms, and legal compliance to protect user privacy. Cyber security business models must evolve to ensure a safe and reliable future for international communications as 6G technology changes the digital world [4].

 DOI: 10.1201/9781003540045-4

4.1.1 Importance of Knowledge Representation

Knowledge representation (KR) is a very important tool when learning, assessing, and navigating complex and changing risks within the organizations' cyber security business models. Specifically, this application of a systematic approach to categorizing elements will be helpful in the different processes and relationships among them in the cyber security frameworks so that it is possible to identify the vulnerabilities and the areas that really need improvement better. This systematic approach enables better decision-making with a comprehensive understanding of the interactions and influence of many variables. Moreover, it becomes easier to integrate leading-edge technologies such as machine learning and AI, which depend on well-defined data structures to identify and react to risks instantaneously [5].

More importantly, KR facilitates stakeholder engagement and communication by standardizing vocabulary and a framework for security strategy discourses. It requires easy understanding for coordination of efforts across departments from information technology (IT) and risk management to executive leadership and external partners. What is more, by providing succinct and comprehensive security measure summaries with effectiveness ratings, it helps ensure regulatory compliance. Finally, strong KR suggests that businesses should have strong cyber security defenses to protect assets and, by extension, confidence from customers through adjustments in the prevailing landscape of digital threats [6, 7].

4.2 NEW TYPES OF CYBER THREATS EXPECTED TO EMERGE IN 6G

4.2.1 Advanced Persistent Threats on Enhanced Networks

A number of novel cyber threats are anticipated to surface once 6G networks are implemented. These threats will take advantage of the new technological developments and complications brought about by 6G, building on the vulnerabilities that already exist. The following are some of the main categories of cyber threats that are probably going to gain prominence in 6G.

The capacity of Advanced Persistent Threats (APTs) to penetrate networks and stay hidden for extended periods of time makes them a formidable challenge to cyber security. These assaults are frequently extremely focused, trying to obtain sensitive data, interfere with operations, or accomplish strategic goals by targeting particular companies or industries. APTs are sophisticated because they are persistent and covert, using cutting-edge methods to get over conventional security measures. Usually, they start with a breach and then gain a foothold in the network from which the attackers systematically increase their access, obtain intelligence, and take out important data [8, 9].

With the introduction of 6G technology, network connectivity will undergo revolutionary changes that will be evident in the greatly increased data transfer rates, decreased latency, and seamless connectivity of a large number of devices. Although these developments hold great promise for a range of applications, they also bring with them new cyber security issues, especially with regard to APTs. Because to 6G's improved connectivity, there is an exponential increase in the possibility of data exfiltration, which makes it possible for hackers to send more data at previously unheard-of speeds. This ability shortens the window of opportunity for detection and response, which in turn speeds up the theft of confidential data. Furthermore, it is probable that the sophisticated methods utilized by APTs will progress in tandem with the technological breakthroughs introduced by 6G [10]. Attackers can employ elaborate evasion strategies, include making use of the greater bandwidth for more secret channels of communication, blending harmful activity into large volumes of normal traffic, and taking advantage of the more intricate network architectures [11]. In order to increase their stealth and persistence, APT actors may also exploit the integration of AI and machine learning in 6G networks, undermining the efficacy of conventional detection techniques.

4.2.2 AI-Powered Attacks

Latest on the cyber security attack list through AI: this method will be used to fuel further attacks by the malicious people who use AI combined with machine learning. These people gain the ability to design phish schemes in much more detailed and persuasive ways but easily get at vulnerabilities and create targeted and even precise strikes of a magnitude and precision never achieved before in history. Such machines have abilities to tailor their assaults around behavioral patterns, analyze vast volumes of data over possible targets, and implement on-time changes based on these analyses to evade traditional security systems. Threatscapes, therefore, appear evermore dynamic and difficult as defenders try to keep the upper hand with a form that rapidly shifts from traditional threats in conventional defense systems [12].

With 6G technology, AI-powered attacks are going to be amplified. This generation of networks is going to support millions of devices with extremely high data transfer rates and an AI-based network optimization and management system. While this brings several advantages, it also reveals new ways for AI-capable cyber threats to be exploited. For instance, embedding AI in 6G networks, into traffic management, resource allocation, and anomaly detection, provides an opportunity for hackers to hijack such systems [13]. Others can hack into the algorithms that AI employs and compromise the right utilization of network resources, lead to poor quality services, or even unauthorized access to private information [14].

As AI is deep rooted in the optimization and management of 6G networks, any compromise to these AI systems would have devastating effects. Hackers may use AI models that subtly alter AI systems but go unnoticed until much damage has been done. This calls for a strong security measure especially crafted to secure AI and machine learning, ensuring they are not manipulated or misused [15].

4.2.3 Quantum Computing Attacks

With the ability to solve complicated problems at speeds that classical computers could never match, quantum computing represents a revolutionary advance in processing capability. Although promising in many areas, this development seriously jeopardizes the security of existing cryptographic techniques. The majority of modern encryption techniques, like Rivest–Shamir–Adleman (RSA) and Elliptic Curve

Cryptography (ECC), rely on the difficulty of computing discrete logarithms and factoring big numbers, which are computationally impossible tasks for traditional computers. Nevertheless, employing methods such as Shor's algorithm, quantum computers can effectively resolve these issues due to their capacity for doing massive parallel calculations. Due to such capabilities, encrypted data that were previously thought to be secure may now be susceptible to quantum computer decoding, potentially resulting in critical data breaches [16].

Quantum computing has a variety of effects on 6G networks. Quantum-resistant encryption techniques are becoming increasingly important as 6G networks are built to protect data from potential quantum assaults [17]. It is anticipated that these networks will use cutting-edge encryption methods built to resist quantum attackers' high processing power. Opponents with access to quantum computer resources, however, might still provide serious threats. They might target data that were encrypted with techniques from pre-6G cryptography, which aren't meant to withstand quantum decoding. This implies that if quantum computing becomes more widely available, enormous volumes of previously encrypted data that are still in use or storage could be vulnerable to decryption. The amount of computer power needed for encryption and decryption procedures is another issue with quantum computing. Since quantum-resistant algorithms usually require more memory and processing power, 6G network performance and efficiency may suffer. A key factor in the design and implementation of these networks is ensuring that they can support the increased computing load while preserving high-speed connectivity and low latency [18].

4.2.4 Edge Computing and Internet of Things Exploits

By decentralizing computational resources closer to the source of data generation, edge computing and the growth of Internet of Things (IoT) devices will be essential elements of the 6G environment, enabling quicker data processing and real-time analytics. However, there are serious security risks associated with this increased decentralization and connectivity. Because edge devices and IoT sensors frequently have low processing and storage capacities and few solid security measures, they are prime targets for assaults [19]. By taking advantage of these devices' vulnerabilities, attackers may be able to gain access to the network and use it as a springboard to compromise more important systems or conduct a variety of other attacks [20]. In a 6G environment, where the number of connected devices is anticipated to expand dramatically, the effect of these vulnerabilities is amplified. Every gadget, be it an advanced edge computing unit or a basic sensor, is a possible point of attack. The sheer number and diversity of IoT devices—from industrial sensors to smart home devices—makes it more difficult to guarantee consistent security standards. Attackers may use these flaws to take control of a device, obtain unauthorized access, or steal confidential information. A single weak point in the network can be compromised to allow for the lateral movement of other compromised devices and systems. The possibility for distributed denial-of-service (DDoS) assaults, which are orchestrated using compromised IoT devices, is one particularly worrying vulnerability in the context of 6G. Attackers can build botnets that are capable of overloading network resources and causing major downtime and service disruptions by seizing control of a large number of vulnerable devices. Such assaults may be carried out faster and on a larger scale than ever before thanks to the high speed and high capacity of 6G networks, which increases their potential impact [21, 22].

4.2.5 High-Frequency and Satellite Attacks

6G technology is going to bring in the large-scale increase of the higher frequency band use and inclusion of satellite communications. This would increase the prospects of global communication and connectivity.

With the growing satellite communications in 6G, hackers will focus more on these systems. The dangers posed include eavesdropping on data transfers, private information interception, and disruptions of communication lines. These attackers may exploit vulnerabilities in security mechanisms of satellite links, and breaches may threaten the availability, confidentiality, and integrity of data [23].

The introduction of more frequency bands in 6G-terahertz, millimeter wave, and millimeter-wave frequencies brings with itself new issues for signal transmission as well as reception. Owing to the fact that they have higher frequencies, these kinds of wavelengths are more likely to get affected by surrounding influences or physical obstructions in the line of sight. Malicious actors can seize this advantage by using a jamming or spoofing technique. The physical characteristics of higher frequency signals could also lead to the development of new attack strategies that exploit scattering, diffraction, and reflection [24].

4.3 THE COST OF CYBER ATTACKS

Cost of cyberattacks in 2023 and targeted companies (Figure 4.1): Globally, ransomware attacks increased by 33% in a single year, from 1 in 13 organizations in 2022 to 1 in 10 in 2023. A cyber security website called "Check Point Research, 2023" claims that there are over 60,000 hacking attempts globally every year, or 1,158 attempted incursions per organization per week. The insurance sector is concerned about this growing trend (Figure 4.2).

Figure 4.2 shows a relationship between the type of data handled and the amount of assaults that occur; the most sensitive industries are determined to be those in education, healthcare, finance, services, IT, and government and military institutions [25]. The government/military, education, research, and healthcare industries are at the top of the list because of the volume of sensitive information they manage (Figure 4.3).

4.4 THEORETICAL FOUNDATIONS IN CYBER SECURITY FOR FUTURE BUSINESS MODELS

4.4.1 What is a Business Model?

Business models describe how companies create and deliver value to their customers, and how they get rewarded for doing that. The business model construct encompasses the product or service, the customer and market, the company's role within the value chain, and the economic engine that enables it to meet its profitability and

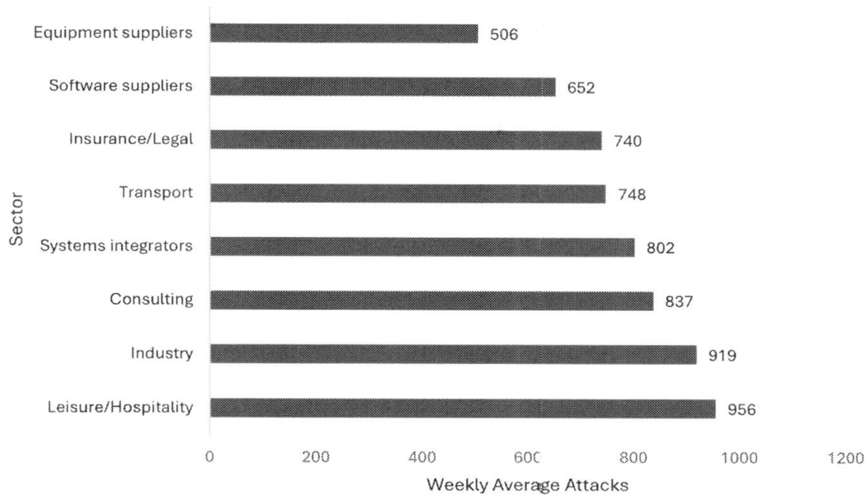

FIGURE 4.1 Cyber Security or Technological Trends.

Source: *Atlas* **magazine.**

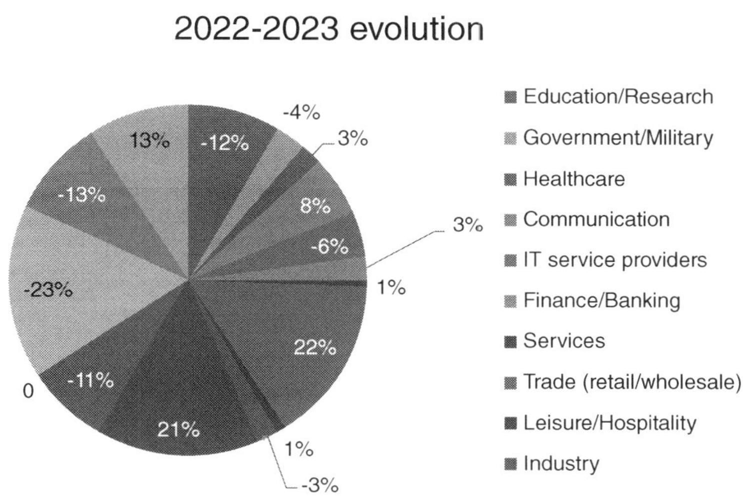

FIGURE 4.2 Cyber Security or Technology Themes.

Source: *Atlas* **magazine.**

growth objectives. Business models are often used by startups as modeling tools to help them design, prototype, and build their new ventures. They are also used by established companies to plan, develop, and support their innovation process. In this chapter, we use the business model construct to predict how companies' architectures and business model development processes will evolve into the future.

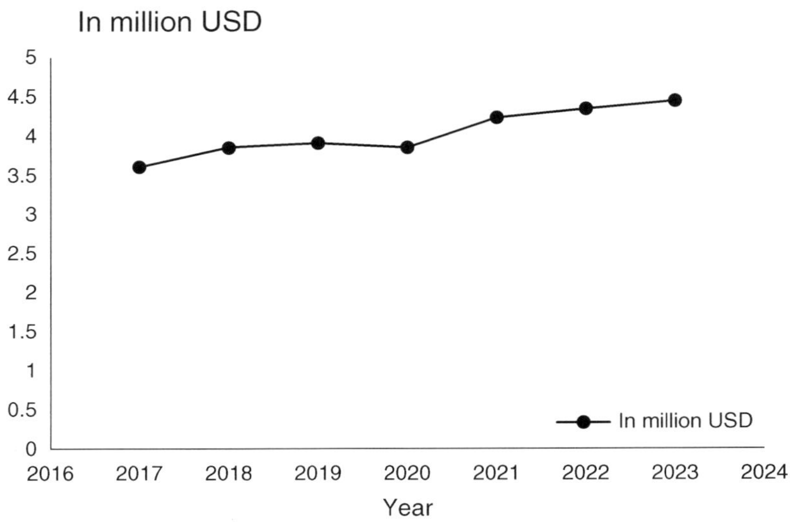

FIGURE 4.3 IBM Security Data Breach Report 2023.

Source: IBM.

Cyber security is a business facilitator that supports the viability and success of predicted business models in the digital age and not only an IT function. Setting the scene, this section, "Theoretical Foundations in Cyber Security for Future Business Models," sets the stage by defining cyber security and going over how it applies to various kinds of businesses, such as traditional companies, digital-native firms, and startups. It introduces the concept of cyber resilience and highlights the significance of businesses succeeding in a world where cyberattacks are a regular occurrence. Cyber threats are dynamic and always evolving. This section looks at the evolution of threats from simple viruses to sophisticated nation-state assaults and the background of cyberattacks [26, 27].

This section investigates how cyber security is evolving in light of future economic models, particularly those driven by cutting-edge technological advancements like 6G networks. First, a basic structure known as *Prevention, Detection, Response, and Recovery* (PDRR) is constructed (Figure 4.4). It is made expressly to address the unique problems that arise from the growth of networked IoT devices and ultra-reliable, low-latency communication that are expected in 6G contexts. Preventive measures include dynamic barriers to entry that adapt in real time based on contextual data and AI-driven intelligence on threats that can identify and proactively mitigate new dangers. Detection techniques swiftly spot irregularities and potential intrusions by utilizing advanced behavioral analytics and machine learning algorithms. The core of response capabilities comprises the AI-powered automated incident response methods, which allow for rapid containment and mitigation of cyberattacks while lowering the risk of human mistake. Recovery strategies primarily focus on recoverable designs that ensure business continuity. Technologies like

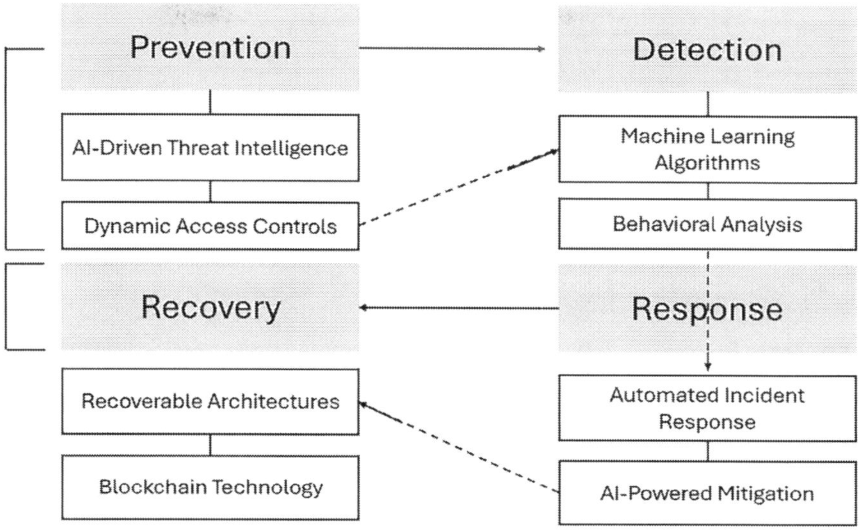

FIGURE 4.4 PDRR Framework for Cyber Security.

blockchain, which maintain data integrity and facilitate safe transactions, strengthen these designs [28].

4.5 FUNDAMENTALS OF KNOWLEDGE REPRESENTATION

The manner in which data, procedures, and ideas are arranged, structured, and conveyed inside an organization's framework is referred to as knowledge representation (KR) in business models. In cyber security, KR is the methodical process of organizing, arranging, and encoding data regarding cyber security risks, vulnerabilities, defenses, and other pertinent entities to make comprehension, reasoning, and decision-making easier. It includes a range of techniques and models for encapsulating intricate cyber security knowledge in a way that is both machine understandable and intelligible to humans.

4.5.1 Concepts and Techniques in KR

Entities, attributes, and relationships are essential parts of KR for cyber security that are used to describe and manage data concerning security threats, weaknesses, assets, and countermeasures. The following is a thorough explanation that includes mathematical illustrations and graphs.

(1) **Entities**

Fundamental components or commodities in the context of cyber security are called entities. They stand for the essential components that require management, supervision, or protection. The typical cyber security entities are as follows:

(a) **Assets**:

Anything that is valuable to the organization and must be protected is considered an asset in the context of cyber security and business. This value might be either material or immaterial, and it could have significance in terms of money, strategy, reputation, or compliance. The foundation of an organization's operations are its assets, which can take many different forms, examples include hardware, software, networks, systems, data, and intellectual property [28].

Significance: To guarantee the duration and integrity of corporate activities, assets must be safeguarded since they are the main targets of threats.

(b) **Threat actors**:

Threat actors are people, teams, or entities with the purpose and ability to take advantage of holes in networks or information systems. They might try to access data without authorization, interfere with services, pilfer intellectual property, or do other harm. Threat actors may be driven by a variety of factors, including monetary gain, political aspirations, and personal convictions. A few instances are nation-state actors, hackers, insider threats, and cybercriminal groups.

Significance: Recognizing threat actors is essential to creating suitable defense plans and anticipating possible points of attack.

(c) **Vulnerabilities:**

Vulnerabilities or weaknesses that can be used by adversaries to penetrate systems, procedures, or configurations. Examples include misconfigured systems, weak passwords, unpatched software, and software defects.

Significance: To lower the likelihood of successful attacks, vulnerabilities must be found and mitigated.

(d) **Events**:

Instances or occurrences pertaining to cyber security are called as events, examples include malware infestations, illegal access attempts, and security lapses.

Significance: Event monitoring and analysis facilitates the identification, handling, and avoidance of security incidents.

(e) **Controls:**

Controls are security procedures used to minimize risks and safeguard assets. Intrusion detection systems, access controls, encryption, and firewalls are a few examples [29].

Significance: In order to minimize vulnerabilities and safeguard assets from harm, controls are necessary.

(2) **Attributes**:

Properties or traits that characterize an entity are called attributes. They enable more thorough analysis and comprehension by offering more context and information about the items. Attributes in cyber security are shown in below representation:

For Assets:
Type: The asset's category (data, system, application, etc.).
Value: The asset's significance or value to the company.
Owner: The person or organization in charge of the asset.
Location: The asset's actual or logical location.
Criticality: The effect a compromised asset might have on company operations.

For Threat Actors:
Level of Skill: The threat actor's proficiency and power.
Motivation: The motivations (such as monetary gain or a political purpose) for the conduct of the danger actor.
Techniques: The threat actor's methods and equipment.
Tools: Specific software or hardware used by the threat actor.

For Vulnerabilities:
Severity: The possible consequences of an exploit of the vulnerability.
Exploitability: The vulnerability's ease of exploitation.
Impact: The possible harm brought forth by taking advantage of the weakness.

For Events:
Time: The precise day and time the incident happened.
Location: The site of the event.

For Controls:
Type: The control's category (preventive, detective, corrective, etc.).
Effectiveness: The control's capacity to reduce hazards.
Status of Implementation: Indicates if the control is planned, in progress, or already in place.

(3) **Relationships**:
Relationships describe the ways in which entities are connected to or interact with one another. They allow a thorough grasp of the cyber security ecosystem by offering context and connectivity across various entities. In cyber security, common relationship types include the following:

(a) **Association:**
Association is the process of connecting entities depending on how they interact or are connected. An illustration would be a vulnerability

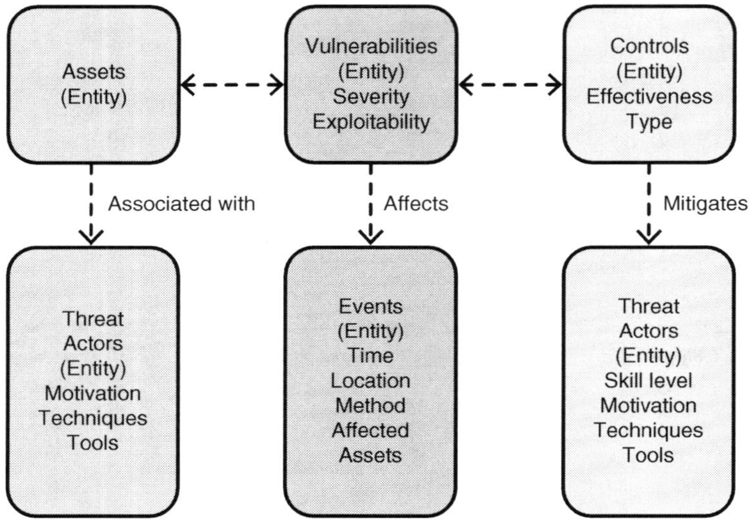

FIGURE 4.5 Entities, Attributes, and Relationships in Cyber Security.

connected to a particular asset (such as a software flaw in a certain program).

(b) **Dependency**:
Dependency represents how one entity relies on another to function correctly. An example of a condition-based control would be a firewall rule that depends on the network setup.

(c) **Impact**:
Describes how one thing affects another. Examples include an occurrence that influences an asset (like a database security breach).

(d) **Mitigations**:
Relationships where one entity lessens the risk provided by another are known as mitigation (Figure 4.5). An illustration of a security measure that reduces a particular vulnerability would be encryption, which lowers the possibility of data theft.

Example: Consider a streamlined cyber security scenario with the following entities and relationships:

1. **Assets**: A_1, A_2
2. **Vulnerabilities:** V_1, V_2
3. **Controls**: C_1, C_2
4. **Threat Actors**: T_1, T_2
5. **Events:** E_1, E_2

Edges can be used to visualize the relationships:

1. (A_1, V_1): Asset A_1 is combined with Vulnerability V_1.
2. (V_1, T_1): Vulnerability V_1 can be exploited by Threat Actor T_1.

3. (C_1, A_1): Control C_1 mitigates risks for Asset A_1.
4. (E_1, A_1): Event E_1 impacts Asset A_1.

4.5.1.1 Techniques in KR

KR techniques are ways to encode and store data so that computer systems may use them for logic, decision-making, and problem-solving purposes. These methods are chosen according to the needs of the application and the type of knowledge being represented, and their levels of complexity vary [29].

KR can be done using four main techniques (Figure 4.6), as follows.

(a) **Logical Representation**
Logical representation represents knowledge through formal logic. First-order and propositional logic are the two primary forms of logic that are employed [30]. As an illustration, logical representation can be used in cyber security to specify access control guidelines.
Propositional logic: Simple statements that can be either true or false are used in propositional logic. For example,

$$\text{Has Access}\left(\text{Server, Alice}\right) \rightarrow \text{True}$$

It is stated here that "Alice has access to the Server."
First-order Logic: By incorporating quantifiers and predicates, propositional logic can be expanded.

$$x\ (\text{User}\ (x) \rightarrow \text{Can}$$
$$\text{Access}\ (x,\ \text{Server}))$$
$$\text{User(x)} \rightarrow \text{Can Access (x, Server))}$$

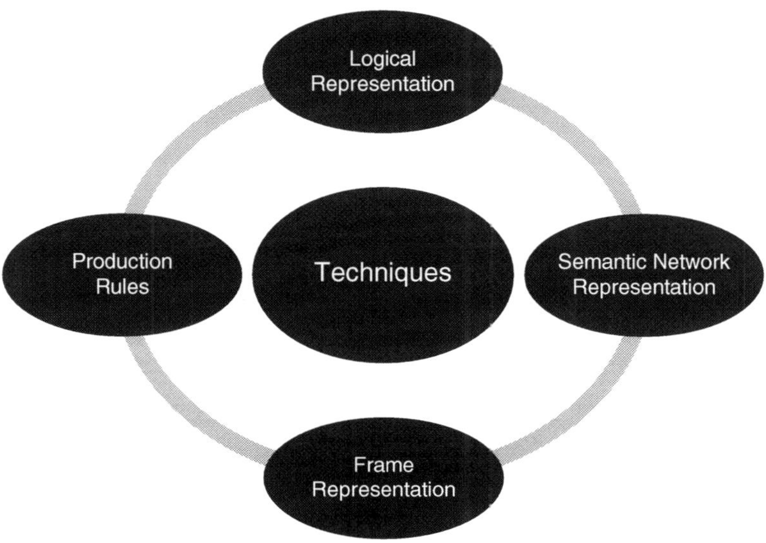

FIGURE 4.6 Techniques Used in Knowledge Representation.

It is stated here that "All users can access the Server."

(b) **Semantic Networks**

Graph structures are used by Semantic Network Representation to express knowledge. Entities are represented by nodes, while relationships between entities are shown by edges. As an illustration, a semantic network in cyber security can depict the connections between various threat categories and their defenses.

Nodes: Symbolize entities such as "Malware," "Firewall," "User."

Edges: Stand for connections like "has access to," "is mitigated by," etc.

Graph Representation:

$$\text{Malware} \xrightarrow{\text{is mitigated by}} \text{Firewall}$$

$$\text{User} \xrightarrow{\text{has access to}} \text{Server}$$

(c) **Frame Representation**

Stereotypical circumstances are represented using organized templates, or frames, in Frame Representation. Slots, or attributes, and their values make up each frame.

Example: An incident response process in cyber security can be represented by a frame.

Frame: Incident Response

Slots:

- Incident Class: Phishing
- Recognition Approach: Email Filter
- Response Action: Quarantine Email

Mathematical Representation:

$$\text{Incident Response} = \{\text{Incident Class: Phishing, Recognition Approach: Email Filter, Response Action: Quarantine Email}\}$$

(d) **Production Rules**

Conditional statements that express knowledge as "if–then" rules are known as production rules. They are employed to deduce judgments or courses of action based on specific circumstances. As an illustration, production principles in cyber security can be applied to intrusion detection.

Rule: An alert should be generated if more than 100 attempts are made to log in unsuccessfully.

$$\text{IF Unsuccessful Login Attempts} > 100 \text{ THEN Trigger Alert}$$

4.6 BUSINESS MODEL FRAMEWORKS

Structured tools known as business model frameworks assist firms in methodically comprehending, creating, and evaluating their business models. Yves Pigneur and Alexander Osterwalder created the Business Model Canvas, which is one of the most popular frameworks. Customers, offer, facilities, and financial viability are the four fundamental components of a business that are covered by the Business Model Canvas, a visual chart with a total of nine essential, interrelated building blocks (Figure 4.7), which are as follows:

1. Customer segments: individuals or groups that the company targets
2. Value propositions: goods and services that add value for clientele groups
3. Channels: ways in which the value proposition is communicated to clients
4. Customer relationships: kinds of connections a business makes with its clientele
5. Revenue streams: the sources of money for every category of customers
6. Key resources: vital resources needed to fulfil the value proposition
7. Key activities: essential steps that the business needs to execute to run well
8. Key partnerships: a network of partners and suppliers that support the viability of the business plan
9. Cost structure: all expenses incurred in running the company.

4.6.1 Business Model Framework in Cyber Security

Organizations can systematically design, analyze, and improve their cyber security services by applying business model frameworks to the cyber security sector. Cyber security businesses can improve their operations, target markets, and value propositions by employing this methodical approach to handle the difficulties associated with safeguarding digital assets. The nine components that comprise the cyber security Business Model Canvas are described further as follows:

- **Customer segments:** Knowing your customer segmentation is essential when it comes to cyber security. Cyber security firms cater to a wide range

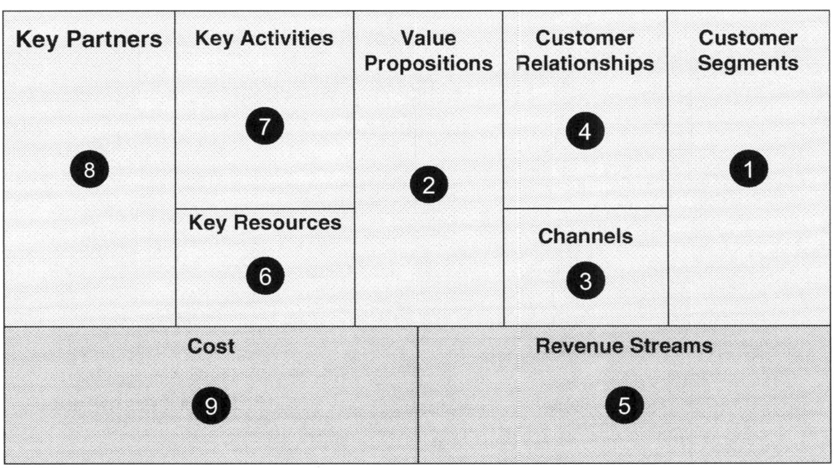

FIGURE 4.7 Framework for Business Model Canvas.

of customers, including government organizations, big businesses, small and medium-sized businesses (SMBs), and private citizens.

- **Value propositions:** Securing the confidentiality, integrity, and safety of digital assets is at the center of cyber security's value propositions.
- **Channels:** Various segments receive cyber security solutions through efficient ways. Online platforms serve individual consumers and SMBs, while direct sales teams provide specialized services to governments and businesses. Relationships with resellers broaden the market, and webinars are a great way to establish credibility and leadership in the field.
- **Customer relationships:** For cyber security organizations, cultivating and sustaining excellent client connections is essential. They frequently use specialized account managers to offer large businesses and government clients individualized support, making sure these clients receive customized solutions and continuous care. Automated services, such self-service portals, provide ease and quick support to individual customers and small and medium-sized enterprises (SMEs).
- **Revenue streams:** Cyber security companies generate income from a variety of sources, including license fees for proprietary technology, consulting charges for advisory services, subscription costs for software and services, and training fees for certification courses.
- **Key resources**: Advanced technology, knowledgeable cyber security specialists, intellectual property, and a strong infrastructure are important resources. Threat detection techniques, security systems, data centers, patents, and system and organization controls (SOCs) are crucial elements.
- **Key activities:** Research and development (R&D) for new security solutions, ongoing threat monitoring, incident response, marketing and sales, and customer service are all considered core tasks. These guarantee innovation, quick attack mitigation, real-time breach discovery, and ongoing client pleasure.
- **Key partnerships:** Strong connections are essential, and these can include those in the fields of technology, business, education, and with hardware/software vendors. These connections facilitate the integration of solutions, knowledge sharing, research assistance, and resource acquisition.
- **Cost structure:** Costs incurred by cyber security companies include personnel wages and benefits, R&D investments, operating costs for SOCs and data centers, sales and marketing expenses, and costs associated with complying with regulations.

4.6.2 Types of Cyber Security Business Models

(a) **Product-based model**

Product-based cyber security businesses create and market hardware, software, or cloud-based solutions that fend off online attacks. Symantec, McAfee, Palo Alto Networks, Cisco, and Fortinet are important companies in this context. These businesses provide a broad range of goods, including

TABLE 4.1
Business Model for a Cyber Security Company

Key Partners (8)	Key Activities (7)	Value Propositions (2)	Customer Relationships (4)	Customer Segments (1)
Technology partners (hardware/software vendors)	Threat detection and incident response	Comprehensive security solutions	Dedicated account managers	Enterprises (large, medium-sized)
Threat intelligence providers	Security solution development and maintenance	Data protection and privacy	24/7 customer support	Government agencies
Regulatory bodies and industry organizations	Customer onboarding and training	Threat intelligence and real-time threat response	Regular security updates and patches	Financial institutions
Academic and research institutions	R&D	User-friendly and scalable solutions	Training and certification programs	Healthcare providers
				SMBs
			Customer success teams	Individual consumers

	Key Resources (6)		Channels (3)	
	Threat intelligence databases		Direct sales force	
	Advanced security technologies and infrastructure		Online sales (website, e-commerce platforms)	
	Research and development team		Managed service providers (MSPs)	
	Intellectual property and patents		Industry events and webinars	

Cost (9)	Revenue Streams (5)
Salaries for cyber security professionals and R&D staff	Subscription-based services (monthly/annual)
Technology infrastructure and maintenance	One-time license fees
Marketing and sales expenses	Managed security service fees
Compliance and certification costs	Consulting and implementation services
	Training and certification fees

sophisticated threat detection systems, firewalls, and antivirus software. Cloud-based solutions and the integration of AI and machine learning for improved threat detection and response are becoming more popular, according to market trends. Product-based models frequently find success when their performance is built on their ability to remain ahead of hackers and innovate continuously, that is:

$$\text{Product Success} = \text{Invention} + \text{Threat Intelligence} + \text{Customer Collaboration}$$

(b) **Service-based models**

Security system and device monitoring and management can be outsourced using service-based models like Managed Security Service Providers (MSSPs). These services include vulnerability management, incident response, and security event monitoring [28, 29]. For businesses without the funds to keep an internal security team, MSSPs provide an affordable alternative. In contrast to product-based models, service-based models provide continuous support and knowledge, responding to new risks and guaranteeing legal compliance. Customized security solutions are what have made MSSPs like SecureWorks and IBM Security so well known. Service-based models, as opposed to product-based ones, frequently entail continuing administration and maintenance by the service provider. The following succinctly describes the comparison with product-based models:

$$\text{Service-Based} \rightarrow \text{Continuing Support}$$
$$\text{Product-Based} \rightarrow \text{One-Time Setup}$$

(c) **Subscription and S**oftware-as-a-Service **Model**

The way that businesses purchase and implement security solutions has changed dramatically with the emergence of subscription-based and software-as-a-service (SaaS) models in cyber security. These approaches offer subscription-based access to protection software and services, frequently housed in the cloud. Reduced initial expenses, scalability, and frequent upgrades are advantages. Nevertheless, issues like dependence on outside providers and worries about data privacy continue to exist. Businesses looking for flexibility and adaptability in their safety record may find the SaaS model to be an appealing alternative due to its ability to expedite implementation and integrate with current systems. The following formula can be used to express the value propositions of membership and SaaS models:

$$\text{SaaS Value} = (\text{Scalability} \times \text{Flexibility}) \,/$$

$$\text{Upfront cost}$$

4.7 HYBRID MODEL

Hybrid models take advantage of the benefits of both product- and service-based approaches. For example, a business may employ a product-based firewall and contract with an MSSP for threat intelligence and security information and event management (SIEM). Successful hybrid model case studies, like Cisco's managed privacy services, show that this strategy may offer complete security solutions while freeing up business owners to focus on their core competencies. The hybrid model's efficacy can be expressed as follows:

$$\text{Hybrid Model} = \text{Product-based solutions} + \text{Service-based solutions}.$$

4.8 CONCLUSION

The depiction of cyber security knowledge and business models is a complex task that requires an integrated approach. Because cyber dangers are dynamic, requiring transdisciplinary knowledge, and requiring constant adaptation and standardization, these models are intrinsically complicated. It is essential to effectively capture and communicate this complexity in order to establish resilient cyber security policies that are capable of keeping up with changing threats and technological developments. R&D in a number of important areas will be necessary in the future to address the difficulties in portraying cyber security business models and expertise. These include creating interdisciplinary frameworks that integrate knowledge from various fields to develop holistic cyber security models, leveraging AI and machine learning to create models that continuously learn and update themselves based on new data and threats, and developing comprehensive and standardized ontologies that can adapt to the rapidly evolving cyber security landscape. Furthermore, standardization efforts are essential for creating industry-wide protocols for threat intelligence and data exchange, and behavioral analyses are essential to improve the efficacy of cyber security strategies by assisting in the prediction and mitigation of human-related security threats.

REFERENCES

[1] Spoorthi, M., R. Hegde, and S. M. Soumyasri. "Social Engineering Threat: Phishing Detection using Machine Learning Approach." In *2023 IEEE 3rd Mysore Sub Section International Conference (MysuruCon)*, Hassan, India, pp. 1–7. 2023. https://doi.org/10.1109/MysuruCon59703.2023.10397016.

[2] Pooja, M. R., and M. Spoorthi. "A Review on Cyber Crimes During Pandemic of COVID-19." *Journal of Network Security and Data Mining* 6, no. 3 (2023): 1–6.

[3] Gururaj, H. L., Tanuja Kayarga, Francesco Flammini, and Dalibor Dobrilovic, eds. *Federated Learning Techniques and Its Application in the Healthcare Industry*. World Scientific, 2024.

[4] Spoorthi, M., H. L. Gururaj, V. Ambika, V. Janhavi, and H. Najmusher. "Impacts of Social Engineering on E-Banking." In *Social Engineering in Cybersecurity*, pp. 85–118. CRC Press, 2024.

[5] Spoorthi, M., and H. L. Gururaj. "Federated Learning and Its Classifications." In *Federated Learning Techniques and Its Application in the Healthcare Industry*, pp. 27–53. 2024. https://doi.org/10.1142/13722

[6] Spoorthi, M., and H. L. Gururaj. "Federated Learning and Its." *Federated Learning Techniques and Its Application in the Healthcare Industry* (2024): 27.

[7] Ambika, V., M. Spoorthi, and A. D. Radhika. "Role of Social Engineering in Cyber Security." In *Recent Trends in Computational Sciences*, pp. 250–256. CRC Press, 2023.

[8] Aranda, Juan, Erwin J. Sacoto Cabrera, Daniel Haro Mendoza, and Fabián Astudillo Salinas. "5G Networks: A Review from the Perspectives of Architecture, Business Models, Cybersecurity, and Research Developments." *Novasinergia* 4 (2021).

[9] Gomes, Julius Francis, Marika Iivari, Petri Ahokangas, Lauri Isotalo, Bengt Sahlin, and Jan Melén. "Cyber Security Business Models in 5g." *A Comprehensive Guide to 5G Security* (2018): 99–116.

[10] Islam, Md Toriqul, and Ridoan Karim. "Cybersecurity and Integrated Business Models." In *Integrated Business Models in the Digital Age: Principles and Practices of Technology Empowered Strategies*, pp. 3–46. Cham: Springer International Publishing, 2022.

[11] Schütz, Florian, Bastian Spierau, Florian Rampold, Robert C. Nickerson, and Simon Trang. "Chasing Cyber Security Unicorns: A Taxonomy-based Analysis of Cyber Security Start-ups' Business Models." (2023). ECIS 2023 Research Papers. 262. https://aisel.aisnet.org/ecis2023_rp/262

[12] Jacobs, P. C., S. H. von Solms, and M. M. Grobler. "Towards a Framework for the Development of Business Cybersecurity Capabilities." *The Business & Management Review* 7, no. 4 (2016): 51.

[13] Atoum, Issa, Ahmed Otoom, and A. Otoom. "A Classification Scheme for Cybersecurity Models." *International Journal of Security and Its Application* 11, no. 1 (2017): 109–120.

[14] Thakur, Kutub, Meikang Qiu, Keke Gai, and Md Liakat Ali. "An Investigation on Cyber Security Threats and Security Models." In *2015 IEEE 2nd International Conference on Cyber Security and Cloud Computing*, pp. 307–311. IEEE, 2015.

[15] Radanliev, Petar, Dave De Roure, Jason R. C. Nurse, Razvan Nicolescu, Michael Huth, Stacy Cannady, and Rafael Mantilla Montalvo. "Integration of Cyber Security Frameworks, Models and Approaches for Building Design Principles for the Internet-of-Things in Industry 4.0." In *Living in the Internet of Things: Cybersecurity of the IoT-2018*, pp. 1–6. IET, 2018.

[16] Rabii, Anass, Saliha Assoul, Khadija Ouazzani Touhami, and Ounsa Roudies. "Information and Cyber Security Maturity Models: A Systematic Literature Review." *Information & Computer Security* 28, no. 4 (2020): 627–644.

[17] Dube, Durga Prasad, and R. P. Mohanty. "Towards Development of a Cyber Security Capability Maturity Model." *International Journal of Business Information Systems* 34, no. 1 (2020): 104–127.

[18] Rea-Guaman, Angel Marcelo, Tomás San Feliu, Jose A. Calvo-Manzano, and Isaac Daniel Sanchez-Garcia. "Comparative Study of Cybersecurity Capability Maturity Models." In *Software Process Improvement and Capability Determination: 17th International Conference, SPICE 2017, Palma de Mallorca, Spain, October 4–5, 2017, Proceedings*, pp. 100–113. Springer International Publishing, 2017.

[19] Kosutic, Dejan, and Federico Pigni. "Cybersecurity: Investing for Competitive Outcomes." *Journal of Business Strategy* 43, no. 1 (2022): 28–36.

[20] Niemimaa, Marko, Jonna Järveläinen, Marikka Heikkilä, and Jukka Heikkilä. "Business Continuity of Business Models: Evaluating the Resilience of Business Models for Contingencies." *International Journal of Information Management* 49 (2019): 208–216.

[21] Spoorthi, S., N. Rakshitha, and K. S. Chandraprabha. "Cost Optimization for Migration of Data in Cloud Data Centers." In *Emerging Research in Computing, Information, Communication and Applications: ERCICA 2020*, Volume 2, pp. 279–287. Springer, 2022.

[22] Bujari, Armir, Marco Furini, Federica Mandreoli, Riccardo Martoglia, Manuela Montangero, and Daniele Ronzani. "Standards, Security and Business Models: Key Challenges for the IoT Scenario." *Mobile Networks and Applications* 23 (2018): 147–154.

[23] Prause, Gunnar. "Sustainable Business Models and Structures for Industry 4.0." *Journal of Security & Sustainability Issues* 5, no. 2 (2015).

[24] Wolter, Christian, Michael Menzel, Andreas Schaad, Philip Miseldine, and Christoph Meinel. "Model-Driven Business Process Security Requirement Specification." *Journal of Systems Architecture* 55, no. 4 (2009): 211–223.

[25] Gururaj, H. L., M. Spoorthi, V. Ravi, J. Shreyas, and K. S. Roy. "Foundations of Cybersecurity." In *Securing the Future. SpringerBriefs in Applied Sciences and Technology.* Cham: Springer, 2024. https://doi.org/10.1007/978-3-031-63781-0_1

[26] Wolter, Christian, Michael Menzel, Andreas Schaad, Philip Miseldine, and Christoph Meinel. "Model-Driven Business Process Security Requirement Specification." *Journal of Systems Architecture* 55, no. 4 (2009): 211–223.

[27] Joshi, James B. D., Walid G. Aref, Arif Ghafoor, and Eugene H. Spafford. "Security Models for Web-Based Applications." *Communications of the ACM* 44, no. 2 (2001): 38–44.

[28] Vlasov, M. P., A. K. Modenov, and O. V. Harchenko. "Modelling of the Supply Chain Planning for the Business and Economic Security." *International Journal of Supply Chain Management* 9, no. 3 (2020): 750–756.

[29] Gururaj, H. L., M. Spoorthi, V. Ravi, J. Shreyas, and K. S. Roy. "Compliance and Governance in Zero Trust." In *Securing the Future. Springer Briefs in Applied Sciences and Technology.* Cham: Springer, 2024. https://doi.org/10.1007/978-3-031-63781-0_5

[30] Ghelani, Diptiben. *Cyber Security, Cyber Threats, Implications and Future Perspectives: A Review.* Authorea Preprints, 2022.

5 Reactive versus Proactive Cyber Security and Real-Time Threat Protection

Subramanya V Odeyar, Thejaswini K M, Lolakshi P K, and Chaithra K N

5.1 INTRODUCTION

Cyber security is the practice of protecting systems, networks, and programs from digital threats [1]. These attacks often target sensitive information, seek financial gain, or disrupt business operations. As technology continues to advance at a breathtaking pace, the landscape in this field also keeps on changing therefore calling for strong security measures.

Cyber security domains include data security, network security, software security, and operational security [2]. Cyber security is a measure of the practice, procedure, and tools implemented to protect the unauthorized access to computers, servers, mobile devices, electronic systems, and entities which store, transmit, and process information of various kinds [3].

As the globe becomes more interconnected, the requirement of cyber security involves numerous key concerns for people, businesses, and governments. Increased reliance on digital systems and the internet has given rise to ways of being more susceptible to cyber threats that are more frequent and sophisticated in nature [4]. Nevertheless, some of the major reasons for the prime place of cyber security in today's society are as follows:

1. **Protection of sensitive data:** Huge amounts of personal, financial, and business data are flowing through cyberspace and online storage facilities; hence, cyber security assumes a prominent place in terms of protecting these against unauthorized access and breaches [5].
2. **Business continuity:** A cyberattack may be disastrous for business operations, with the sufferers incurring huge losses, both in terms of finance and reputation. Effective cyber security is required to sustain business processes.
3. **Compliance and legal requirements:** Protection concerns have stringent laws and standards that regulate the industries involved. Cyber security helps an organization to abide by the legal provisions through reducing the possibility of fines.

 DOI: 10.1201/9781003540045-5

4. **National security:** Cyber security is key to protecting those critical infrastructures, government systems, and national security interests from the ever-present dangers of cyber espionage and cyber warfare.
5. **Technological advancements:** The more innovative IT gets, the more vulnerabilities will be opened up for exploitation. Cyber security methods can protect these innovations and ward off risks associated with IoT, AI, and cloud computing as they continue to surge forward very fast.

Due to the sudden increase in information security breaches, organizations across all industries are facing difficulties in protecting themselves from an ever increasing variety of threats. In healthcare, there has always been a concern for patient data that is rich with personal information. With federal funding enacted under the Health Information Technology for Economic and Clinical Heath (HITECH) Act, more patient data are now stored electronically in electronic medical records (EMR) making concerns about healthcare information security grow deeper [6, 7]. There exist a number of cases within the United States that demonstrate how robbers make use of patients' details while engaging in either medical or financial identity theft. These worries have led to state and federal laws on breach notification. Healthcare providers are now required by regulations such as the Health Insurance Portability and Accountability Act (HIPAA) and HITECH Act together with different state laws to disclose breaches according to certain guidelines.

This chapter aims to offer a thorough exploration of cyber security concepts and practices, emphasizing the contrasting strategies of reactive and proactive approaches, alongside real-time threat protection.

5.2 REACTIVE VERSUS PROACTIVE

Reactive cyber security operates through defense mechanisms that respond to and mitigate cyber issues and problems after their actual occurrence. It detects, assesses, and responds to security breaches to ensure minimum damage and prevent further exploitation [8]. Thus, the major goal of reactive cyber security becomes the prevention of and recovery from assaults, returning systems and data to a secure state. Figure 5.1 provides a comparison between Proactive Cyber Security and Reactive Cyber Security.

This proactive approach to security is designed to be agile so as to enable security teams to act proactively and prevent any cyberattack before it happens. This proactive approach calls for the use of diverse tools and technologies in controlling, supervising, monitoring, and reporting potential security issues within an organization.

A proactive security strategy consists of tracking and doing away with potential vulnerability that can be exploited by malicious actors within the organization's information technology (IT) infrastructure [9].

A reactive security strategy is applied to support security teams to act fast immediately after a cyberattack has occurred. Principally, it entails prompt fixing of damages and reducing the harmful effect of threats. Figure 5.2 shows the detailed components of cyber security, highlighting the differences between proactive and reactive approaches.

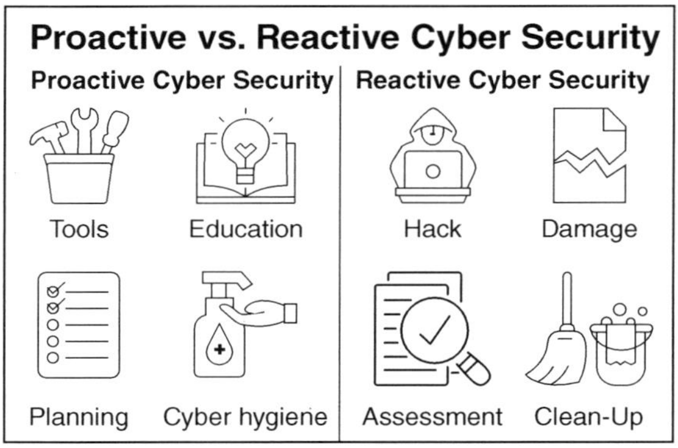

FIGURE 5.1 Proactive versus Reactive Cyber Security.

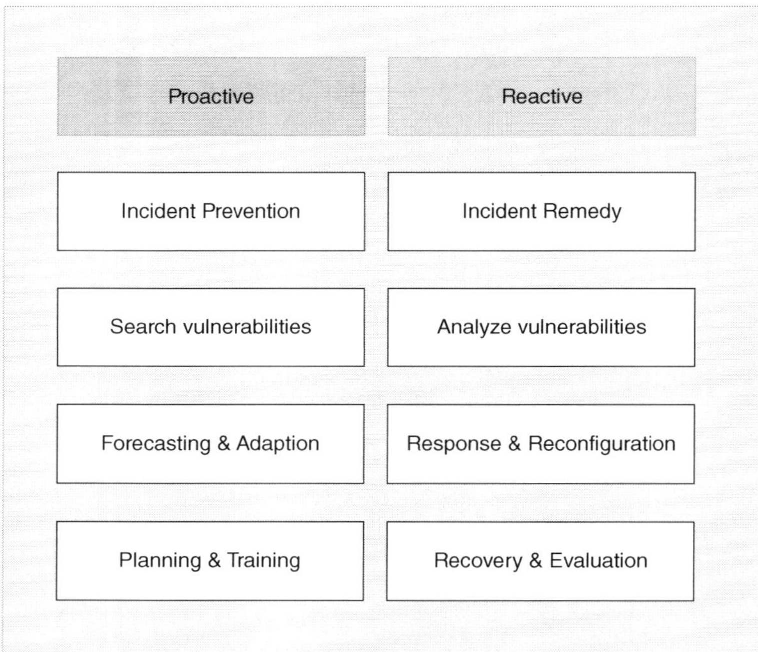

FIGURE 5.2 Components of Cyber Security.

Traditionally, cyberattack detection has relied on reactive methods using which pattern-matching algorithms aid human experts in scanning system logs and network traffic for known virus or malware signatures. Recently, effective machine learning (ML) models have started to automate the detection, tracking, and blocking of malware or intruders. They, however, focused less on predicting beyond hours or days of cyberattack occurrences. Longer-range attack prediction provides the defender more time to develop and share defensive strategies [10].

Currently, long-term attack predictions are heavily dependent on subjective insights made by experienced human experts, often constrained due to lack of specialized cyber security expertise. This chapter presents a state-of-the-art ML-driven methodology that derives an estimate of cyberattack trends years ahead from unstructured big data and logs. It uses a monthly dataset covering key cyber incidents across 36 countries over the last 11 years, with additional new features extracted from scientific research, news, blogs, and social media (tweets) [9, 11]. This automated approach will not only identify future attack trends but also outline a threat cycle comprising five phases that are part of the life cycle of 42 recognized cyber threats.

For so many organizations, security sprawl poses an enormous challenge in view of the rapid growth and complexity of networks and limited security resources. Your organization is probably like most companies that have built a wide variety of perimeter defenses within their network infrastructure over some period. These devices mostly act in isolation, fending off particular threats at different points of entry. You keep your antivirus and antimalware systems up to date and patch and update your systems frequently, watching for new threats.

You could have rolled out all the key insider threat detection tools and set filters and password protections to prevent any rogue actions from employees. In this scenario, should a breach occur, the processes you have in place will permit rapid containment, followed by restorations of the systems and setting them up for forensic investigations with lessons learned to help improve your security posture.

This is a very typical reactive security strategy—one that strengthens defenses so cybercriminals cannot exploit new vulnerabilities, or responds to alerts to signal a network breach. This mode of constantly attending to incident responses is a common position for security teams to find themselves in. Yet, more often than not, this is how organizations establish and maintain their security posture.

In contrast, proactive security identifies the vulnerabilities and possible threats to an organization before these vulnerabilities can be used against it, and takes the necessary actions to ensure that those particular risks never materialize. This enables the organization to stay ahead of threats and avoid falling into the reactive scramble. Some of the critical components that really help in ensuring a tight security posture include next-generation firewalls, antivirus software, spam filters, multifactor authentication, and a good breach response plan.

That means by disabling a traditional Layer 2–3 firewall, a network is put at immediate risk, hence underlining the important role these very foundational security measures play. Usually, the effectiveness of security strategies depends on the proper implementation or mere existence of essential security measures.

5.2.1 Key Concepts of Proactive Cyber Security

Specifically, information security has taken very tedious and sometimes even outright redundant processes. Such efforts could yield useful results, but with significant necessity for streamlining and consolidating cyber security under a coherent strategy [12]. This proactive security strategy will aim to bring all security dimensions into one umbrella for the most complete solution possible, focusing on the needs of both startups and large enterprises alike. In such a strategy:

- Both the target security state and the existing posture are included;
- A wide range of cyber security measures, such as firewalls and user authentication policies, are addressed;
- Measures are intended to be flexible and updated over time;
- The main goal is to identify and fix security flaws; and
- Popular tools and technology are considered.

5.2.2 Reactive Cyber Security Approaches

Organizations usually focus on reactive cyber security measures, but in today's setting these measures are simply not good enough to manage the acuteness of the threats. Reactive strategies take care of the solutions after the fact of an attack, and this policy is not going to help much in protection against the changing nature of cyber threats.

5.2.2.1 Firewalls

Firewalls have become an integral part of the reactive strategy in cyber security [13]. They help in managing network traffic and ensuring that any future threats do not have a chance to infect the network.

5.2.2.2 Anti-Malware Software

Exactly! Reactive security is when you allow malware to get into your network and then try to get rid of it using anti-malware tools that detect and delete. On the other hand, proactive security focuses on not letting these bad tools invade your systems and networks in the first place, which again improves the effectiveness of your cyber security.

5.2.2.3 Password Protection

In fact, password protection has become of paramount importance in today's digital world. Strong password policies are very essential to ensure that users do not configure easily crackable passwords. Software developers can play a big role in putting mechanisms in place for password strength enforcement and educating users to create strong passwords. This kind of proactive measure will radically minimize the chances of unauthorized access and enhance the general cyber security posture.

5.2.2.4 Spam Filters

Spam filters are used quite a lot in reactive cyber security because they aid in the identification of denial and virus-infected messages mailed to email boxes [14]. By filtering out possibly unsafe content or material before it gets to its destination or user, spam filters avoid the safety hazard involved with attachments or links in pernicious emails. This proactive filtering approach becomes very important for protecting organizational networks or systems against several forms of cyber threats.

5.2.2.5 The Growing Importance of Proactive Cyber Security

A proactive cyber security strategy minimizes an organization's reliance on reactive cyber security measures alone. It is through the implementation of proactive and reactive capabilities that an organization can achieve effective security threat management and mitigation. From this perspective, a proactive strategy avoids threats from occurring, and a reactive plan works as a contingency to quickly handle such situations if they arise. In these ways, dual approaches secure robust overall cyber security resilience and end-to-end protection and preparedness against new emerging cyber threats.

5.2.2.6 Preventing Threats and Disruptions from the Get-Go

While proactive cyber security measures are essential for the detection and mitigation of potential vulnerabilities, so that no exploitation can occur to bring down or breach an institution's informational infrastructure, small security lapses may result in huge breaches, exposing sensitive data. Hence, organizations that have proactive plans could work systematically over the vulnerabilities that crop up and thereby reduce the chances of security incidents, enhancing overall resilience to cyber threats.

5.2.2.7 Simplifying Reactive Security

A robust proactive security plan can, in reality, reduce the impact of expending a huge part of your cyber security budget on reactive security measures. Applying proactive strategies puts one in better stead to have identified and dealt with most vulnerabilities and threats before they become incidents, hence drastically reducing incident counts and their impacts. This approach makes incident response easier and improves the cyber security stance through prevention and readiness.

5.2.2.8 Reducing Clean-Up Costs

When an organization experiences a data breach or other security issues, there are unavoidable costs involved in remediation. These costs may encompass fines, settlement expenses, and business disruptions. However, proactive cyber security approaches can mitigate these losses by reducing the severity and impact of breaches. Investing in proactive security measures like strong defenses, routine audits, employee training, and comprehensive incident response plans can lower the likelihood of breaches and minimize potential financial and reputational damages.

5.2.2.9 Staying on Top of Emerging Threats

A good cyber security strategy in its totality allows organizations to be proactive about cyber threats within the industry and a step ahead of ill-minded actors in the threat landscape. The all-rounded strategy includes leading monitoring and analytics tools that enable the tracking of minor and major vulnerabilities in an organization's infrastructure on a continuous basis. This is a measure of being proactive toward threat detection, allowing remediation of vulnerabilities in a timely manner before attackers can exploit them. It can also provide monitoring and analytics at granular levels, enabling organizations to continue improving the overall maturity of cyber security and resilience to emerging threats.

5.2.2.10 Maintaining Compliance

An effective proactive cyber security strategy is one that propels your organization toward critical security framework compliance to build trust, safety, and compliance within your industry. Organizational trust can be built with customers when the entity can proactively establish and maintain appropriate security controls that guarantee protection of sensitive information, ensure minimum business risk, and elaborate compliance with the industry norms. Not only are potential threats reduced at this point but such a move also enhances confidence in the relationship between organizations and their stakeholders, based on a culture of security and reliability.

5.2.2.11 Building Customer Trust

Proactive strategies in the implementation and maintenance of security would help your institution indicate that data security is not just another requirement to meet but indeed a priority. You give your institution a competitive edge in the industry since you are better positioned to protect sensitive information and maintain business operations. Besides, proactive security measures will foster trust with customers over some time since they will be assured that their data are safe. Cyber security comes to the front line of organizational priorities: by it, not only are risks mitigated, but also a differentiation is made for organizations in being among those that are dependable and trustworthy within the digital ecosystem.

5.2.2.12 Assessing the Return on Investment Rate

This requirement translates the security needs of the business by developing proactive cyber security plans, and it is, therefore, easier to explain how the cyber security budget is allocated and used. The betterment of the Return on Security Investment (ROSI) undermines reactive strategies and leads to the use of preventive and mitigation strategies in the proactive approach [14]. It calls for a conveyance of more resources to the preventive side as a measure to prevent costly cyberattacks rather than to take steps after an attack has happened to deal with the incident. Proactive security measures, such as investment in the right protection and defenses, employee training, use of threat intelligence, and continuous monitoring, will obviously support any organization to streamline and optimize expenditure toward cyber security while further reducing the latent financial and reputational impacts of the cyber threats.

5.3 THE BEST PRACTICES FOR IMPLEMENTING PROACTIVE SECURITY METHODOLOGIES

The expected damage from a data breach indeed can be huge, running into millions of dollars for small to medium-sized enterprises and businesses and can even run into billions for the larger ones. Unlike a simple "undo" button like CTRL+Z, there is no quick reversal once a cyberattack has taken place. Substantial disruption, financial losses, reputational damage—the attackers can create all of it, leaving it for the attacked organization to manage a complex aftermath [15].

5.3.1 Cyber Risk Assessment and Vulnerability Scanning

One has to measure the level of risk before the incidents occur, which is particularly true in the case of online businesses; this is where the very significant role of vulnerability scanning comes into play, by helping in identifying the already existing vulnerabilities among the assets. In these cases, the scans enable the security teams to take proactive measures on vulnerabilities that might be exploited by bad actors, thus reducing potential problems and increasing the overall cyber security posture. The steps involved in cyber threat intelligence are shown in Figure 5.3.

5.3.2 Continuous Monitoring and Threat Detection

Network monitoring no doubt plays a critical role in every cyber security strategy, more so in proactive strategies [5]. This will help the cyber security team keep continuous tabs on network traffic, system logs, and user activities for possible anomalies or weak points that might be concealed within a network or an IT system. This way, early detection of vulnerabilities can be identified, and security teams would have enough time to proactively respond and reduce risks before they change into other grave security incidents. This proactive stance has significantly enhanced overall cyber security defenses and protected organizational assets against probable threats.

5.3.3 Patch Management for Software and Systems

This means updates to software utilities, drivers, and firmware should be an essential part of proactive cyber security. Successful patch management ensures that all such components are up to date with the latest security patches and updates. This will

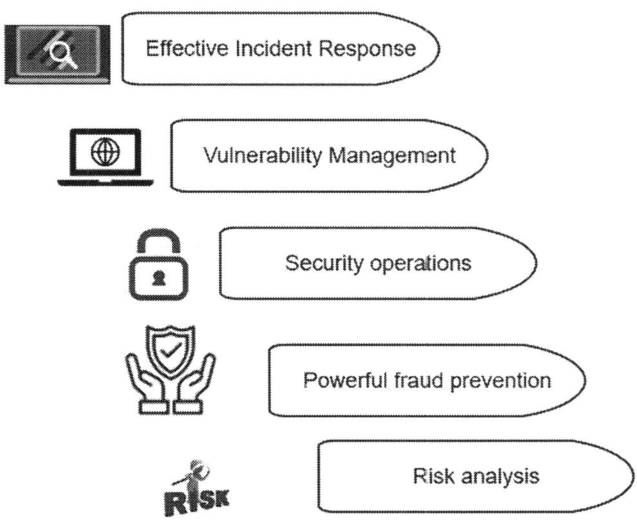

FIGURE 5.3 Cyber Threat Intelligence Processes.

assist in the closing of known vulnerabilities, strengthening general defenses in cyber security by shrinking possible attack surfaces for threats.

5.3.4 Developing Strong Incident Response Plans

Despite all the efforts that cyber security specialists take to secure systems and networks, there are some attacks that can rarely be prevented from touching some part of an online business. However, an organization can prepare for and minimize the effect of such incidents by the use of a strong incident response plan as guided in this chapter.

Endpoint security, otherwise referred to as endpoint protection, is the process of proactively taking measures in safeguarding endpoints like desktops, laptops, and mobile devices. Endpoint security management is a kind of centralized platform that allows cyber security teams to monitor, manage, and protect endpoints and critical devices from hazardous threats and cyberattacks. Strong endpoint security measures should be put in place to beef up an organization's overall cyber security posture. It safeguards sensitive data and systems that are vulnerable to these endpoints. Taking a proactive approach, this implementation helps prevent security breaches and ensures asset integrity and availability.

5.3.5 Promoting Security Awareness Among Insiders

Addressing insider threats is paramount for any comprehensive security strategy because these threats can pose significant risks to organizations. Insider threats originate from authorized users, employees, and business partners who may intentionally or unintentionally breach security protocols or misuse access privileges. Implementing measures to detect, monitor, and mitigate insider threats is essential for safeguarding sensitive data, intellectual property, and critical systems. This proactive approach helps organizations mitigate potential risks and fortify cyber security defenses against both external and internal threats.

5.3.6 Strengthening Data Protection with Proactive Metrics

A robust data protection plan is essential for effective cyber security strategies. Without a suitable data protection policy in place, organizations and their clients face substantial risks, including breaches of confidentiality and integrity. Implementing data encryption is crucial for ensuring data security, as it makes sensitive information unreadable to unauthorized parties even if intercepted. Additionally, organizations should use secure data transmission methods and protocols such as Hypertext Transfer Protocol Secure (HTTPS), Virtual Private Networks (VPNs), and secure file transfer protocols to protect data while it is in transit. By prioritizing data protection measures, organizations can build trust with clients, comply with regulatory requirements, and strengthen their overall cyber security defenses.

5.3.7 Encryption and Information Privacy Measures

Encryption plays a vital role in cyber security by transforming data into an unreadable format, thereby protecting it from unauthorized access or interception by malicious actors [8]. There are several dependable encryption solutions available that organizations can use to secure sensitive data both during storage and transmission. These solutions employ strong encryption algorithms to ensure that only authorized parties with the correct decryption key can access and decipher the encrypted data. Implementing encryption is essential for maintaining data confidentiality and integrity, especially when handling sensitive information such as personal data, financial records, and intellectual property.

5.3.8 Regular Data Backups and Disaster Recovery Planning

Backup and data recovery plans ensure we have an excellent proactive cyber security strategy. For several reasons, online businesses and small organizations require a data backup and recovery plan [3]. These plans can assist you in recovering your data quickly and preventing disruption in the event of cyberattacks or other issues.

5.3.9 Human Threat Hunting

Threat hunting is a proactive cyber security technique aimed at identifying and mitigating cyber threats that might otherwise go undetected within a network or IT infrastructure. This approach involves actively searching for indicators of compromise (IOCs), suspicious activities, or anomalies that could indicate potential threats or ongoing attacks. By proactively hunting for threats, cyber security professionals can detect and respond to them before they escalate and cause damage to the organization's network and IT systems. Threat hunting plays a critical role in enhancing overall cyber security resilience by enabling early detection and swift mitigation of emerging threats.

5.3.10 Penetration Testing

Penetration testing, or pen testing, is indeed crucial for proactive cyber security efforts. It involves systematically probing networks, systems, and applications for vulnerabilities that could be exploited by malicious actors. By conducting regular and rigorous penetration tests, organizations can identify weaknesses and security gaps before they are exploited [4].

A well-defined pen testing plan outlines the scope, objectives, methodologies, and frequency of tests. It ensures that testing is comprehensive and conducted in a structured manner to effectively assess the organization's security posture. Regular pen testing helps organizations stay ahead of evolving threats, enhance their resilience to cyberattacks, and maintain robust cyber security defenses by enabling them to prioritize and implement patches, updates, and other security measures.

5.3.11 Integrating a Security-First Mindset into Your Organization

Cyber security awareness training provides a foundation for improving the information security of data within an organization by making employees aware of the potential consequences of their actions and how minor errors might lead to significant security breaches. Indeed, research indicates that more than 70% of data breaches are due to the human factor and, equally generally, the negligence of an employee [2]. In this regard, creating a security mindset among employees is of essence in protecting sensitive organizational data from exposure.

5.3.12 Involvement of Leadership in Cyber Security Initiatives

Indeed, leadership is decisive for the integration of cyber security concepts within an organization. Leaders are supposed to provide clear expectations and goals, a sound policy and procedure framework, and a culture of security awareness and resilience. Above all, leaders at all levels organize necessary resources and support for the implementation of cyber security measures so that these can be enacted and their efficiency enhanced to safeguard the various strata of the organization from emerging threats.

5.3.13 Leveraging Technology for Proactive Cyber Defense

With these new technologies and advanced tools, security professionals, analysts, and engineers can push ahead and invent new solutions that are going to be effective against the contemporary cyber security threats [1, 3]. Then there is AI, which is positively transforming the cyber security space, with an array of tools and techniques at its disposal wanting to bring in the difference in several dimensions of cyber security operations.

5.3.14 Automated Security Solutions for Real-Time Protection

Security at perceptive levels requires real-time monitoring and protection—things AI does exceedingly well for teams. AI helps teams keep vigilant on new threats and supports an organization's ability to monitor, analyze, and comprehensively report on cyber security threats as one tool.

5.3.15 Integrating Proactive Security into Business Operations

AI is going to integrate with the already-used security tools inside an organization to largely improve operational security. The integrated tools would then go on to actively monitor network traffic, analyze data transfers in real time, and hence empower cyber security teams to detect and subsequently respond to any potential threats in good timing. This will increase the general effectiveness of cyber security via AI's capabilities by supplementing and streamlining existing security measures.

5.3.16 Predictive Analytics and Detecting Emerging Threats

Data gathered from past incidents or other sources is, of course, very instrumental in proactive cyber security. It would give expert teams an insight into those attack patterns and formulate effective response strategies. AI thus has a very important role here in making predictive analytics possible and thereby helping to detect emerging threats before they turn into actual attacks. In this regard, using AI and data analytics

TABLE 5.1
Differences Between Reactive and Proactive Cyber Security

Aspects	Reactive Cyber Security	Proactive Cyber Security
Definition	Responds to incidents after they occur	Anticipates and prevents incidents before they occur
Time of Action	Before the incident	After the incident
Focus	Detection, response, and mitigation	Prevention, risk assessment, and continuous monitoring
Tools and Techniques	Incident response plans, forensics, patch management, and recovery tools	Threat intelligence, vulnerability assessments, penetration testing, and security audits
Cost	Can be costly due to damage control, recovery, and potential downtime	Initial investment might be high, but can save costs by preventing incidents
Approach	Curative and damage control	Preventive and risk management

in such a proactive process automatically enhances preparedness toward cyber security and enables organizations at large to better mitigate the risks by anticipating and preempting any threats likely to occur [9].

5.3.17 Wrapping Up

Proactive measures within cyber security are very essential in protecting the data. These proactive measures include various effective strategies that make one integral approach. This is mostly useful in trying to stop, at an initial stage, cyber threats from establishing themselves and then causing chaos. Run through proactive protection measures involving systematic security evaluation, vulnerability management, threat hunting, and employee training to a great extent. This will help an organization efficiently protect its critical information from any external threats and sustain continuous business operations. The difference between reactive and proactive cyber security approaches are presented in Table 5.1.

5.4 STRENGTHS AND WEAKNESSES

The strengths and weaknesses of both proactive and reactive cyber security are shown in Figures 5.4 and 5.5.

5.4.1 Situational Suitability

1. Reactive Cyber Security
   The small business enterprises typically have little or no capability to perform proactive cyber security. Also, entities recovering from recent breaches and companies managing legacy systems are usually in the early development phase of their cyber security framework.

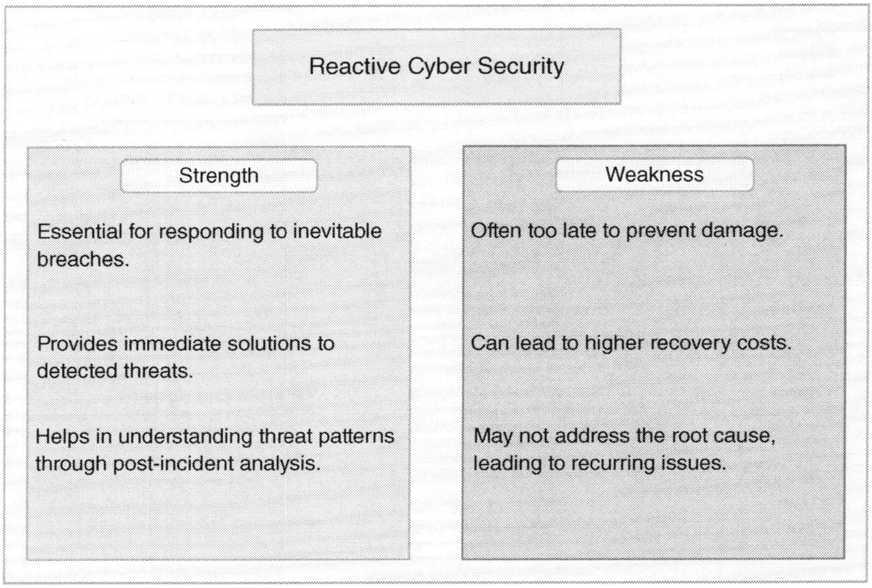

FIGURE 5.4 Reactive Cyber Security.

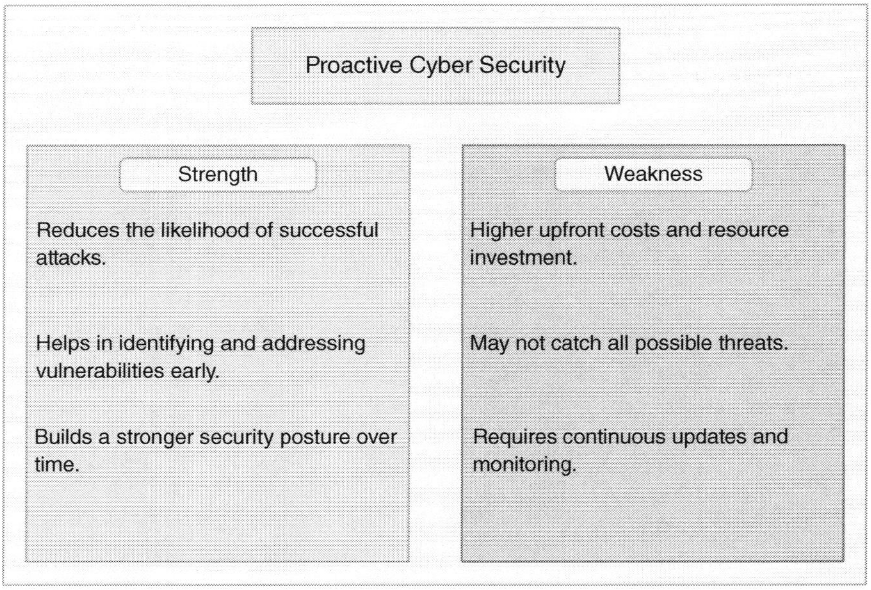

FIGURE 5.5 Proactive Cyber Security.

2. Proactive Cyber Security
   These include well-entrenched cyber security practices that have put in place protection that is effective 24 hours a day, 7 days a week for critical data and assets such as financial institutions, healthcare providers, government agencies, and large enterprises.

5.4.2 Integration of Both Approaches

1. Holistic Strategy
   These security measures add up to both reactive and proactive elements of defense. It means that proactive steps, such as continuous monitoring, threat intelligence, and regular security audits, can be taken to deal with and reduce threats as early as possible. Incident response plans prepared in advance will ensure effective and timely response to security breaches or incidents.
2. Layered Security
   Employing a multilayered security approach includes implementing proactive measures to prevent incidents, alongside reactive measures to effectively manage breaches that may occur despite these preventive efforts.
3. Automation and AI
   The use of automation and AI significantly boosts proactive and reactive cyber security functionalities. Automated tools for identifying and addressing threats, alongside predictive analytics powered by ML, provide a comprehensive strategy for cyber security. This combined approach helps organizations detect threats promptly, react quickly, and continually enhance their defenses against evolving cyber risks.
4. Continuous Improvement
   One should update proactive and reactive cyber security strategies regularly, keeping in touch with threat intelligence and incident analysis. Lessons learned from past incidents could be implemented to enhance prevention strategies, making them capable of mitigating new evolving threats. In this way, such constant fine-tuning will help an organization retain resilience and adaptiveness of its cyber security strategy.
5. Training and Awareness
   Staff have to be trained on proactive and reactive cyber security practices regularly. As such, frequent training forms another key ingredient in generating security awareness and preparedness within an organization. This continuous education will help employees develop skills required in the detection of potential threats, taking precautionary measures against them, and developing response skills to security incidents in a manner that enhances overall cyber security resilience.

   Therefore, effective cyber security calls for such an integration of reactive and proactive measures that an organization will develop the ability to regain its balance quickly with this defense system if it ever finds itself thrown off by an attack. The main objective of this approach would always remain risk mitigation, as it helps organizations foresee and prevent attacks, and easily respond to incidents with great efficiency and effectiveness. This strategy gives maximum possible protection to critical assets and data against cyber threats, therefore enhancing cyber security preparedness and resilience.

5.4.3 Case Study: The Equifax Data Breach

In 2017, Equifax, a prominent US credit reporting agency, suffered a substantial data breach compromising personal information of about 147 million people. This case study analyzes the breach's causes, the company's reactive and proactive cyber security actions, and the insights gleaned from the incident. The case of Equifax, with data on over 800 million individuals and 88 million businesses globally, underscores the critical importance of cyber security due to the sensitive nature of its data.

Timeline of Events

March 2017: Equifax's IT team was informed of a critical vulnerability in the Apache Struts web application framework that they used.
May–July 2017: Hackers exploited this vulnerability, gaining access to Equifax's systems.
July 29, 2017: Equifax discovered the breach.
September 7, 2017: Equifax publicly disclosed the breach.

5.4.4 Reactive Cyber Security Measures

1. Incident Response
   Detection: Equifax's internal security team detected the breach upon noticing unusual network activity.
   Immediate actions: Equifax promptly responded to halt unauthorized access and minimize impact, which involved patching the vulnerability and launching an internal investigation.
   Public disclosure: Equifax publicly acknowledged the breach over a month after discovery, facing considerable backlash for the delayed disclosure.
2. Forensic Analysis
   Equifax enlisted a cyber security firm to conduct a comprehensive forensic investigation aimed at assessing the extent and repercussions of the breach.
3. Recovery Efforts
   The company provided complimentary credit monitoring and identity theft protection services to all impacted individuals. Significant resources were allocated to the repair and enhancement of the affected systems.

The Equifax data breach underscores the crucial role of both reactive and proactive cyber security tactics. Reactive strategies are essential for addressing and minimizing immediate threats, while proactive measures are critical for establishing a robust security framework capable of averting future incidents and lowering overall risk. By integrating these approaches, organizations can develop a comprehensive defense strategy that addresses both immediate response requirements and long-term security objectives. The lessons gleaned from Equifax's breach underscore the importance of ongoing enhancement, rigorous security protocols, and a steadfast commitment to safeguarding sensitive data.

5.5 CONCLUSION

In conclusion, reliance on either reactive or proactive cyber security measures is insufficient in dealing with cyber threats. A balanced approach will adapt both strategies, positioning an organization to mitigate immediate risks through a harmonized avenue and foster long-term resilience. Organizations truly effective at protecting their assets, mitigating risk, and earning/maintaining stakeholder trust will do so by prioritizing proactive initiatives while driven by robust reactive capabilities.

REFERENCES

1. Rosiek, Travis. "Chief information security officer best practices for 2018: Proactive cyber security." *Cyber Security: A Peer-Reviewed Journal* 1, no. 4 (2018): 361–367.
2. Collins, Raymond Martin Luther. "Proactive cybersecurity through active cyber defense." Master's thesis, Utica College, 2017.
3. Smith, Jane, and Patrick Thomas. *Cybersecurity in the Age of AI: A Proactive Defense Approach*. No. 13306. EasyChair, 2024.
4. Hyder, Muhammad Faraz, and Muhammad Ali Ismail. "Securing control and data planes from reconnaissance attacks using distributed shadow controllers, reactive and proactive approaches." *IEEE Access* 9 (2021): 21881–21894.
5. Fuertes, Walter, Francisco Reyes, Paúl Valladares, Freddy Tapia, Theofilos Toulkeridis, and Ernesto Pérez. "An integral model to provide reactive and proactive services in an academic CSIRT based on business intelligence." *Systems* 5, no. 4 (2017): 52.
6. Abdi, Nima, Abdullatif Albaseer, and Mohamed Abdallah. "The role of deep learning in advancing proactive cybersecurity measures for smart grid networks: A survey." *IEEE Internet of Things Journal* 11, no. 9 (2024): 16398–16421.
7. Kipling, Lesley. "The industrial internet of things: From preventive to reactive systems – redefining your cyber security game plan for the changing world." *Cyber Security: A Peer-Reviewed Journal* 4, no. 2 (2020): 102–110.
8. Bhuyan, Soumitra Sudip, Umar Y. Kabir, Jessica M. Escareno, Kenya Ector, Sandeep Palakodeti, David Wyant, Sajeesh Kumar et al. "Transforming healthcare cybersecurity from reactive to proactive: Current status and future recommendations." *Journal of Medical Systems* 44 (2020): 1–9.
9. Miller, Kevin L. "What we talk about when we talk about" reasonable cybersecurity": A proactive and adaptive approach." *Florida Bar Journal* 90, no. 8 (2016).
10. Kuraku, Sivaraju, Dinesh Kalla, Fnu Samaah, and Nathan Smith. "Cultivating proactive cybersecurity culture among IT professional to combat evolving threats." *International Journal of Electrical, Electronics and Computers* 8, no. 6 (2023).
11. Chen, Hong-Mei, Rick Kazman, Ira Monarch, and Ping Wang. "Can cybersecurity be proactive? A big data approach and challenges." (2017). *Proceedings of the 50th Hawaii International Conference on System Sciences*. http://hdl.handle.net/10125/41885
12. Xu, Shouhuai. "Cybersecurity dynamics: A foundation for the science of cybersecurity." *Proactive and Dynamic Network Defense* (2019): 1–31.
13. Moholth, Ole Christian, Radmila Juric, and Karoline Moholth McClenaghan. "Detecting cyber security vulnerabilities through reactive programming." (2019). *Proceedings of the 52nd Hawaii International Conference on System Sciences*. http://hdl.handle.net/10125/60157
14. Almahmoud, Zaid, Paul D. Yoo, Omar Alhussein, Ilyas Farhat, and Ernesto Damiani. "A holistic and proactive approach to forecasting cyber threats." *Scientific Reports* 13, no. 1 (2023): 8049.
15. Greidanus, Mateo D. Roig, Gab-Su Seo, and Sudip K. Mazumder. "A Proactive–Reactive Methodology for Cyber-Resilient Inverter Control System." *IEEE Access* (2024): 69051–69065. Electronic ISSN: 2169-3536 DOI: 10.1109/ACCESS.2024.3400768.

6 Exploring the Importance of Incident Management in Modern Organizations

Smitha G Prabhu, Divya C D, Hong Lin, and Asha R

6.1 INTRODUCTION

The phenomenon of globalization has undergone a meteoric rise since the mid-1990s and has resulted in the emergence of a borderless world. It has unlocked new horizons, thereby creating an era of habitual change for mankind. The advent of the internet has acted as a powerful catalyst for the globalization momentum. The telecommunication/information technology (IT) revolution spread digital technology to every nook and corner of the world within a short span of time.

Globalization has transformed the world into a borderless cyber community, paving the way for a new economic ecosystem. It has inaugurated the era of cooperation and competition in an interconnected world [1]. Under such a paradigm, opportunity and exploitation coexist. Nations with socioeconomic disparities have become equally vulnerable to disasters in the world's financial markets. Globalization is a double-edged sword. It may create new avenues and opportunities for national and global interests or cause peril to countries and institutions [2]. The effects of globalization transcend national borders and have widespread repercussions on the financial markets, infrastructure, and the larger populace of nations and economies [3, 4].

A professional banker by profession will ensure that the national economy of the country does not erode and is intact, irrespective of the potential disaster in the world financial markets, and that globalization does not become a curse [5]. To meet this challenge, brings afresh the concept of active incident management and strategic reconstruction of the Banker's Diagnostic and Resilience Model for the national economy to resist changes in the world's financial markets/globalization and continue to be a competitive world country (CWC) [6]. Emerging multinationals must pool their strengths, and policymakers are required to preemptively manage the development of the financial markets [7]. The growth of evolving multinational enterprises (MNEs) into global service markets is currently driven by capital market teams and the need for emergency financial accounts. Incident management life cycle is presented in Figure 6.1.

 DOI: 10.1201/9781003540045-6

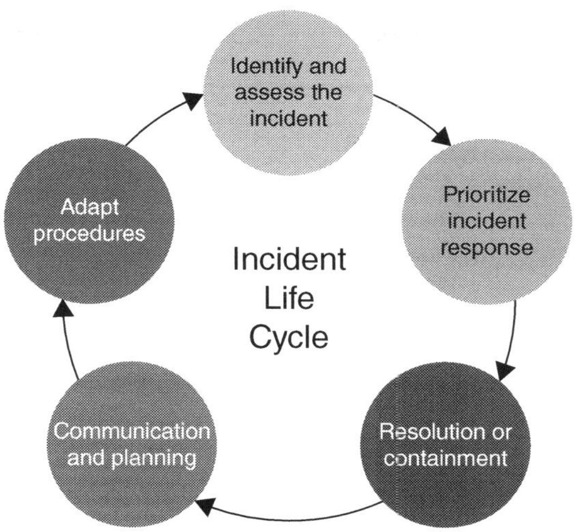

FIGURE 6.1 Importance of Incident Management.

6.2 THE CONCEPT OF INCIDENT MANAGEMENT

There is a growing demand for organizations to increase their productivity and service availability. This demand has led organizations to respond by increasing the size and complexity of information systems, hardware, networks, application software, and data [8]. However, this growing complexity makes them more prone to disruption and incident involvement. Incident management processes are established to minimize disruption and restore services to normal as quickly as possible [9]. Incident management is a holistic concept that considers the entire organization, including people, processes, technologies, and culture. [10]

An incident can be defined as an unplanned interruption to an IT service, a failure of a component of an IT service that has not yet impacted service, or an unanticipated reduction in the quality of an IT service. There are three scopes of incident management processes: within a single organization, with multiple organizations involved in the value chain, and interfaces to the customer [11, 12]. An incident management process comprising four subprocesses—incident detection and recording, incident classification and initial support, investigation and diagnosis, and resolution and recovery—has a wider scope that includes resources from all involved organizations [13, 14]. Existing frameworks guide organizations in establishing incident management processes, such as Information Technology Infrastructure Library (ITIL) and Control Objectives for Information and Related Technologies (COBIT) [15]. However, these frameworks primarily focus on only one organization, omitting escalating issues spanning multiple organizations [16].

The discussion of the concept of incident management is based on literature study and interviews with four incident management practitioners. To enhance the understanding of incident management, a framework with five dimensions is proposed: levels, scopes, processes, conceptual model, and infrastructure. Within these five dimensions, a further description is presented of key components of incident management in modern organizations [17]. Practitioners are interested in the inventory or overview of existing models regarding incident management processes. A well-known collaborative incident management process is the telecommunications Global Roaming Services (GRS) process. With respect to literature, there are some initiatives to model incident management processes [18, 19]. The published models mainly concern a single organization involved in the value chain. A random-access model, illustrating the incident management process with respect to a single organization, is discussed.

6.2.1 Definition and Scope

Incident management encompasses the principles and practices utilized by organizations for the assessment, investigation, and governing of incidents. The normative process of incident management will be encapsulated, alongside examination of the specific applications of incident management within organizations. The entities, incidents, and timeframes detailed herein are fictional, designed solely for illustrative purposes [10, 20].

A common definition of an incident is a deviation from the norm, the type and extent of which may vary greatly between organizations. Even within the same organization, incidents may be perceived in different ways depending on the perspective of the person tending to the incident. Therefore, organizations will often refer to certain notable encounters as incidents, regardless of whether there is consensus on this, or regard the same incident as two distinct incidents, by viewing one as an incident and another as a consequence of that incident. Even with the common understanding of what incidents are, one may still question what constitutes a notable incident meriting management.

A dangerous or potentially dangerous incident, incidents involving considerable injury or potential injury to personnel, contamination or potential contamination of the environment, or large monetary loss are some examples of incidents that appear not to be the subjects of mutual dispute within organizations [21]. Other incidents may constitute notable and manageably large workloads on personnel. On the contrary, incidents may also be dealt with on the basis of discretion, where incidents are disregarded unless otherwise directed by someone with influence over the organization's activities. Thus, the organizational perception of what constitutes an incident varies across and within organizations [22, 23].

Similar to the variety with known incidents, the unknown incident space surrounding organizations is equally extensive. Even the organization's own personnel may conduct acts of malice or negligence against it [24]. Incident management is in the deterministically conceivable nature of organizations, since their existence, space for interpretation, and subsequent action may be referred to as the incident management area [25]. Covering only the detected incident space of an organization is tantamount to ignoring all relocations, internal and external, that a means of transport may undertake in its life cycle. And again, a means of transport may be an example of an entity in reference to the incidents related to the activities of organizations [26].

6.2.2 Key Components

Incident management consists of several interconnected components that contribute to its effectiveness and efficiency. Organizations can minimize the occurrence and impact of incidents by addressing these components, ensuring critical business activities continue unhindered [27]. This mission is achieved by minimizing service downtime and returning services to normal operation as swiftly as possible, mitigating disruptions to normal operations of people, processes, and technology [28].

There are six key components for implementing incident management successfully. The first component is a clear definition of purpose, outlining what incident management involves and what it does not, creating common understanding among stakeholders [29]. The second is a documented and communicated policy that formalizes a clear statement of all stakeholders' commitments, guiding behavior and actions. For example, an incident management policy should specify the organization's commitment to returning services to normal operation as quickly as possible while minimizing adverse impact on the business [30].

The third component is defined roles and responsibilities so all relevant stakeholders know their responsibilities and accountability concerning incident management. The fourth is an incident management program that details the activities planned and scheduled for the ongoing implementation of incident management within the organization [31, 32]. An incident management program is typically a multiyear program encompassing the gradual implementation of several components and several phases per component. The fifth component is appropriate organization and resources, specifying the organization and resources required for incident management to be effective [33, 34]. The sixth and final component is systems for the control and joining of all activities, using, for instance, a management information system and a dedicated tool in this regard [35].

6.3 INCIDENT MANAGEMENT PROCESS

Incidents can occur at any moment and can result from various issues, such as hardware or software failures, physical disasters, or human actions. Thus, it is essential to be ready to respond to incidents appropriately. When dealing with interruption in service, every organization should adopt procedures to recover the condition of normal business as quickly as possible while minimizing negative impact [36]. The following process outlines the steps to be taken during an incident.

1. Detection and Reporting
   The first step in the incident management process is to detect incidents and understand their impact. This can include monitoring software applications, networks, and alerts regarding unusual event occurrence. Users can report incidents through telephone, email, or a web-based portal. Providing clear guidelines to users to assist them in reporting incidents is vital. Ideas or questions to incorporate in a call include what happened, what should have happened, and if there were any changes made in relation to reports of the incident. At this stage, it is necessary to gather further information about the

FIGURE 6.2 Incident Management Process.

incident to assess whether calling it so is warranted. This includes gathering logs, talking to users, and verifying monitoring alerts [37, 38]. All contacts with users should be recorded to minimize disruption. An initial assessment should be made regarding the priority of the incident. Assessment is usually conducted by service desk or Tier-1 support staff. Priorities are determined based on the severity of the impact on the organization and the number of users impacted. Priority categories are as follows:

- Major incident: critical systems down affecting the entire organization;
- Urgent: important systems down affecting several users or an entire department;
- High: systems down affecting one user; and
- Medium: question or request for clarifications.

2. Response and Resolution
   In this step, the responsibility for resolution is assigned to a person or team based on the impact and priority of the incident. Work is conducted to resolve the incident and restore normal service. Updates should be provided regularly regarding actions taken to resolve the issue [39, 40]. Regular escalation should be conducted to ensure focus on resolution and ongoing communications with the users affected. Transparency is essential. Updated and relevant information should be shared but avoid communicating assumptions or facts that are not confirmed.
3. Documentation and Communication
   All incidents should be documented. This is important for showing statistics for regulatory compliance and for identifying trends. This documentation can result in a "lessons learned" report detailing what happened so it can be

avoided in the future [41, 42]. Regularly review and share key metrics with the organization, including average resolution time, trends, and problem categorizations. This information can assist in decision-making regarding future investments, such as improved training or hardware upgrades. The process of incident management is as shown in Figure 6.2.

6.3.1 Detection and Reporting

Incident detection and reporting are the critical first steps in the incident management process. An incident can be detected using automated tools, through routine operational checks, by means of customer feedback or complaints, via help desk requests, and by alert notifications from monitoring and probe equipment [43]. It is now common for organizations to use system-generated alerts that immediately inform operators of equipment and network problems. These alerts are usually prioritized but need to be analyzed further in order to classify the incident [44]. The introduction of electronic monitoring and customer databases has increased the workload for operators, who are now inundated with event alerts and prompted cases [45]. As a result, operators need to filter through these alerts, with many of these not requiring action. Operators also need to extract useful information from these alerts to classify them accurately [46]. Successful classification will ensure that the incident is directed to the most appropriate staff for resolution, thereby optimizing the use of the workforce [47].

After the incident has been detected and classified, it is reported and logged. All relevant information regarding the incident is compiled into a report and forwarded to the relevant personnel [48]. There are usually two types of reports submitted, namely, a telephone report and a written report. Written reports can take various forms such as incident reports, investigation reports, and cause analysis reports [49]. The report includes a description of the incident as well as the initial response measures taken. In order to provide sufficient information to understand the nature of the incident, reports on severe incidents are usually much more detailed than reports on less problematic incidents [50]. There will also be a telephone report submitted first, and this can provide sufficient information on the severity of the incident and consequent management and technical actions taken [51].

The information contained in the initial report should include details such as the time of the occurrence, the nature of the incident, the groups affected, the instigation of the incident, recovery measures taken, and recommendations if further work is required [52]. The purpose of the initial report is to save time by alerting incident management personnel to the potential seriousness of the incident prior to receipt of full details. Further investigation, remedial measures, and the gathering of more information will usually begin following the initial report.

6.3.2 Assessment and Prioritization

Upon detection and reporting of an incident, it is essential that critical information about the incident is systematically collected. This information is then evaluated to determine the appropriate response, a scale of priority, and the incident categorization. Decisions about escalation and the assignment of incident solvability are also made at this stage. The initial assessment is generally executed by the helpdesk, using a selection of automated inquiries about the system or the affected component.

Assessment is essential for identifying and understanding the information regarding the incident, such as what has occurred, how the incident occurred, and what consequences it has had. The main goal of assessment is to verify eligibility for resolution, prioritize the incident, and warrant necessary support resources. During assessment, the following questions need to be answered: Is the incident valid? Is the incident repeating? Is there interference with business-critical functions? What are the equivalents or possible workarounds? Who will be in charge of the resolution?

The results of the assessment are used for categorizing the incident and determining a feasible priority. The type of categorizing and available priority levels varies with organizations, but the main purpose is to direct resources to the most important incidents. As a general rule, incidents that are business-critical have a greater priority than others. It is also essential to identify the incident service category to ensure that help is provided by the right support teams. The categorization of the incident, along with the criteria used for prioritization, are documented in a short text and saved into the ticket.

6.3.3 Response and Resolution

Incident response refers to the actions taken by an organization to mitigate the impact of an incident and recover from it as quickly as possible. The response will often include a combination of immediate actions, such as implementing workarounds and restoring services, as well as longer-term actions to address the root cause of the incident and prevent it from happening again in the future.

The resolution of an incident refers to the completion of the actions needed to restore services to their normal state and minimize any negative impact on the organization. A resolution can involve partial or full restoration of service, completion of a workaround, or the decision to terminate an incident if no further action is deemed necessary.

For incidents that need further investigation, either a working diagnosis is undertaken to analyze the underlying problem of an incident, or a full-root cause investigation is launched if it is beyond the capabilities of the service recovery teams. It is critical that the service recovery teams fully understand the problem before any fix is implemented, or if at all.

In addition, criteria for detecting incidents must be established. Contextual information must also be gathered to understand the nature of the incident. Only once these actions are undertaken can a resolution or a workaround be fully developed and the incident dealt with.

All efforts must be made to revert to a working state as quickly as possible. Ideally, fixes should be tested under controlled conditions prior to implementation. If this is not possible, the consequences of implementation must be understood and plans must be in place for further escalation or rollback should an implemented fix not work. If this is not done, control of the incident will generally be lost and the situation could spiral out of control.

In the case of incidents affecting more than one service, a coordination team must be assembled. This team must have an oversight role and should be assigned a key individual who has authority over the parties involved and has the experience and skills to bring the incident to a resolution.

Time is critical and information must be released regularly. Rapidly sharing information on the status of the incident is essential, fostering an environment of trust and camaraderie among those involved. In the absence of information, there is a tendency for rumors and speculation, which can lead to chaos.

6.3.4 Documentation and Communication

Documentation and communication, which represent the final two stages of the incident management process, are essential activities that must immediately follow the implementation of a resolution and recovery effort and should be completed before the incident is formally closed. Documentation, which represents the record-keeping aspects of the incident management process, includes the development of service reports, tracking changes in status, and formatting and distributing correspondence. Communication involves more personal mediums of parley, such as face-to-face meetings, phone calls, and other forms of video, audio, and electronic interactions.

Documentation and communication occur together and entail the same steps, such as documenting the service, identifying the complainant, and determining when the complaint was initiated. However, each stage also has its own specifics, such as identifying if the call is terminated or putting it on hold, which make the process more complex. Each of these elements is discussed in the following to help clarify the steps in this activity, which is depicted in the documentation and communication process model.

Documentation Business Rule:

1. The complaint type shall consist of one, and only one, of the following:
    - Record Retention/Research
    - Performance
    - Configuration
    - Command Syntax/Usage
    - Oracle Software Version
    - Remote Command Execution
    - Surveillance Functions
    - Software Problem
    - Device Driver Problem
    - Networking and Transport Protocols.
2. The severity level shall consist of one, and only one, of the following:
    - Severity Level 1 (Highest): Business is severely affected.
    - Severity Level 2 (High): Business is significantly affected.
    - Severity Level 3 (Medium): Business is affected but manageable.
    - Severity Level 4 (Low): Business is not affected.
    - Severity Level 5 (Lowest): Clarification of product capabilities with no impact on business.

6.4 BENEFITS OF EFFECTIVE INCIDENT MANAGEMENT

An effective incident management process also helps to prevent problems from happening, enhance the company's image to customers, reduce risk and losses, handle incidents efficiently and professionally, increase productivity and avoid interruptions, save costs, and analyze problems, risks, and incidents quickly to increase overall operational effectiveness.

An incident can be defined as a disruption of normal business functions, whereas incident management, as the name implies, is dealing with incidents. An effective incident management process should help organizations respond to incidents quickly, thus making it possible to recover from disruptions as quickly as possible.

With an effective incident management process in place, companies become accustomed to dealing with incidents. Investigation of problems and incidents may be automated, such that problem management tasks take place automatically when incidents arise. Normal operations are suddenly restored in response to a number of indicator changes. The company is thus well-prepared to deal with serious problems and incidents, which reduces operational risks. Systems producing and dealing with the report have been made more reliable and are perceived to be more reliable because the number of unacceptable incidents that cause disasters has been minimized.

By bringing the reports into the hands of the users, the company also enhances its image before customers. Automated initial responses to incidents make the system appear competent and organized and may fool the users into just waiting and doing nothing. Hence, a good incident management process can prevent problems from happening or occurring too often. The risks of the other system components have been estimated by investigating the history of events for a certain group of components. Taking this information into consideration, actions will be prioritized, which will contribute to an improved situation with respect to these risks.

An effective and thus beneficial incident management process also leads to a more rapid analysis of problems, risks, and incidents with respect to the IT system and its impact on the business process. Various indicators of events happening in the IT system and business processes are being monitored. These indicators, which monitor the critical functions of the business processes and IT systems, are reported on predefined time intervals. Sophisticated computer systems have made it possible to gather a lot of different information concerning the incidents happening in a company.

6.5 CHALLENGES AND BARRIERS TO SUCCESSFUL INCIDENT MANAGEMENT

The automation of technology, coupled with increased interaction between machines and individuals, has led to the increased complexity of information systems, networks, and applications. Developing and growing organizations, as well as trends related to the global exchange of information, call for more complex services and an increased demand for technology. As a result, managing incidents and dealing with risks (external or internal) has become even more important. However, there are several barriers and challenges concerning incident management.

First, the incident management process is cross-organizational and involves collaboration between several business entities. Stakeholders have diverse requirements for incident prioritization and are concerned with the privacy and confidentiality of incident data. Next, security information and events are generated in vast quantities and require real-time investigation. Large volumes of data can also lead to information overload, making it difficult for users to concentrate on a small number of high-priority incidents.

Last, individuals' knowledge is often contradicted by proper security procedures. An ad hoc attitude can spread a negative security culture and threaten an organization's infrastructure. Moving from a reactive perspective to a proactive stance implies much important change within the organization. Incident management cannot be treated as a general support service and is instead a highly specialist service that impacts all other services.

Barriers include organizational silos and cultures, limited prioritization of threats and attacks, limited adoption of common incident management or response frameworks, and limited flexibility and adaptability of certain security solutions. Furthermore, in many organizations, the incident management process is perceived as a breach detection exercise only, with more emphasis placed on post-analysis strategies. This restricts the ability to respond in real time or in an agile manner.

Addressing these barriers requires a commitment to long-term investment in and dedicated ownership of incident management strategies. Once there is an awareness that processing incidents across the local area network impacts business operations, productivity, and profitability, the first steps toward establishing a structured approach can be made.

6.6 BEST PRACTICES IN INCIDENT MANAGEMENT

Adopting industry standards and best practice models for incident management facilitates transparency, structure, consistency, and improvement for both operational services and customer relationships. The strictest models could guard against risk investigations or problems associated with personal injury and economic loss damaging high technology installations, such as utilities, refineries, airports, or banks. In less strict environments, similar approaches protect the wheeling and dealing of smaller workers using mobile communication or embracing work-from-remote schemes. Procedures in those models can range from scalable and simple approaches documented in spreadsheets to extensive, expensive enterprise solutions filled with analytical intelligence, adding countless extended flowcharts in thousands of web pages.

Disasters or incidents can be customers packing and taking their business elsewhere, employees not entering the office at all, or the media reflecting upon a leading story against the organization. Thus, responding to critical events efficiently, accurately, and in the organization's best interests is important. Rather than deferring dealing with incidents for more important operational activities or ignoring their occurrence and risk to current business plans, proactive approaches should be embraced, and informed handling of events outside the ordinary line of business should be prioritized. Successful installations apply time-outs and dedicate resources to logically and efficiently address extraordinary incidents as they occur.

Documentation is key to organize the effort, keep individuals accountable, and improve future performance by consecutively reviewing past experiences. In its simplest form, a template listing items to remind, notify, verify, investigate, resolve, analyze, review, and the like is sufficient to achieve earlier success with incidents, later replicable to other scales and environments. Easy to use, this template should be introduced alongside others such as coding events or responses. By using carefully restricted spreadsheets and maintaining simple recordkeeping, organizations can foster interest and engagement while preserving a strong and proactive culture around incident management, investigations, and outcome-focused analysis. Thus, adopting standardized and simple templates and approaches early would be better than holding data in some inadequately defined structure for later use.

Performance metrics scale with the capacity and capability of the crew. In the most limited endeavors, counting interesting events or reactions, analyzing their consequence ranks, and categorizing language against class of event is sufficient to acquire knowledge.

In larger teams, metrics on both recent and historically significant events—along with outcomes from team-based versus instructor-led activities, individual expertise and attitude during discussions or debates, knowledge acquisition, and the sharing of best practices within classes or alternative settings—can effectively complement basic growth statistics.

Prompt Action Reports (PARs) are similar but longer and generally involve multiple incident classes under investigation. Avoidance of repeating earlier mistakes, improvement of simulator design or modeling techniques, and attitude to begin exploring frantic party options could be pursued in PARs.

6.7 INCIDENT MANAGEMENT TOOLS AND TECHNOLOGIES

Incident management tools and technologies are essential in modern organizations to prevent downtime, reduce recovery time, minimize damages, and restore normalcy in business operations. Early incident detection using real-time log monitoring tools helps organizations ensure business continuity. Centralized logging tools, such as security information and event management (SIEM) systems, are widely adopted by organizations to collect the logs of all equipment operations and analyze them. Log files, events, queries, actions, reports, alerts, and tasks related to the security of system resources, data, and networking equipment are recorded. Analyzing logs helps detect issues, track operations, ensure compliance, and prevent unfounded disputes with partners or customers.

The first task in addressing any incident is its detection and classification. Automated tools and technologies can assist with monitoring well-known incidents and examining log files. Early detection is crucial for preventing small incidents from escalating. Automated methods include analyzing system logs, process logs, and network traffic. Log analysis involves searching for patterns of commands that correlate with a network attack. These patterns identify processes generally associated with an attack. Commercial tools for log analysis systems include Recoverix, Stat Monitor, and Netrecon.

Commercial tools for incident management are often costly, difficult to tune, and develop unrealistic expectations among security personnel due to the low number of false positives. The implementation of a monitoring system can create a situation of backfilling the report, instead of backfilling the actions, leading to the so-called security turn where more and more reports are generated with no effect on improved security. Behavior monitoring can be classified as pattern-based, statistical, and transaction-based, each with its own mathematical foundation and requirements for the analyzed system. Some organizations develop their own monitoring tools. Free tools are also available, such as Snort, Tripwire, Network Flight Recorder, and Tcpdump. Some networking equipment vendors offer free monitoring tools, but they are often generic and require considerable resources to tune for effective use.

Rebuilding incidents by replaying log files is a new approach to forensic analysis of breaks of confidentiality or integrity. For investigating certain types of incidents, it can be useful to analyze log files of various equipment types in conjunction with traffic files captured from workstations and network segments where the incident occurrence is suspected. Analyzing workstations log files may help confirm or refute hypotheses about how an incident occurred, how an attacker achieved access to the system, how a backdoor was installed, and how the malware was transmitted. To perform a complex analysis of log files regarding an incident, in most scenarios it is necessary to use a versatile tool. As with analyzing logs of the packets captured from networks and history files of monitoring tools generating alerts, the analysis of these files should be performed using scripts or specifically designed programs since they cannot be analyzed manually in a reasonable time frame.

6.8 INCIDENT MANAGEMENT IN DIFFERENT INDUSTRY SECTORS

Organizations across various industries face incidents that can disrupt normal operations, result in loss of infrastructure, compromise safety measures, devastate brand image, and drain resources and funds. Therefore, effective planning for incidents is vitally important. Incident management is the process of managing, evaluating, and reducing incidents in an organization. In recent years, it has gained popularity in both academia and industry. Organizations have continued to deal with various incidents, creating a focus on assessing, analyzing, and managing these events. This interest has led to an increased need to adopt, implement, and formalize incident management in many organizations.

Airlines and aviation services are continuously threatened by accidents and incidents due to their antiquity, vastness, complexity, and interorganizational relationships. Reasons for concerning incident management in airlines and aviation services include incidents such as the Lockerbie Air Crash, Swissair Flight 111, American Airlines Flight 587, the Concorde disaster, the loss of over 20 aircraft, and the September 11 attacks. Therefore, these organizations constantly strive to improve their incident management systems and learn lessons from incidents.

The rail industry utilizes railways to transport passengers and goods. Recently, governments have encouraged competition in rail operations, allowing the establishment of various Train Operating Companies (TOCs) to provide passenger transport services. However, such competition has resulted in increased safety levels and incidents. To comply with legal requirements, maintain a focus on safety, and implement a positive safety culture, TOCs need to retrieve circumstances around incidents and encourage staff to submit detailed reports. This requirement underlines the use of incident management systems in this industry.

Healthcare organizations comprise a variety of public and private testing centers, hospitals, laboratories, and pharmacies. Healthcare providers constantly investigate incidents that have led to performance problems, loss of trust, and brand image. Organizations offering healthcare continuously strive to learn from incidents and recover as soon as possible. IT is a key enabler of healthcare functions; hence, incidents occur that affect the entire organization, such as prolonged database unavailability and malicious hackers gaining access to tamper with private patient records. Therefore, a focus on incident management in the healthcare sector is warranted.

6.9 RESULTS

Table 6.1 and Figure 6.3 present the features of effective incident management. Effective incident management enhances operational efficiency by rapidly detecting issues, minimizing downtime, and reducing financial losses, ensuring a swift, structured response. It also fosters customer trust, strengthens regulatory compliance, boosts employee morale, and drives continuous improvement, all while enhancing the organization's reputation and long-term success.

TABLE 6.1
Effective Incident Management

Feature	Description	Accuracy/ Efficiency
Quick Incident Detection	Rapid identification of issues reduces response time and mitigates impact	Very High (90–95%)
Efficient Response Coordination	Structured response processes help coordinate resources efficiently during an incident	High (85–90%)
Minimized Downtime	Faster incident resolution limits downtime and reduces operational disruptions	Very High (90–95%)
Improved Customer Trust	Swift and transparent incident handling builds customer trust and confidence	High (85–90%)
Data-Driven Decision-Making	Incident data help in analyzing patterns and making informed decisions for future improvements	High (80–90%)
Reduced Financial Losses	Minimizing impact through effective management reduces overall costs associated with incidents	Very High (90–95%)
Enhanced Regulatory Compliance	Ensures adherence to industry standards, reducing risks of fines and legal issues	High (85–90%)
Continuous Improvement	Post-incident analysis and improvement strategies prevent similar incidents in the future	Very High (90–95%)
Boosted Employee Morale	Effective incident management fosters a safe, well-prepared work environment, improving morale	High (80–90%)
Strengthened Reputation	Efficient incident handling enhances the organization's reputation for reliability and preparedness	Very High (90–95%)

TABLE 6.2
Sectors in Incident Management

Industry Sector	Common Incidents	Key Focus Areas in Incident Management	Special Requirements	Estimated Effectiveness of Incident Management
Healthcare	Data breaches, equipment malfunctions, patient safety issues	Patient data security, equipment reliability, compliance with health regulations	HIPAA compliance, fast incident response for patient safety	**90–95%**
Finance	Cyberattacks, fraud, system outages	Cyber security, fraud detection, service continuity	High data security standards, regulatory reporting (e.g., SOX)	**95–98%**
Retail	Supply chain disruptions, point-of-sale (POS) system failures, data breaches	Customer data protection, supply chain resilience, payment processing reliability	PCI compliance for payment systems, real-time monitoring	**85–90%**
Manufacturing	Equipment failures, safety hazards, supply chain issues	Equipment maintenance, worker safety, supply chain continuity	Safety protocols, quick recovery to avoid production delays	**90–93%**
Telecommunications	Network outages, data breaches, service disruptions	Network uptime, data privacy, quick customer communication	High service reliability, customer service level agreement (SLA) management	**92–96%**
Energy and Utilities	Power outages, equipment failures, cyberattacks	Grid reliability, safety protocols, environmental impact	Critical infrastructure protection, regulatory compliance	**94–97%**
Education	Cyber security threats, data privacy breaches	Student and staff data protection, digital infrastructure reliability	FERPA compliance, frequent cyber security assessments	**85–88%**
Government	Cyberattacks, data leaks, critical infrastructure failures	National security, data integrity, service continuity	High security standards, transparency with public	**93–97%**

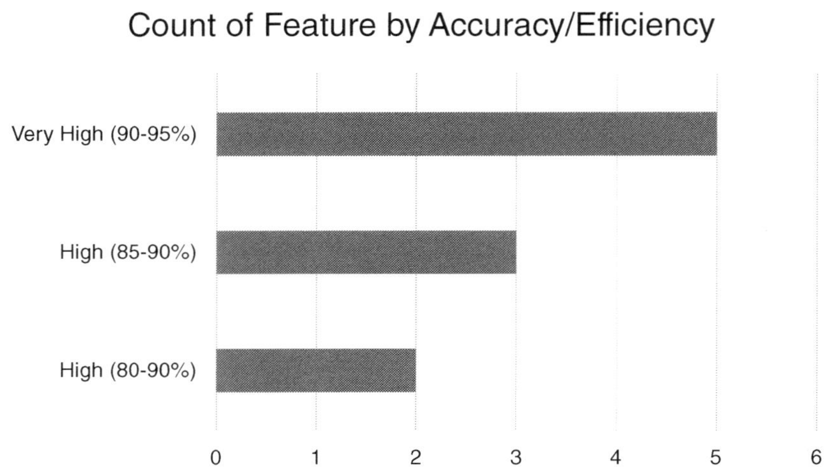

FIGURE 6.3 Effective Incident Management.

Incident management effectiveness varies across sectors, with healthcare, finance, and energy benefiting from high response rates and regulatory compliance. Key focus areas include data security, system reliability, and industry-specific requirements such as the Health Insurance Portability and Accountability Act (HIPAA) compliance as presented in Table 6.2.

6.10 CONCLUSION

Organizations need incident management capabilities and resources. They should have a comprehensive framework, invest in training, and use incident information for improvements. Sharing communication with all management levels shows a proactive approach and assures stakeholders participation. Incident management is crucial for organizational resilience. It reduces the impact of unexpected events and improves competitiveness. It focuses on reducing uncertainty and securing the business. Well-managed incidents prevent further damage to the organization.

REFERENCES

1. A. Hermawanto and M. Anggraini, "Globalization and locality: Global communication and digital revolution in the borderless world era," *Proceedings of LPPM UPN*, 2020. researchsynergypress.com
2. F. O. Usman, A. J. Kess-Momoh, and C. V. Ibeh, ". . . Trends: A global review: Examining emerging trends, challenges, and opportunities in the field of entrepreneurship, with a focus on how technology and globalization . . . ," *International Journal of . . .* , 2024. ijsra.net
3. A. O. Zeitz and D. A. Leblang, "Migrants as engines of financial globalization: the case of global banking." *International Studies Quarterly*, vol. 65, no. 2, pp. 360–374, 2021.
4. C. O. Udeagwu and I. E. Nnubia, "Globalisation and transnationalism: Impact and implications for Nigeria," *Journal of African & . . .* , 2024. nigerianjournalsonline.com

5. D. W. Arner, E. Avgouleas, and E. C. Gibson, "COVID-19, macroeconomic and sustainability shocks, moral hazard and resolution of systemic banking crises: Designing appropriate systems of public support," *European Business Organization Law Review*, 2022. Springer. springer.com
6. A. Ahmad, S. B. Maynard, K. C. Desouza, and J. Kotsias, "How can organizations develop situation awareness for incident response: A case study of management practice," *Computers & Security*, 2021. Elsevier. qut.edu.au
7. R. Van Tulder, S. B. Rodrigues, and H. Mirza, "The UN's sustainable development goals: Can multinational enterprises lead the decade of action?" *Journal of International . . .*, 2021. nih.gov
8. H. Benbya, N. Nan, H. Tanriverdi, and Y. Yoo, "Complexity and information systems research in the emerging digital world," *MIS Quarterly*, 2020. umn.edu
9. D. A. McEntire, *Disaster Response and Recovery: Strategies and Tactics for Resilience*. John Wiley & Sons, 2021.
10. W. Health Organization, "Patient safety incident reporting and learning systems: Technical report and guidance," 2020. who.int
11. Z. Chen, Y. Kang, L. Li, X. Zhang, H. Zhang, and H. Xu, "Towards intelligent incident management: Why we need it and how we make it," in *Proceedings of the 28th . . .*, 2020. google.com
12. J. Chen, S. Zhang, X. He, Q. Lin, H. Zhang, and D. Hao, "How incidental are the incidents? characterizing and prioritizing incidents for large-scale online service systems," in *Proceedings of the 35th . . .*, 2020. github.io
13. O. M. Agbede, "Incident handling and response process in security operations," 2023. theseus.fi
14. T. Ruskojärvi, "Cyber security incident management process in NOC/SOC integration," 2020. theseus.fi
15. D. Schlette, P. Empl, and M. Caselli, "Do you play it by the books? A study on incident response playbooks and influencing factors," in *IEEE Symposium on . . .*, 2024. researchgate.net
16. P. Jarzabkowski, R. Bednarek, K. Chalkias, et al., "Enabling rapid financial response to disasters: Knotting and reknotting multiple paradoxes in interorganizational systems," *Academy of Management*, 2022. city.ac.uk
17. A. Georgiadou, S. Mouzakitis, and D. Askounis, "Assessing mitre ATT&CK risk using a cyber-security culture framework," *Sensors*, 2021. mdpi.com
18. N. Schulenkorf, J. W. Peachey, G. Chen, and A. Hergesell, "Event leverage: A systematic literature review and new research agenda," *European Sport Management Quarterly*, vol. 24, no. 3, pp. 785–809, 2024.
19. A. Errida and B. Lotfi, "The determinants of organizational change management success: Literature review and case study," *Journal of Engineering Business Management*, vol. 2021, 2021. sagepub.com
20. P. R. Schulman, "Organizational structure and safety culture: Conceptual and practical challenges," *Safety Science*, 2020. e-tarjome.com
21. R. L. Brauer, "Safety and health for engineers," 2022. solumanu.com
22. H. Lee, "Changes in workplace practices during the COVID-19 pandemic: The roles of emotion, psychological safety and organisation support," *Journal of Organizational Effectiveness: People and Performance*, vol. 2021, no. 1, pp. 1–15, 2021. researchgate.net
23. A. Anand, P. Centobelli, and R. Cerchione, "Why should I share knowledge with others? A review-based framework on events leading to knowledge hiding," *Journal of Organizational . . .*, 2020. hal.science
24. S. Yildiz, Ö. Uğurlu, J. Wang, and S. Loughney, "Application of the HFACS-PV approach for identification of human and organizational factors (HOFs) influencing marine accidents," *Reliability Engineering & System Safety*, vol. 202, pp. 1–10, 2021. ljmu.ac.uk

25. R. Fucà and S. Cubico, "Undecidability and the evolution of ideas in an emergency event: An example of how to systemically test organizational effectiveness (OE) in university groups," *Education Sciences*, 2020. mdpi.com
26. M. A. Waddell, "Repeat audit findings: How FEMA responds to feedback." *International Journal of Disaster Risk Reduction*, vol. 100, p. 104157, 2024.
27. S. Kisely, N. Warren, L. McMahon, C. Dalais, and I. Henry, "Occurrence, prevention, and management of the psychological effects of emerging virus outbreaks on healthcare workers: Rapid review and meta-analysis," *BMJ*, 2020. bmj.com
28. S. S. Wang and U. Franke, "Enterprise IT service downtime cost and risk transfer in a supply chain," *Operations Management Research*, 2020. springer.com
29. A. Y. Alqahtani and A. A. Rajkhan, "E-learning critical success factors during the covid-19 pandemic: A comprehensive analysis of e-learning managerial perspectives," *Education Sciences*, 2020. mdpi.com
30. I. H. Sawalha, "Views on business continuity and disaster recovery," *International Journal of Emergency Services*, vol. 10, no. 3, pp. 351–365, 2021.
31. S. Morandini, F. Fraboni, M. De Angelis, and G. Puzzo, "The impact of artificial intelligence on workers' skills: Upskilling and reskilling in organisations," *Informing . . .*, 2023. unibo.it
32. T. C. Greenwell, L. A. Danzey-Bussell, and D. J. Shonk, *Managing Sport Events*. Human Kinetics, 2024.
33. A. A. Mughal, "Building and securing the modern security operations center (SOC)," *Journal of Business Intelligence and Big Data*, 2022. tensorgate.org
34. M. Yazdi, F. Khan, R. Abbassi, and R. Rusli, "Improved DEMATEL methodology for effective safety management decision-making," *Safety Science*, vol. 127, p. 104705, 2020.
35. K. Corsi and B. Arru, "Role and implementation of sustainability management control tools: Critical aspects in the Italian context," *Accounting*. emerald.com
36. I. Keshta and A. Odeh, "Security and privacy of electronic health records: Concerns and challenges," *Egyptian Informatics Journal*, 2021. sciencedirect.com
37. S. Anson, *Applied Incident Response*. John Wiley & Sons, 2020.
38. E. Salfati, E. Salfati, and M. Pease, "Digital forensics and incident response (DFIR) framework for operational technology (OT)," 2022. cyber0cloud.com
39. A. K. Skidmore, N. C. Coops, E. Neinavaz, et al., "Priority list of biodiversity metrics to observe from space," *Nature Ecology & Evolution*, vol. 5, no. 5, pp. 1–10, 2021. unibo.it
40. M. Izadi, K. Akbari, and A. Heydarnoori, "Predicting the objective and priority of issue reports in software repositories." *Empirical Software Engineering*, vol. 27, no. 2, p. 50, 2022.
41. F. Salguero-Caparrós and M. C. Pardo-Ferreira, "Management of legal compliance in occupational health and safety. A literature review," *Safety Science*, 2020. Elsevier. uma.es
42. J. M. Soon, A. K. M. Brazier, and C. A. Wallace, "Determining common contributory factors in food safety incidents–A review of global outbreaks and recalls 2008–2018," *Trends in Food Science & Technology*, vol. XX, pp. YY–ZZ, 2020. uclan.ac.uk
43. T. Elsaleh, S. Enshaeifar, R. Rezvani, and S. T. Acton, "IoT-Stream: A lightweight ontology for internet of things data streams and its use with data analytics and event detection services," *Sensors*, vol. 20, no. 10, 2020. mdpi.com
44. A. Stanimirović and M. Bogdanović, "Low-voltage electricity network monitoring system: Design and production experience," *Sensor Networks*, 2020. sagepub.com
45. D. Donadoni Santos, "Cybersecurity incident response in eHealth," 2023. upc.edu
46. P. Palanque, A. Cockburn, and C. Gutwin, "A classification of faults covering the human-computer interaction loop," *Computer Safety, Reliability, and . . .*, vol. 2020, 2020. Springer. hal.science

47. C. R. Kovesdi, R. M. Spangler, J. D. Mohon, and P. Murray, "Development of human and technology integration guidance for work optimization and effective use of information," 2024. osti.gov
48. A. Ahadh, G. Vallabhasseri Binish, and R. Srinivasan, "Text mining of accident reports using semi-supervised keyword extraction and topic modeling." *Process Safety and Environmental Protection*, vol. 155, pp. 455–465, 2021.
49. Y. Xue, Y. Fan, and X. Xie, "Relation between senior managers' safety leadership and safety behavior in the Chinese petrochemical industry." *Journal of Loss Prevention in the Process Industries*, vol. 65, p. 104142, 2020.
50. P. A. Coventry, N. Meader, H. Melton, and M. Temple, ". . . and pharmacological interventions for posttraumatic stress disorder and comorbid mental health problems following complex traumatic events: Systematic review and . . . ," *PLoS*, 2020. plos.org
51. Advanced Life Support Group (ALSG). *Major Incident Medical Management and Support: The Practical Approach at the Scene*. John Wiley & Sons, 2012.
52. N. Askitas, K. Tatsiramos, and B. Verheyden, "Estimating worldwide effects of non-pharmaceutical interventions on COVID-19 incidence and population mobility patterns using a multiple-event study," *Scientific Reports*, 2021. nature.com

7 Issues, Challenges in E-Banking

Case Study

Gurushankar H B, Francesco Flammini, Vinayakumar Ravi, and Jhanjhi N Z

7.1 INTRODUCTION

E-banking or electronic banking, known also as internet banking or simply online banking, involves the provision of banking services using digital means, whereby customers can remotely access internet platforms to conduct financial business. With the growth of the internet, mobile devices, and the needs for greater convenience, e-banking has become a vital aspect of modern financial systems. It ranges from simple activities such as checking an account balance and transferring money to more complex ones like applying for a loan, making international remittances, and so forth. All these have made banking much easier and efficient for the customer. However, despite all these advantages, the following are issues associated with e-banking on both bank and customer levels [1].

However, despite all these advantages, there are major challenges associated with e-banking at both bank and customer levels [1]. The shift of finances from classical physical branches to new online platforms introduces risks that generate new complexity in services constantly for innovation and risk management strategies. Figure 7.1 describes the challenges facing the banking sector related to cyber security. The rapid development of digital technology also calls for continuous adaptation from banks, as well as their users, on issues ranging from security breaches to regulatory compliance, which act ultimately as great obstacles to the growth of e-banking services. There are some core issues and challenges that banks and users are facing in banking.

7.2 SECURITY CONCERN

One of the most significant challenges that confronts e-banking is transaction safety. The more transactions move online, the more risk factors increase from cyberattacks. The hackers target the sites because they can find login passwords, personal identification numbers (PIN), and account numbers. Among the common methods used are phishing, malware, and social engineering, which lead to such losses and identity theft.

Phishing is one of the methods used by cybercriminals to dupe the user, making him disclose his login credentials or credit card numbers or even other personal details.

 DOI: 10.1201/9781003540045-7

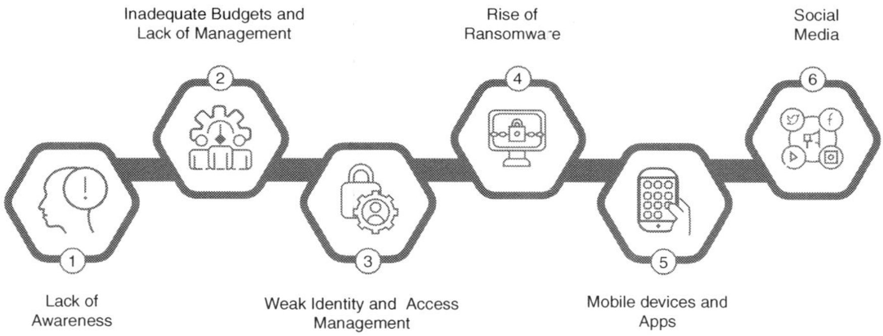

FIGURE 7.1 Challenges in the Banking Sector Related to Cyber Security.

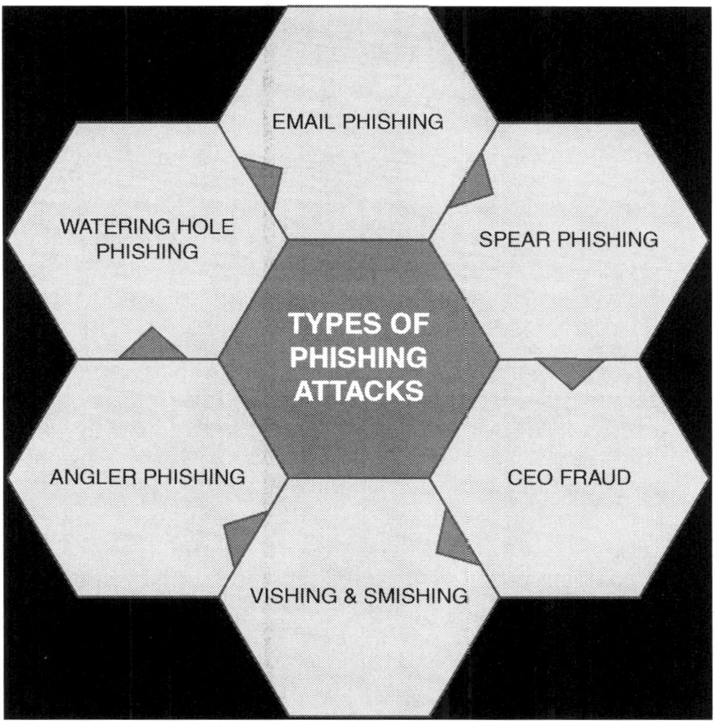

FIGURE 7.2 Types of Phishing Attacks.

The types of phishing attacks are presented in Figure 7.2. Most often, attackers pretend to be a legitimate institution and send a fake email or message looking almost like the original from a reputed organization such as a bank [2]. Generally, these messages contain links to some fraudulent sites through which customers unknowingly enter their details whereby the attacker makes money by stealing that information.

Malware includes viruses, worms, and Trojans that can infect the user's personal computer or mobile device to capture sensitive information such as keystrokes, login details, and banking account details. Malware keyloggers record all the keystrokes that the user types in, which would allow an attacker to steal the usernames, password and PIN when entered on an e-banking platform. Many users opt for weak, easily guessable passwords like "123456" or "password," which makes them vulnerable to brute-force attacks. Others may also use the same password for multiple services, and a breach of one service may likely compromise access to their e-banking account.

In a Man-in-the-Middle (MitM) attack, the attacker intercepts communications between the user and the bank's server. The attacker can then steal information, alter the content of messages, or manipulate the transaction without the user or the bank being aware of the interference. This is particularly dangerous when users are connected to insecure networks, such as public Wi-Fi networks. In a distributed denial-of-service (DDoS) attack, attackers flood a bank's servers with excessive traffic, overwhelming the system and causing it to slow down or crash. While a DDoS attack may not directly steal sensitive data, it can disrupt e-banking services, causing inconvenience to customers and potentially masking other malicious activities, such as data breaches.

Insider threats are risks that come from employees or contractors who, in their positions, have access to banking systems with sensitive information. These people might use the advantage that they have to steal information or commit fraud by using their privileges. Insider threats users are usually hard to identify because they are authorized users who understand all the mechanisms of concealing themselves.

7.3 TECHNICAL INFRASTRUCTURE AND RELIABILITY

As demonstrated in Figure 7.3, the success of e-banking depends much on robust technical infrastructure that will ensure smooth, real-time, and simultaneous transactions. But managing such systems is usually quite challenging because too many banks fail to have enough system capacities to meet heavy volumes of traffic mainly during peak times such as during salary pay dates or tax deadline submissions. Downtime, service outages, or slow processing speeds chafe customers, and lost business is a common net result.

The largest concern in e-banking is that the system has to be up 24 hours a day, 7 days a week with minimal or zero down time. Therefore, scheduled or unscheduled system downtime, because of technical failures or cyberattacks, would result in significant interruption to the banking service delivery process and eventually in lost transactions, frustrated customers, and damage to the reputation of the bank. As the number of customers adopting the e-banking services is increasing and more transactions are being carried out, the bank's system must cope with the growing demand. Scalability refers to the system's ability to accept an increased number of transactions and user loads without any form of performance degradation. Inability to have adequate scalability may cause the e-banking platforms to be slow in response, crash, and shut down when demand is high.

The third factor has to do with legacy systems—the information technology (IT) infrastructure in banks that is so old that it does not interface very easily with newer

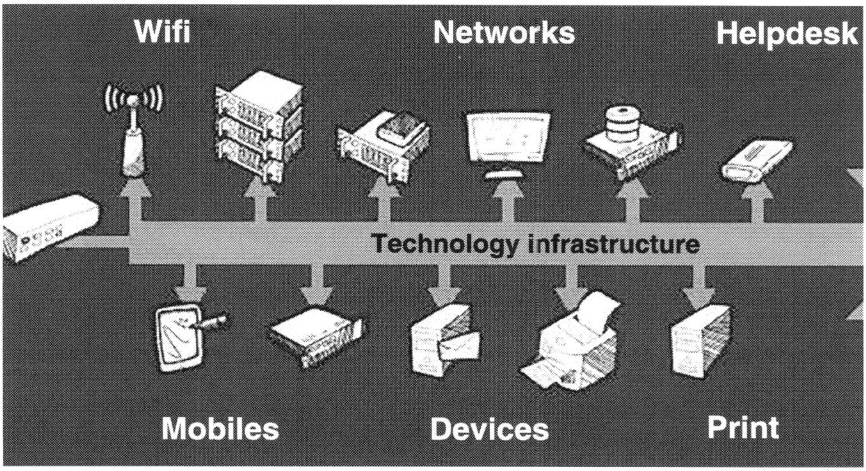

FIGURE 7.3 Technical Infrastructure Architecture.

technologies and platforms. Legacy systems can be less flexible, hard to maintain, and also prone to failure, lessening their reliability for most e-banking needs. It also becomes challenging in the integration of e-banking platforms with other financial services and fintech applications with the outdated underlying infrastructure. Data volumes relating to transaction records, customer details, and even financial statements are involved in e-banking systems. It is fundamentally important to secure all the data stored, retrieve it quickly, and manage it effectively for smooth running of e-banking services. But technically, it is difficult to manage voluminous data in real time when a system needs to honor local laws and place such data under General Data Protection Regulation (GDPR) or other regional laws for the sake of protecting sensitive data privacy.

The technical infrastructure has to be established in ways that are resistant to constant cyber security attacks, as experienced by DDoS attacks, ransomware, and others. An e-banking platform is an easy target for cybercrime due to the sensitive nature of the information it involves and the prospects of gain in terms of money. It therefore needs to ensure that it is secured with a high level of cyber security infrastructure strength and resilience. In this context, mobile banking applications are one of the primary touchpoints for customers. So reliability and silky smooth operation are very important. Mobile applications need to be able to function across a wide range of device specifications, operating systems, and network conditions. This means erratic performance of the app could result in slow transaction times or crashes and even data loss, all of which impact the customer experience negatively.

7.4 CUSTOMER SERVICE AND USER EXPERIENCE

As the number of e-banking transactions is rising, online platforms must garner customer support, as depicted in Figure 7.4. In the traditional context, the touchpoint for the delivery of customer support services was through the branches of banks, but

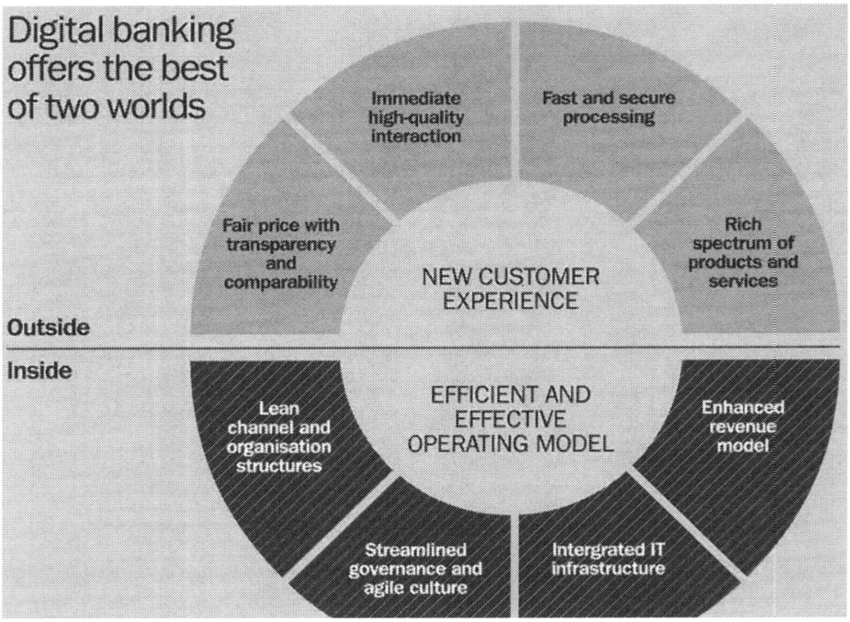

FIGURE 7.4 Customer Service and Experience.

with the advent of e-banking, more customers seek support through chatbots, online frequently asked questions (FAQs), and call centers [3]. One of the most critical facets toward retention is that users expect a smooth and intuitive experience with the product as most people think that whatever problem they are faced with should be resolved instantly during transactions. Poor designs of user interface (UI) will otherwise bring frustration, as will slow response times from the customer service team.

The backbone of a good user experience is an efficient user interface. Therefore, e-banking platforms must be accessible, intuitive, and visually pleasing to both desktops and other portable devices like mobile phones and tablets. The usability and user experience offered by the interface would cause annoyance if it were clumsy, messy, or simply incomprehensible; it will enhance user engagement and satisfaction in the case of an effective, seamless, and easy-to-use interface. Most important for a digital-first banking environment is inclusivity.

An online banking platform must be accessible to all customers. Disability access has to ensure that for the visually impaired, it includes screen reader support, large text options, and high-contrast color schemes while maintaining an easy-navigating feature for ailing minds.

Effective customer support is critical to e-banking as most customers face technical malfunctions, security risk concerns, or even issues with transactions. In this regard, the bank offering several support channels such as phone, live chat, email, and social media for the help of customers in real time helps to increase the overall experience with the customer. Customer support is really important because, in the digital age, a customer needs prompt and efficient support when financial matters are involved. Poor customer service is one reason for dissatisfaction, frustration, and loss of trust, which may lead customers to switch to other competing providers.

Today, customers require more experiences that are in tune with the choices and requirements they make. E-banking platforms using customer data effectively can now offer services designed to the needs of customers and recommendations on products could be provided with a real-time alert. Personalization refers to using data analytics and AI for the analysis of the behavior of customers and forecasting such behavior and more so the provision of customized products along with timely relevant information. Mobile banking is growing fast and so optimizing the mobile experience is the need of the hour. Thus, customers are increasingly asking to be able to work on their mobile phones like on the desktop, performing the same banking functions: to pay, to check balance, and to manage investments. Bad experience of mobile banking such as slow loading and crashes or failure in accomplishment of a task will "painfully" affect customer satisfaction. To many customers, mobile banking has actually become the primary source for accessing banking services. Poor experience on the mobile is often associated with increased churn rates because a significant number of clients will switch banks and look for other banks that provide better mobile services.

Trust is, by nature, the key to e-banking since customers hand over sensitive financial information and depend on the platform for safe transactions. Thus, security aspects such as multifactor authentication (MFA), encryption, and fraud detection are significant for trust building, but very complex security procedures can become a challenge to experience, hence the need for creating a balance between security and convenience. Feedback gathering and acting upon it remain significant elements in enhancing the service of e-banking. This will allow banks to fine-tune their platforms according to user pain points, preferences, and suggestions with continuous refinement and attention to any usability or service issues that may be found.

7.5 REGULATORY COMPLIANCE AND LEGAL CHALLENGES

The multinational nature of e-banking poses a legal challenge because banks are expected to abide by the laws of several country where they operate. Data privacy law, Anti-Money Laundering (AML) rules, and Know Your Customer (KYC) are the regulatory requirements for prevention of fraud activities and money laundering. However, it can be quite challenging to keep track of the change in the regulation of multiple jurisdictions, especially regarding cost-related fines as well as damages to the banking reputation caused by the failure of compliance. Figure 7.5 shows the benefits of regulatory compliance and the legal challenges.

Because of digital banking, the customers' sensitivity to their data managed by banks, such as personal identification information (PII), financial records, and transaction histories, increases, thus leading to increased demand in security over such kinds of information [4]. Data security in the digital economy is a crucial issue since it is not just a component for building customer trust but also for complying with national and international data protection regulation. In the European Union (EU),

FIGURE 7.5 Benefits of Regulatory Compliance.

the GDPR handles the manner in which personal data will be collected, processed, and stored. Banks must ensure that customer data are dealt with lawfully, with clear consent from the customers, and the banks must also give customers the opportunity to allow them access, to correct or delete their data. Generally, the California Consumer Privacy Act empowers California residents to understand what personal data are collected, to opt out of the sale of that data, and to require the businesses to delete those data in the United States.

AML and KYC are regulatory requirements made for banks to prevent their services from being misused, specifically for money laundering, terrorist financing, and fraud. Banks should determine who their customers really are, monitor transactions in the activity of suspicious transactions, and report suspicious activities to the law enforcement authorities. The Financial Action Task Force (FATF) is an international body outlining the standards in combating money laundering and financing of terrorism. Its recommendations are usually enacted into the national laws of many countries. The Bank Security Act (BSA) of the United States, for instance, requires financial institutions to keep records of cash purchases, report transactions above specific amounts, and file reports of suspicious activities.

The other important concern of e-banking is its cyber security since most banks have been targeted or are a target for cyberattacks such as data breaches, hacking, and phishing. Cyber security, therefore, relates to specific regulations set by governments and regulatory bodies to ensure that banks implement appropriate defenses to protect not only their systems but the customers' information as well. The Federal Financial Institutions Examination Council (FFIEC) oversees financial institutions in the United States and provides a guideline by which financial institutions should design their cyber security strategies and risk management processes. In the EU, for instance, the Network and Information Security (NIS) Directive presents a framework of protection for network and information systems engaged in the provision of essential services in areas such as banking.

The services cross countries, especially when banks serve international clients or facilitate cross-border transactions. Legal issues will in this case arise due to the difference in regulations of tax laws and consumer protection standards between the various countries. Banks are supposed to ensure compliance with laws of all the countries in which they carry out their businesses. Noncompliance by the banks may result in fines, legal cases, and some restrictions on operations in foreign jurisdictions. Consumer protection is a key issue when it comes to e-banking as customers are entrusting their money and personal information with banks. Many regulatory frameworks will hence contain provisions designed to prevent unfair practices and fraud as well as the misuse of data. Besides this, there will always be clear terms and conditions, transparent pricing, and access to procedures for dispute resolution. In the United States, the Dodd-Frank Wall Street Reform and Consumer Protection Act gives protection to consumers from unfair or deceptive acts or practices. At the EU level, the EU Directive on Consumer Rights protects consumers by giving them information concerning their rights and an apparatus for dispute resolution.

7.6 FRAUDULENT ACTIVITIES

E-banking platforms are usually the doorway through which fraudsters try to exploit vulnerabilities. Fraud can basically take many different forms, either credit card fraud, identity theft, or account takeovers. Fraud detection systems may not keep pace with increasingly sophisticated tactics deployed by fraudsters. Additionally, customers can inadvertently assist fraud by becoming victims of a scam or failing to secure their devices and accounts [5, 6]. Types of frauds in banking are shown in Figure 7.6.

Identity theft is one form of financial fraud. The identity thieves steal the victim's personal information—Social Security numbers, addresses, or bank account details—and consequently open new accounts, apply for loans, or make unauthorized purchases in the name of the victim. Since it usually becomes extremely difficult to detect and effectively resolve this type of scam, this makes identity theft especially destructive. The aftermath of identity theft is usually financial and reputational. Victims lose, and a bank may also face some financial losses due to such a failure. The reputation of a bank is also likely to be hurt because of the inability to protect customers' sensitive information. Here fraudsters steal bank credentials belonging to legitimate users and acquire unauthorized access to their accounts. After that, the perpetrator can carry out transfers, withdrawal of funds, or amendment of information for account details to keep the rightful owner from gaining access to the account.

Card Not Present (CNP) is a fraud in which the facts of the credit or debit card stolen by fraudsters are used to make purchases online or even over the phone. Because the actual card itself is not needed for the purchase, the fraudster hardly has a chance of being noticed until the transactions are done. CNP fraud is perhaps the

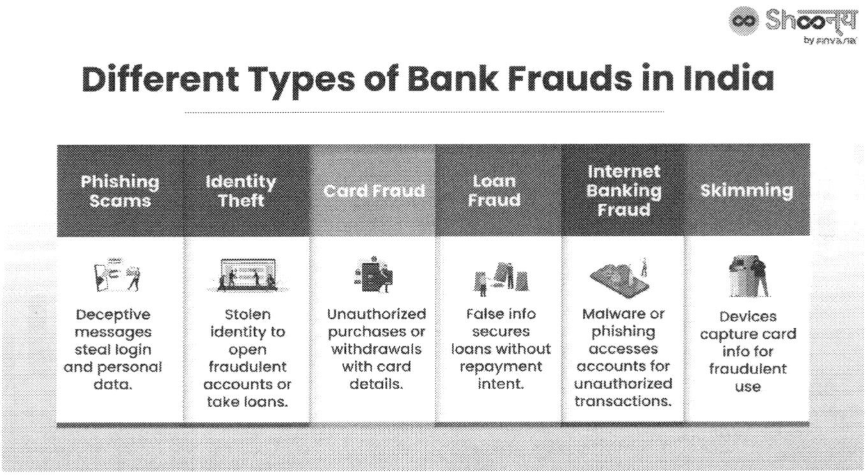

FIGURE 7.6 Types of Frauds in Banking.

most common type of internet fraud and can result in huge losses for customers as well as merchants in monetary terms. Banks will end up paying back the customers in case of any fraudulent transaction, which may turn out to be costly. A money mule is an individual who, sometimes unknowingly, enlists to assist criminals transfer illegitimate funds obtained. In an e-banking system, actions of money mules primarily comprise the process of executing one transfer from one account to another. As such, it is very challenging to track down the source of money that happened to be stolen, making fraud untraceability a critical tactic in this process of money laundering. Money mules allow fraudsters to hide the source of the money that had been stolen. That puts the banks at risk of involvement in illegal activities, by mere innocence.

Synthetic identity fraud is when fraudsters gather actual and fake information to create a completely new, fictitious identity. Being harder to detect, it surprisingly does not put real people's names behind the identity, but it still passes through most checks on verification. Synthetic identities allow fraudsters to indeed make different kinds of accounts with banks, take loans, get credit cards, and run away with that money before the fraud is identified. Since synthetic identities often pass traditional verification processes, like credit checks, banks may not be aware of such fraud until it's already wrought a lot of damage.

7.7 ADOPTION BARRIERS FOR CERTAIN DEMOGRAPHICS

Even as e-banking has gained momentum in metros, there are groups in the population that will not embrace it as easily, especially the older generation or rural dwellers. This could be due to a lack of availability of high-speed internet, unfamiliarity with digital platforms, or other fears regarding security. Among the biggest challenges that banks will face in the future is to make e-banking accessible and responsive to every stratum of society [6].

The elderly and low-income groups lack technological literacy and digital competencies for the easy and convenient access of e-banking services. Again, this is above general computer or smartphone use, as taken for granted by people, but includes access to websites or mobile applications, online account administration, and identification of security risks. Without the appropriate digital literacy, one may feel puzzled or hesitant to employ internet banking. Hence, they may avoid e-banking entirely. Older generations who have never grown up with digital technology may find it difficult to embrace e-banking. Sometimes, a lack of access to education and technology leaves the individual less prepared to connect with digital mediums.

People in rural areas, low-income communities, or developing countries suffer from limited access to reliable internet, smartphones, or computers for the proper implementation of e-banking. The "digital divide" can cause these individuals not to be able to take full advantage of the digital economy, including e-banking. Access to technology and the internet is fundamental for e-banking. Without it, people are deprived of the advantages of digital banking, such as accessibility, financial inclusion, and remote management of finances. Internet infrastructure can be inadequate in rural or far-flung locations for a stable connection, thus preventing the usage of e-banking. Banks can inform their customers about Unstructured Supplementary Service Data (USSD) banking, which offers an opportunity for basic phone users sans internet to engage in a variety of banking operations. It has been found that acquiring smartphones, computers, and internet connectivity is a significant outlay for low-income households and, therefore, a barrier to adoption. To overcome this limitation, public access can be arranged by governments or local organizations at libraries, community centers, or post offices, so that e-banking services can be accessed.

Perhaps many, especially the elderly and the not digitally literate, have really deep security concerns. A fear of fraud, hacking, identity theft, among others, prevents one from embracing e-banking. Some may need face-to-face banking as that seems to feel secure and safe for them about their finances. Trust is very essential in financial matters. If users perceive e-banking as unsecure, they would not adopt it, no matter how convenient and efficient it is to use. Most users will feel too vulnerable if they cannot understand how security features like encryption, MFA, and fraud detection work. To assure customers, banks need to implement strong, visible security features, such as biometric authentication (fingerprint or facial recognition), two-factor authentication, and real-time alerts for any activity in their accounts.

Cultural attitudes toward money management, banking, and technology impact the adoption of e-banking. Some cultures highly value face-to-face interactions and personal relations with the bank staff. Hence, they would not want to shift to digital banking platforms even if that is convenient and inexpensive. Banking is an intensely personal activity, and preferences in culture may powerfully influence people's way of managing finances. Failure to recognize these cultural factors will ensure that there is no acceptance of e-banking in some communities. There are some cultures that build trust through relationships with a bank and, hence, view digital banking as impersonal and untrustworthy. Hence, it is important for banks to provide a hybrid model where customers can do some kind of banking online but maintain access to personal services while in-branch.

Access to e-banking is restricted by financial inclusion issues for several people, especially in developing countries or low-income communities. These include denial of access to the formal banking systems, lower levels of income, and informal financial setups. For people with no access to the basic banking systems, e-banking is irrelevant or inaccessible. E-banking allows for the possibility of providing financial services to less served audiences, although this population might lack access or even economic stability, which are useful to take advantage of via digital services. Individuals who do not hold a traditional bank account are very frequently found in developing countries or areas where fewer services are provided; therefore, they hardly access e-banking services. For instance, people using informal financial systems, such as cash-based transactions, may see little value in embracing e-banking services. Banks can launch mobile money services. This must allow subscribers the opportunity to conduct banking transactions not necessarily through opening a traditional bank account but through their mobile phones via USSD codes.

7.8 INTEGRATION WITH THIRD-PARTY SERVICES

Many of the e-banking services are based on integrations with third-party providers, which could be payment processors, fintech platforms, or mobile wallets. Although such integrations are added for convenience and expand the services being offered, they add technical complexity as well as safety risks. Seamless integration is important to avoid transactional errors, data breaches, or customer dissatisfaction [7]. Despite the growing popularity of e-banking through convenience, efficiency, and access, not all demographic groups adopt e-banking services at the same pace. Various barriers prevent certain groups of people from using them effectively, ranging from technological challenges to socioeconomic, cultural, and psychological factors. Understanding these barriers is crucial in banks offering differential services, thereby closing a significant digital divide.

Without it, customers are denied the convenience, financial inclusion, and remote management of finances brought about by digital banking. Deep rural or remote areas may lack internet infrastructure to provide stable internet connections, thus e-banking cannot be applied. Banks can create e-banking applications optimized for low-cost smartphones, and also ensure that they consume minimal data to operate.

Some groups prefer face-to-face banking contacts in which they feel safer and more in control. Trust is a major factor in financial transactions. If the users do not feel that e-banking is secure, they will not use it, no matter how convenient or efficient it is. Unless users understand how security measures such as encryption, MFA, and fraud detection work, they may feel too vulnerable to adopt e-banking. Banks can implement strong, visible security features, such as biometric authentication (fingerprint or facial recognition), two-factor authentication, and real-time alerts for account activity to reassure customers. Targeted communications educate the user on the safety of e-banking, such as an easy-to-understand tutorial on how to protect their accounts.

Cultural attitudes are influences which impact the adoption of e-banking technology because most people in certain cultural groups emphasize face-to-face relations and personal relationships as that they share with the bank staff. This might keep them from digital banking portals, though they provide convenience and cost economies. Banking is a very sensitive affair, and cultural mores play a big part in how people handle banking matters. Not taking these cultural aspects into consideration would, therefore, make the introduction of e-banking impossible in those communities. There are other communities, especially those located in some Asian, African, and Middle Eastern regions, which emphasize a relationship with bankers rather than having a convenient digital use. For such a culture that becomes dependent on a relationship-based trust building toward the banks, it can become hard to trust online banks as they are not personalized enough. Banks can therefore provide a hybrid model whereby customers are given room to do a portion of their banking through online services but always have access to personal in-branch facilities.

People those who come from developing countries or low-income communities, would be the first obstacles in opening the avenue to e-banking for people. This might include formal banking services not being available, the lower income, or informal financial systems. For people without even the most basic access to traditional banking, e-banking often seems irrelevant or entirely out of reach. E-banking can reach unprovided populations, but those people may not have the necessary initial access to banking services or economic security to actually profit from electronic services. People who use informal financial systems in general, such as cash-based transactions, are likely to show very little interest in using e-banking services.

7.9 DATA PRIVACY AND PROTECTION

With greater digitization in the storage and transfer of personal and financial information, the issue of privacy and security of customer information gains importance. Legal consequences of a breach in any form, loss of customer confidence, and declined business are some of the implications of data breach. Banks have to follow strict data protection laws like GDPR by the EU or similar ones in other countries [8]. Data privacy in e-banking is the right of customers to have their private data and financial information processed confidentially and protected against unauthorized access, misuse, and exploitation. A good amount of data is collected in digital banking, for instance, names, addresses, Social Security numbers, and birthdates.

A data breach occurs when unauthorized persons or organizations break into highly secured sensitive information, usually through hacking or some form of negligence. This means that a customer's financial details may be exposed to malicious activities including identity theft and fraud. Data breaches wear down the trust customers develop with banks and can result in severe financial and reputational losses for banks [9]. The fraudsters perpetrate their scams by phishing attacks. Here, they pretend to be a bank or some other legitimate organization and demand login information or other confidential details from the customer. They use that information to access bank accounts without authorization. Most probably, the most common and efficient method by which cyber crooks circumvent data security measures is through phishing against less technically savvy people. There is malicious software akin to malware, which hackers use when breaching into a banking system to steal some information or even tamper with transactions. In this category of malware, there is a form known as ransomware, which encrypts an organization's data and later demands a ransom for its release.

Malware will look into compromised sensitive information and even banking services, while ransomware attacks might freeze the whole operation of the bank. Insider threats are another form of security risk involving people within, such as employees, who have legitimate access to the bank's systems and misuse their authorized privileges to steal or leak sensitive information. This might be deliberate, such as by disgruntled employees, or accidental, as through carelessness. Internal data leakage can be as destructive as external attacks, and it is hard to identify since internal users are trusted. A possible solution is encryption, which is the change of secret information into code to deny access to unauthorized people. Weak encryption or very old security protocols, however, open doors to a level of vulnerability of that data to cyber-attacks. Strong encryption prevents hackers from reading sensitive customer information that is transmitted or stored.

E-banking involves numerous data privacy regulations and statutes to protect customers' details. Failure to abide by those regulations attracts heavy financial penalties and reputational damage. The GDPR in Europe decrees some stringent regulations in the collection, processing, and storage of personal data. This entitles a person to rights over his or her data, such as the right to access, correction, and erasure. Banks operating in the EU or serving EU customers must comply with GDPR.

The Payment Card Industry Data Security Standard (PCI DSS) is the international standard for payment card information. It applies to all organizations that process credit and debit cards, even when it comes to e-banking. Several data privacy laws exist across countries, such as Brazil's Lei Geral de Proteção de Dados, India's Personal Data Protection Bill, and Canada's Personal Information Protection and Electronic Documents Act. These regulations apply to internationally operating banks, and failure to adhere to them may attract penalties. Encryption protects secret information both at the time of transmission and storage. Masking data can also be applied whereby certain secret information, such as credit card numbers, cannot be revealed unless a specific user has a right to see the full data. Banks can encrypt customer information starting with entering of information into the e-banking platform to the time it reaches a bank's server.

MFA requires two or more proofs of identity (for example, password and one-time verification code) before logging into an account. Even with stolen login credentials, this will reduce the chance of unauthorized access. Biometric data such as fingerprints or facial recognition can be used for a more secure and convenient authentication process. In this sense, sending an OTP to the customer's mobile or email for identity verification has become an important prerequisite before proceeding with any transactions. Continuous security audits and penetration testing help detect vulnerabilities in e-banking systems, giving banks an opportunity to fix potential weaknesses before they could be exploited. Data minimization refers to collecting data only if necessary for carrying out banking services; it does not expose sensitive information at risk of breaching it. Banks can comply with the Data Retention Policy to ensure data are retained only for as long as necessary. It follows that when data are no longer needed, they will be erased securely.

7.10 CONCLUSION

Most of the people enjoy the benefits of convenient operation, yet a number of problems continue to stand before their doors. They range from primary security to infrastructure management, the delivery of services with efficiency to customers, and fulfillment of set regulations. Overcoming these will enable e-banking to be secure, efficient, and accessible both to customers and to financial institutions.

REFERENCES

1. Mbaidin, Hisham O., Mohammad A.K. Alsmairat, and Raid Al-Adaileh. "Blockchain adoption for sustainable development in developing countries: Challenges and opportunities in the banking sector." *International Journal of Information Management Data Insights* 3.2 (2023): 100199.
2. Vinoth, S., et al. "Application of cloud computing in banking and e-commerce and related security threats." *Materials Today: Proceedings* 51 (2022): 2172–2175.
3. Emmanuel, Baffour Gyau, et al. "Transforming banking: Examining the role of AI technology innovation in boosting banks financial performance." *International Review of Financial Analysis* (2024): 103700.
4. Akinbowale, Oluwatoyin Esther, et al. "Development of a policy and regulatory framework for mitigating cyberfraud in the South African banking industry." *Heliyon* 10.1 (2024).
5. Shabbir, Aysha, Maryam Shabir, Abdul Rehman Javed, Chinmay Chakraborty, and Muhammad Rizwan. "Suspicious transaction detection in banking cyber–physical systems." *Computers & Electrical Engineering* 97 (2022): 107596.
6. Saheb, Tahereh, and Faranak Hosseinpouli Mamaghani. "Exploring the barriers and organizational values of blockchain adoption in the banking industry." *The Journal of High Technology Management Research* 32.2 (2021): 100417.
7. Kim, Long, Kanyanit Wichianrat, and Sook Fern Yeo. "An integrative framework enhancing perceived e-banking service value: A moderating impact of e-banking experience." *Journal of Open Innovation: Technology, Market, and Complexity* 10.3 (2024): 100336.
8. Wang, Shuang, et al. "Data privacy and cybersecurity challenges in the digital transformation of the banking sector." *Computers & Security* 147 (2024): 104051.
9. Chang, Victor, et al. "Towards data and analytics driven B2B-banking for green finance: A cross-selling use case study." *Technological Forecasting and Social Change* 206 (2024): 123542.

8 Cyber Security for Machine Learning Systems in Business Data

Vidyashree K P, Shivani T J, Shilpa K S, and Vinayakumar Ravi

8.1 INTRODUCTION TO MACHINE LEARNING IN BUSINESS DATA

The critical area that would need the protection of machine learning (ML) systems is cyber security for an ever-changing digital landscape. In particular, if ML systems deal with sensitive commercial information, then this aspect gains much importance. The more companies are dependent on ML to make their data-driven decisions, the greater need to protect private data. Corporations' ML algorithms work on enormous amounts of data including, but not limited to, financial transactions and customer information that are very attractive to cybercriminals. Some of the most viable threats for these systems include model inversion, data poisoning, and adversarial attacks. This kind of incursion might disrupt the operations or leads to unauthorized access to confidential business information. This chapter will detail how cyber security can be included in the development and deployment of ML models for protection of corporate data. Important topics include specific threat models for ML systems, best practices in handling data securely, encryption techniques, and adversarial defense strategies providing strong security for critical ML applications. Furthermore, it will accentuate the rise of significance of compliance standards and frameworks over legal rights to ensure safe operations of ML-driven business processes from cyber threats and violators. Chapter This chapter gives insights into safeguarding ML systems from evolving cyberattacks and therefore is a preliminary guide toward understanding the synergy among business data, cyber security, and ML.

8.2 OVERVIEW OF ML IN BUSINESS

With so many ever-emerging cyber threats like malware, phishing, ransomware, DoS attacks, and zero-day vulnerabilities, it's already clear that traditional security protocols and defense mechanisms have the uphill task of trying to keep pace with such changes. Such changes show, at best, that today's security strategies rely so heavily on the intervention of the analyst. Not only is this manual method inherently slow and often prone to human error but it also complicates the detection of and timely response to the increasingly sophisticated and ever-evolving threats.

DOI: 10.1201/9781003540045-8

ML now emerges as a transformative technology that facilitates automation within security systems, empowering security teams to more effectively navigate the complex threats of the present day. In contrast to the traditional rule-based detection methods, ML algorithms truly excel at identifying subtle anomalies and nefarious activities. They achieve this through the meticulous real-time analysis of vast datasets, revealing intricate patterns of attack. The capability for intelligent and automated decision-making not only enables swifter response times but also enhances adaptability to the ever-evolving landscape of cyber security. It thus identifies threats better through addressing known as well as unknown dangers and, hence, provides a more proactive kind of defense when it is integrated into cyber security frameworks. In terms of changing security policies and responding to newly emerging threats, it is a significant leap in safeguarding highly dynamic networks, particularly in areas where traditional defense mechanisms cannot protect against modern cyberattacks [1].

Companies like Netflix use ML to make personalized recommendations. This technology is important for the optimization of business operations since it automates tasks, enhances decision-making, and improves customer experiences. For instance, Netflix applies deep learning algorithms in its recommendation engine to analyze user behavior, preferences, and content trends, thus allowing it to recommend tailored movies and series [2, 3]. The system will make an accurate prediction of what users are likely to love by integrating deep learning models with collaborative filtering. In this sense, it creates much better quality recommendations by exploiting large amounts of user interactions and advanced neural networks, which are responsible for intricate relationships between users and the content. For example, Amazon applied ML toward dynamic pricing and optimized the supply chain. These models serve the function of predicting demand, optimizing inventory, and allowing real-time price adjustments. This means that they ensure smooth operations and significant profits. With the advancement of science, its application in the commercial world increases in scope and complexity. It can be inferred that in this fast-moving market, an efficient supply chain management is facilitated by companies using predictive analytics and by offering customer support through chatbots and self-service kiosks. Data-driven insight is now at the core of business acumen and operational efficiency, in large part because of automation of process through ML. These algorithms greatly contribute to the development of commercial applications because they make decision support data driven and optimize operations. Figure 8.1 shows several ML strategies, including reinforcement, supervised, and unsupervised learning, all fine-tuned to serve specific needs in business.

For example, classification tasks may improve fraud detection systems and customer churn analysis, while supervised learning can be applied to regression tasks like population growth prediction and weather forecasting. Conversely, unsupervised learning helps with focused marketing, data-driven market segmentation, and structure discovery. Reinforcement learning is one of the many ways that ML is being used to drive efficiency and creativity in business. It also helps to construct sophisticated chatbot agents and optimize operational procedures [4].

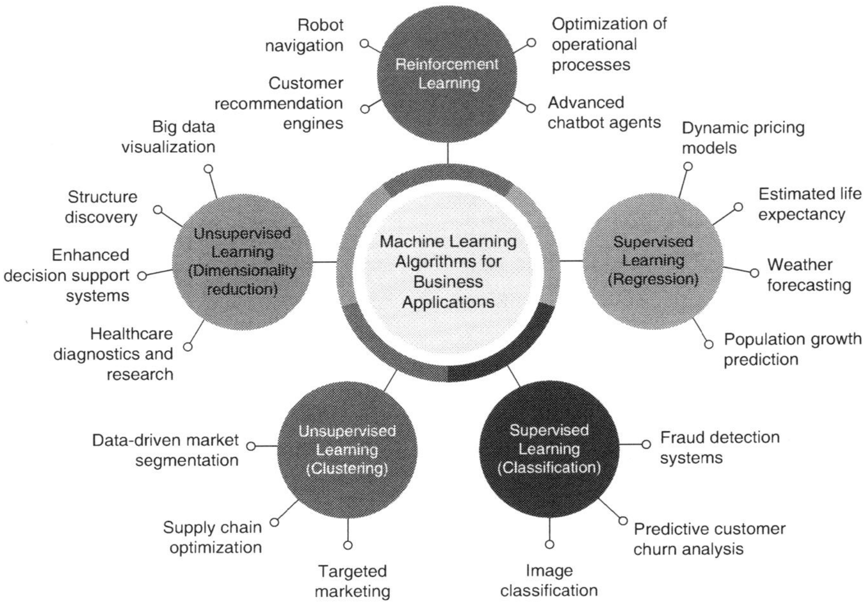

FIGURE 8.1 ML Algorithms for Business Applications.

8.3 TYPES OF BUSINESS DATA LEVERAGING ML

ML has greatly improved the ways in which companies use data to make decisions and derive insight. Critical to this are customer lists, which may include demographic information, purchase history, and interaction histories. Utilizing ML algorithms makes it possible to analyze data in ways that can create more personalized marketing initiatives and more granularly defined client profiles. Personalized recommendations and predictive analytics allow companies to forecast what the customer may need or want, and this is helpful for the service delivery of customers [5]. The operational data comprise indicators in resource allocation, industrial processes, and supply chain logistics. Predictive requirements for maintenance can be achieved with ML algorithms; therefore, such an action would minimize the costs and maximize the operational efficiency. Automating some activities will keep businesses having relatively simple functions and focusing on strategic objectives [6].

Businesses also require financial data, which includes market trends, transaction histories, and financial records. By evaluating past financial data to predict market moves, ML can improve fraud detection systems, automate credit scoring procedures, and optimize investment portfolios. This makes it possible for businesses to handle risks and make well-informed financial decisions [7–9].

8.4 IMPORTANCE OF SECURING BUSINESS DATA IN ML SYSTEMS

According to the author [10], Figure 8.2 highlights several important facets of data management and its importance to companies. The removal of redundant data is one of the main advantages mentioned. Businesses may keep clean and consistent datasets by avoiding redundant or unneeded data by putting strong data management systems in place. Since redundant data might result in inconsistent reporting and decision-making processes, this improves data quality and increases operational efficiency. Stricter data privacy and security regulations are another crucial element. Businesses must place a high priority on protecting sensitive data in the face of growing cyber risks and stringent regulations like the California Consumer Privacy Act (CCPA) and the General Data Protection Regulation (GDPR). By providing restricted access, encryption, and routine audits of stored data, data management systems aid in the maintenance of high security standards by guaranteeing that only authorized individuals have access to sensitive data.

8.5 CYBER SECURITY CHALLENGES IN ML

The array of problems accompanying ML integration is very decisive to the effectiveness of cyber security. An obvious problem is susceptibility of the ML model to adversary attacks, where, under some situations, attackers secretly change some input data items and use them to produce outputs for the model manipulated. For instance, in a very interesting example, the researchers were able to manipulate an image recognition system to misclassify a stop sign as a yield sign with just a few pixel changes in the image [11]. This kind of vulnerability underscores the importance of developing strong countermeasures against such attacks because they can have serious implications for security-related applications. There is a significant aspect of the dependency on high-quality data. Training data used when developing the ML algorithm are key to the accuracy it produces. When the train data have some error and bias, then the accuracy of predictions would be terrible. For example, a biased dataset would make a facial recognition system less optimal for performance for users in certain demographics, leading to ethical implications and jeopardizing

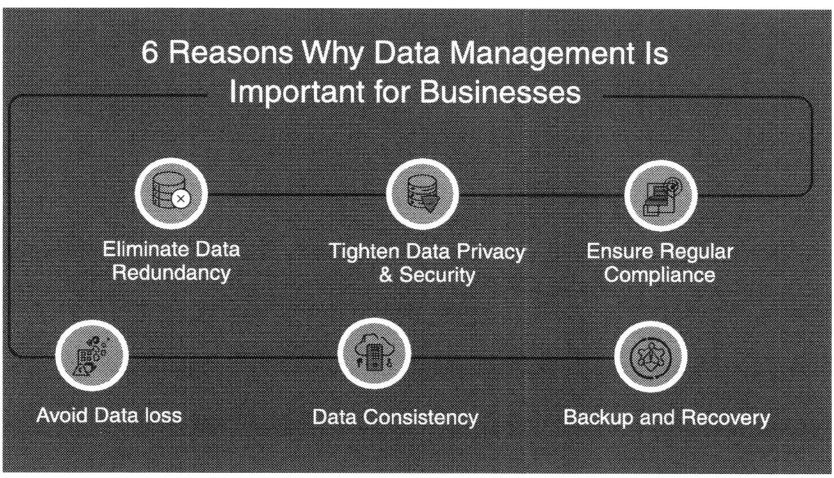

FIGURE 8.2 Reasons Why Data Management is Important for Business.

the integrity of the security protocols in place [12]. Furthermore, an adversary may compromise the training set through data poisoning techniques by injecting malicious data into it, which only serves to further degrade the model's performance [13].

Moreover, ML application development is highly threatened as cyber threats are dynamic, meaning that attackers keep changing their plans and strategies. This results in the need for upgrading models and retraining models about recent changes. For example, ransomware attacks are advancing rapidly, and they also now utilize advanced encryption techniques to defeat those systems that have ordinary methods of detection. Organizations may find themselves vulnerable to attack vectors that had previously been mitigated if ML models are not adapted to these evolving threats [14]. Lastly, the issue of interpretability continues to pose a significant challenge.

For cyber security experts, it becomes very challenging to understand the decision-making processes that govern the outputs of many ML models. Deep learning algorithms are even harder to understand because they work like "black boxes" [15]. Due to the lack of transparency, security teams find it very difficult to trace the actual cause of a failure or an attack, thus restricting their response capabilities in incidents. For instance, if a model incorrectly labels a benign file as dangerous without offering a clear reason, analysts could spend time chasing false positives while real threats remain undiscovered. In conclusion, while ML presents a promising avenue for improving cyber security, the effective implementation of ML in security applications necessitates tackling certain issues, including adversarial attacks, data quality, adaptation to changing threats, and model interpretability.

Table 8.1 presented by the author [16] lists crucial resources, including Apache Spark, a potent big data processing framework. If not adequately secured, using such tools can reveal weaknesses. Because Apache Spark, for example, can manage big datasets, hackers looking to expose confidential company information find it to be a desirable target. Another tool on the list, Apache Kafka, is also commonly used for real-time data processing and streaming. Due to its dispersed structure and complexity, security issues including incorrect authentication and data leakage during transit may arise. Attackers can take advantage of these flaws in weak security protocols, intercepting data streams and gaining access to private data. Furthermore, whereas technologies like R and Elasticsearch offer strong analytics capabilities, they also come with strict access constraints that need to be monitored to keep out unwanted access. For instance, if Elasticsearch is set incorrectly, it may expose data, making it possible for attackers to take advantage of security holes and run arbitrary queries, which might result in data breaches.

8.6 DATA PRIVACY CONCERNS IN BUSINESS ML APPLICATIONS

Figure 8.3, adapted from [17], illustrates the importance of data privacy and confidentiality. In digital era, data have become an essential resource that drives innovation, informs decisions, and facilitates the smooth running of modern civilization. But the abundance of data has led to previously unheard-of issues with privacy and confidentiality. The safeguarding of data from unauthorized access, breaches, and exploitation has become increasingly imperative due to the massive generation and sharing of sensitive information by individuals and companies. This increasing

TABLE 8.1
Tools for Data Lakes Conversion

Tool	Brief Description
Apache Spark	Open-source cluster computing framework
Spark Core	Provides distributed task dispatching, scheduling, and basic input/output (I/O) functionalities
Spark Structured Query Language (SQL)	Presents Spark module for structured data processing
Spark Streaming	An extension of the core Spark application programming interface (API) to perform streaming analytics
Spark MLib	Spark's machine learning library
GraphX	Graph processing API
Akka	Implementation of the Actor Model on the Java Virtual Machine
Apache Cassandra	Open-source database management system
Apache Kafka	Open-source stream-processing software platform
Kafka Streams	A client library to build applications and store in Kafka clusters
Kafka Connect	Enables data processing capabilities between Apache Kafka and other data systems
Elasticscarch	A search and analytics engine
11	Statistical and computing programming language and software environment
Scala	General-purpose programming language
Python	Programming language
MQ Telemetry Transport	Simple and lightweight messaging (ISO/IEC 20022) protocol

concern has led to the development and application of state-of-the-art technologies, especially ML, to improve data confidentiality. This introduction lays the framework for a detailed examination of ML methods for preserving data securely by providing a broad overview of the evolving data privacy landscape and highlighting the crucial role of ML. An unprecedented quantity of data is being gathered, stored, and shared because of the digital revolution of our environment. These data are extremely profitable targets for hackers since they contains intellectual property, financial information, healthcare data, personal information, and more. Effective data privacy measures are desperately needed, as seen by the numerous data breaches and privacy violations that have occurred. Both individuals and organizations are working to find solutions to the dual challenges of protecting sensitive information from hostile actors and unintended exposures while simultaneously reaping the benefits of data-driven insights [17]. According to the author, the digital era has made data privacy extremely important, and maintaining secrecy now depends on integrating ML tools. Over the course of our inquiry, we have looked at several elements of ML-enhanced data privacy. The ability to detect and neutralize emerging threats in real time is made possible by ML techniques. They can quickly respond to possible breaches because of their extraordinary ability to identify anomalies and dangerous tendencies. In the ever-changing landscape of cyber security today, these systems

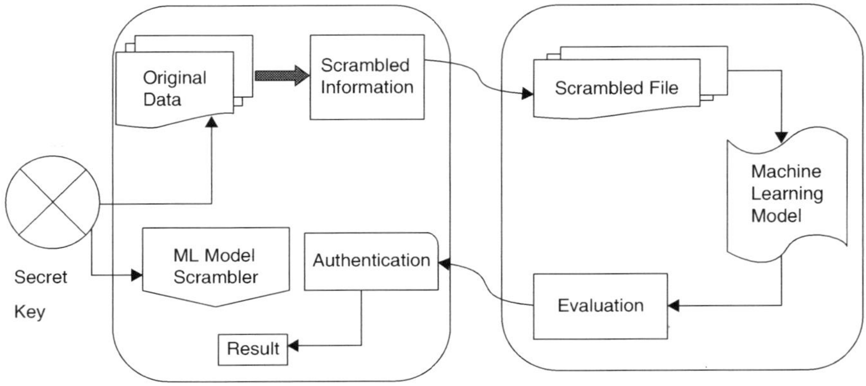

FIGURE 8.3 Representation of a Data Privacy and Confidentiality Model using ML.

must also be able to adapt and alter as threats do. Multifactor authentication (MFA) solutions, which secure sensitive data better, depend on ML as well. ML simplifies data encryption, ensuring that malicious actors are unable to decode the data even if they are intercepted. Because of the sophisticated encryption techniques used, it is very difficult for unauthorized individuals to access confidential data. In the digital age, ML technologies are a valuable ally in the ongoing battle to safeguard data confidentiality and privacy. Crucially important are their abilities to boost encryption, enhance authentication, and detect threats. In order to safeguard our most valuable digital assets as technology advances and cyber threats evolve, ML will always be necessary. Continuous adaptation and improvement of these solutions is necessary to maintain a competitive edge and ensure that data privacy is a top concern in the dynamic digital world.

8.7 VULNERABILITIES IN ML PIPELINES

While ML pipelines are essential to many applications, they are subject to vulnerabilities at different phases of development. Improving system robustness requires an understanding of these hazards through relevant case studies and established methodology. One of the main weaknesses is the quality of the training data, which might result in biased results. Mehrabi et al.'s [18] work, for instance, demonstrated how skewed datasets can produce discriminatory outcomes, especially in applications like recruiting algorithms, which unfairly disfavor minority candidates [19]. This emphasizes how important it is to have diverse datasets and rigorous data auditing procedures to successfully reduce bias.

The possibility of adversarial assaults, in which malevolent parties might alter input data to trick ML models, represents another serious vulnerability. The study in [11] demonstrated that even slight modifications to images can cause machine learning models to misclassify them, leading to inaccurate predictions. The study in [20] further explored this area by developing sophisticated methods for generating adversarial examples capable of bypassing existing defense mechanisms. In response, methods like adversarial training—which include training models with adversarial inputs to increase their resilience—have been proposed [21].

Risks also arise during the deployment phases, especially in relation to unauthorized access to models. The possibility of using reverse engineering deployed models was demonstrated by [22], who emphasized the significance of putting security measures like secure enclaves and model encryption into place to safeguard sensitive data and intellectual property. According to [23], algorithmic biases can have negative effects in crucial domains like criminal justice, reinforcing systemic disparities. This highlights the equally important ethical issues. Algorithmic audits and transparency initiatives are two approaches that have been proposed to solve these ethical issues and guarantee accountability and equity in automated decision-making systems [24].

To summarize, the mitigation of vulnerabilities in ML pipelines requires a comprehensive strategy that integrates strong data practices, adversarial defenses, and ethical considerations. Stakeholders can greatly increase the resilience of their ML systems against potential vulnerabilities by utilizing tried-and-true approaches and learning from case studies. This promotes confidence and reliability in ML applications. For deeper insights and a more comprehensive exploration of these topics, refer to the studies presented in [19], [11], and [22].

8.8 ADVERSARIAL ATTACKS (POISONING, EVASION, AND INFERENCE ATTACKS)

With three primary categories—poisoning, evasion, and inference attacks—adversarial attacks pose serious risks to ML systems. When attackers insert malicious data into the training dataset, it's known as a poisoning attack. When a model is deployed, this may distort the learning process and result in subpar performance. In a spam detection system, for instance, a malicious party could inject emails that are not spam but seem like spam, fooling the model into misclassifying additional spam messages.

According to [25], the general workflow of a deep learning system is illustrated in Figure 8.4, which consists of multiple crucial steps that work together to allow the model to learn from data and generate predictions. To guarantee quality and relevance, data are first gathered and preprocessed, which may include feature extraction, augmentation, and normalization. After that, an appropriate deep learning architecture is chosen, such as recurrent neural networks (RNNs) for sequential data or convolutional neural networks (CNNs) for image processing. The prepared dataset is then used to train the model, which modifies its parameters based on optimization algorithms such as stochastic gradient descent and the loss function. The model is evaluated using a different validation dataset after training to gauge its generalization and performance. Lastly, the trained model can be used in real-world settings where it is constantly exposed to fresh data to improve its forecasts, enabling continuous learning and condition adaption. In deep learning systems, this approach emphasizes the significance of model selection, data integrity, and iterative improvement.

In ML, according to the author [25], Figure 8.5 shows the adversarial attacks that mainly try to reduce the efficacy of models by tampering with training datasets or

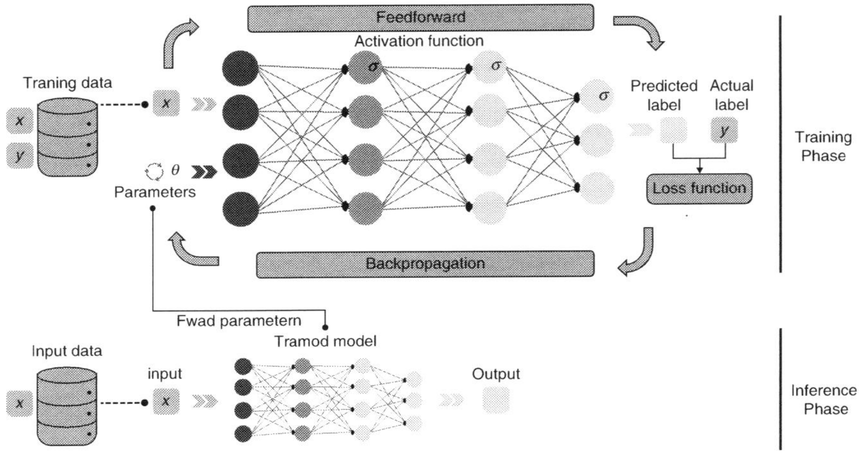

FIGURE 8.4 The General Workflow of a Deep Learning System.

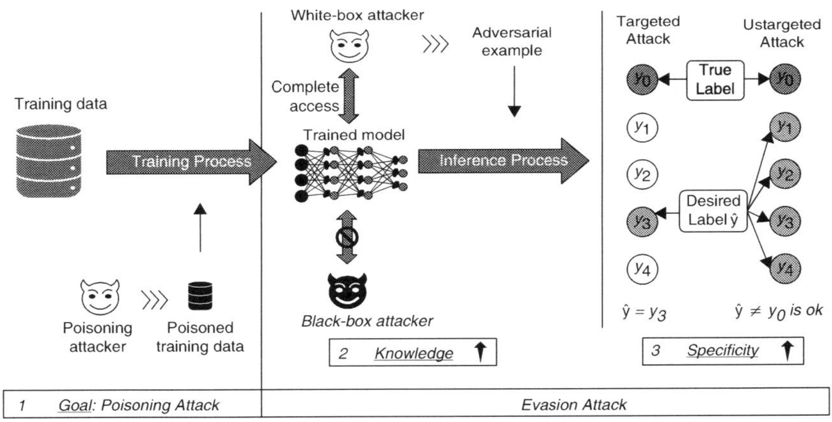

FIGURE 8.5 Threat Models in Adversarial Attacks, Illustrating the Adversary's Goal.

input data. Attackers that obtain unauthorized access to the training dataset through poisoning assaults can modify it by introducing phony samples. This intentional modification, which is similar to "poisoning" the dataset, frequently causes the model's accuracy to significantly decline or misclassifies test samples. These assaults are primarily meant to interfere with the model's learning process, which will provide outputs that are not trustworthy.

Evasion assaults, on the other hand, function differently. Without changing the model's parameters, these assaults target deep neural networks (DNNs) that have already been trained. Rather, the adversary creates deceptive test samples that the model is unable to identify, thus enabling the attacker to avoid discovery. Evasion attacks are particularly hard to fight against in this scenario since the attacker does not need access to the training dataset.

Depending on the attacker's goals, adversarial attacks can be categorized according to their level of specificity. The main objective of untargeted attacks is to trick the model into generating a false prediction without thinking about the kind of erroneous output that results from the manipulation. Targeted attacks, on the other hand, are more complex; the attacker's goal is not simply to cause a false prediction, but also to influence the model to produce a particular inaccurate outcome. Because targeted attacks are inherently more precise and complicated than untargeted ones, they typically have lower success rates.

An adversary's degree of model knowledge has a big influence on how successful an attack is. With complete control over the model's architecture, parameters, and gradients, an attacker can create highly customized adversarial samples through white-box attacks. This thorough comprehension enables more efficient input manipulation. Black-box attacks, on the other hand, are distinguished by a lack of in-depth understanding of the target model. In this case, attackers learn by making mistakes, interacting with the model, and deriving conclusions from its outputs to create their tactics. Szegedy et al. [26] initially introduced the concept of evasion attacks, demonstrating that adversarial examples can mislead a machine learning model into making incorrect predictions during the inference stage. To find hostile samples with the least amount of distortion that could be mistakenly identified as a targeted label, they created a mathematical framework. This framework works by introducing subtle perturbations to innocuous input data, which, when confronted with adversarial examples, cause the trained models to exhibit considerable misbehavior.

Poisoning attacks, in contrast to evasion attacks, take place during the training phase and entail corrupting the dataset to negatively impact the model's performance. Attackers do this by changing pre-existing samples in the training set or by inserting malicious data. These attacks fall into two general categories, namely, availability violations, which try to reduce the model's overall accuracy, and integrity violations, which concentrate on tricking the model about samples while keeping it functional in other domains.

8.9 DATA BREACHES IN BUSINESS CONTEXT

Businesses may suffer significant repercussions from data breaches; numerous well-known incidents highlight this possibility. The 2017 Equifax data breach is a prominent instance, wherein the personal details of over 147 million consumers—including addresses, birth dates, and Social Security numbers (SSNs)—were compromised. Their software's known vulnerability was not patched, which resulted in the breach, and cost them dearly in terms of money and damaged customer confidence. In order to compensate impacted parties and enhance security procedures, Equifax settled for $700 million after facing legal action and regulatory scrutiny.

The data breaches that occurred in different corporations and the resulting consequences are summarized in these tables, which offer a comprehensive picture of the data security difficulties that businesses confront.

TABLE.8.2
Summary of Notable Data Breaches

Company	Year	Records Affected	Type of Data Compromised	Consequences
Equifax	2017	147 million	SSNs, birth dates, addresses	$700 million settlement, loss of trust
Target	2013	40 million	Credit/debit card information	$18.5 million settlement, enhanced security investments
Yahoo	2013/2014	3 billion	Email addresses, security questions	Decreased acquisition price by Verizon, reputational damage
Marriott	2018	500 million	Passport numbers, email addresses	$124 million settlement, regulatory scrutiny
Facebook	2019	540 million	Usernames, passwords, comments	$5 billion fine by FTC, enhanced privacy measures
Capital One	2019	106 million	Credit card applications, SSNs	$80 million fine, improvement of security practices

TABLE.8.3
Consequences of Data Breaches

Consequence	Equifax	Target	Yahoo	Marriott	Facebook	Capital One
Financial Settlement	$700M	$18.5M	-	$124M	$5B (fine)	$80M
Regulatory Scrutiny	Yes	Yes	Yes	Yes	Yes	Yes
Reputational Damage	Yes	Yes	Yes	Yes	Yes	Yes
Investment in Security Measures	Yes	Yes	Yes	Yes	Yes	Yes
Legal Actions	Yes	Yes	Yes	Yes	Yes	Yes

TABLE.8.4
Data Breaches by Year

Year	Company	Records Affected	Major Impact
2013	Target	40 million	Holiday shopping season disruption
2013	Yahoo	3 billion	Largest breach, trust erosion
2017	Equifax	147 million	Significant regulatory fines
2018	Marriott	500 million	Major hotel chain vulnerability
2019	Facebook	540 million	Major Federal Trade Commission (FTC) fine
2019	Capital One	106 million	Compromised credit applications

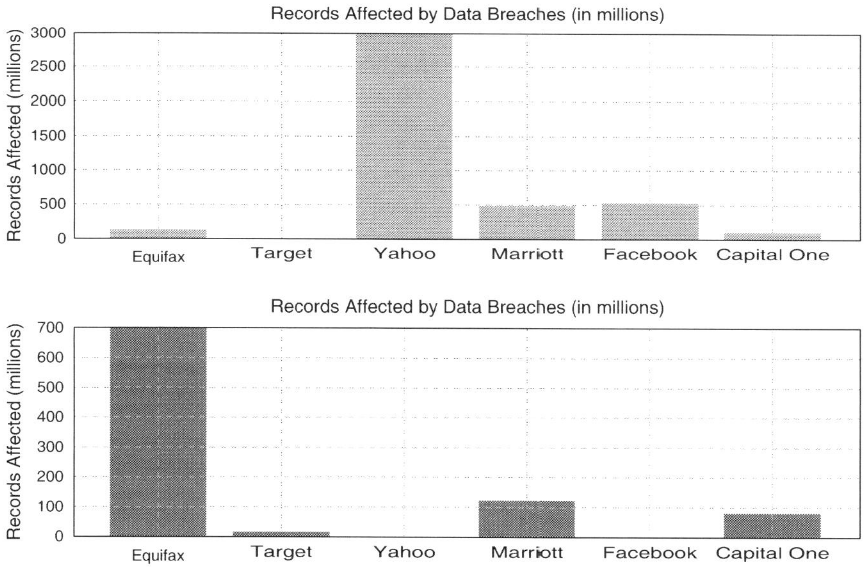

FIGURE 8.6 Bar Graphs on Data Breaches in Business Context.

In Figure 8.6, the frequency and financial impact of data breaches in different sectors are provided as bar graphs. The first graph provides an overview of the most vulnerable business as calculated from the sum total of breaches reported in technology, healthcare, retail, and finance business industries. The second graph reveals the financial implication of the data breach. Taken together, the plots paint a picture of the risk business landscape and financial impact for the data breaches.

Figure 8.7 pie chart illustrating the distribution of various data integrity threats faced by organizations

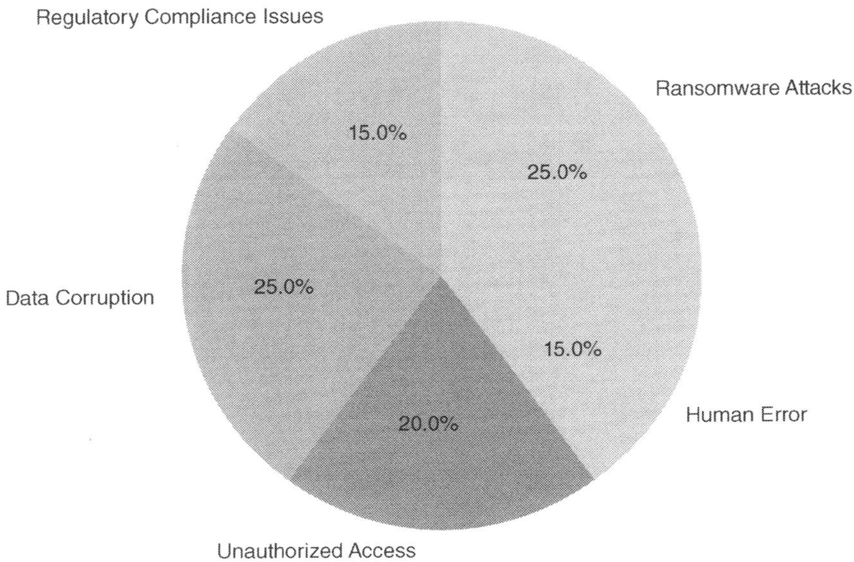

FIGURE 8.7 Graphically depicts the distribution of different types of data integrity threats that organizations are vulnerable to, as a pie chart. Every portion defines the proportionate degree of varied dangers, which is reflected through the lens of their criticality in the broader scheme of data integrity risks. This could be an example of insider threats, where danger from contractors or insiders can be categorized as being threats as they have access to some sensitive information. In contrast, there are quite a few depictions of external threats, like cyberattacks and data breaches, and the urgency is to have some serious security measures in place in order to combat these issues. The whole analysis focuses on internal as well as external issues in order to completely safeguard data integrity and continue the operations of the business.

8.10 EXAMPLES OF ATTACKS AND DEFENSES IN REAL-WORLD BUSINESS SCENARIOS

8.10.1 Scenarios

8.10.1.1 Malware

Malware is a software that gains unauthorized access to a system. Malware could be considered a spyware, ransomware, viruses, or worms, which can damage or block the functioning of a system. A malware can make a system inoperable by disrupting the normal functioning of certain parts of the system or by installing harmful software. Different types of malwares are as follows:

i) **Viruses:** A virus is a program that will have another legitimate program attached to it and the program runs when clicked, spreading and infecting the entire or part of the system and making the system inoperable. To defend a virus, the system should be periodically updated and have a good antivirus installed.

ii) **Worms:** A worm is a malware that is self-replicating and spreads across a system rapidly deleting the files, adding extra payload to the system. A worm doesn't require any program attached to it and it can operate independently. To protect the system from worms, it is always good to have the firewall updated. Additionally, the system should be updated and a strong antivirus should be installed in the system.

iii) **Trojan:** It is often called Trojan Horse. It is a malware that acts as a legitimate software by using social engineering techniques. Once a trojan is installed in a system, it will not affect the system but it will steal the personal data, it may provide a backdoor entry for remote access to the system, or it may even download and install additional malwares. Trojans always look harmless. To avoid getting attacked by a trojan, one should always be cautious while opening attachments in the mail, and downloading software from untrusted sites should be avoided. Additionally, it is always good to have a good antivirus to identify the malicious sites or software before downloading.

iv) **Ransomware:** Ransomware is a malware that encrypts the user's file and asks for a ransom amount for decryption. Ransomware could be installed in the system while a user downloads software from some malicious websites or clicks on a link attached in the mail, and so on. To protect files against ransomware, it is always good to take a backup of the data periodically, stay vigilant to the mails that are received from some phishing mail id, and to have a strong security password for the system or the file itself.

v) **Spyware:** This is a kind of malware that gathers personal information or device information without the notice of the user. The spyware gathers the data of a person based on their browsing habits and keystrokes. The following are the common spywares:

    a) **Keyloggers:** It is a spyware technique where the information is gathered based on the keystrokes made by the user.
    b) **Adware:** Information is gathered through targeted advertisements.
    c) **Tracking cookies:** The browsing pattern of users is checked by tracking cookies. Pop-ups are generated on a website, and when users click the pop-ups, their personal information stored on the computer can be gathered.

To avoid spyware attack, therefore, it is advisable to use pop ups blockers, be cautious while clicking any website links, avoid using the public Wi-Fi, always connect to the company VPNs while doing the jobs related to an organization, and beware of any free software.

2) **Denial-of-Service (DoS) Attacks [27]:** DoS is a cyber security attack where the cybercriminals flood the network with server requests and do not give space to any legitimate requests. Here the cybercriminals attack the network to which the hijacked device is connected. There could be multiple attacks from a single system spread out in the distributed environment.

When the network is flooded with traffic, there is the probability of the system crashing. In DoS, the hacker uses the IP address of the network to send fraudulent traffic to flood the user's network, which can crash the network or even shut down the network completely. Types of DoS attacks are as follows:

a) **Volumetric attacks:** Overflooding the network with massive floods of requests.
b) **Protocol attacks:** Recognizing the weakness of certain protocols and exploiting it.
c) **Application Layer attacks:** Identifying specific applications in the device and targeting them.
d) **Distributed denial of service (DDoS):** In the DDoS attack, multiple systems send fraudulent traffic to the single network where the hijacked device is present.
e) **Resource exhaustion:** In this attack, the cybercriminal repeatedly sends request for a single resource in the network resulting in application overload and finally the application slows down or crashes.
f) **Reflective attacks:** These are extended DDoS attacks where the cybercriminal spoofs the IP address of a network, sends the request to the server, and gets his request served, hence accessing the required information.

3) **Man-in-the-Middle Attack:** It is an attack where an attacker eavesdrops on the traffic and impersonates himself as another to steal the information from the target. In general terms, a man in the middle tries to grab the data that flows between the endpoints. The attack not only targets the flow but also the data integrity and the confidentiality of the data [28].
4) **SQL injection:** SQL injection exploits the database with injected SQL queries to steal sensitive data from a database or to modify the data by inserting, deleting, or updating the data. Basically, the SQLi executes all the access rights of a database administrator. This attack typically targets web applications. Most of the web applications store users' personal data. With the growth of the internet and increased use of web applications for various purposes, the security of the data used by applications holds top priority. Typically, the communication between the database and the user occurs by the user inputs and hence altering the SQL queries to reach the database would fetch the attackers a lot of information about the user trying to accessing the database [29].
5) **Phishing:** Phishing is a cyberattack where the cybercriminals spam the inbox with the social engineering mails attaching links to websites that are very similar to the original. Most common phishing attacks create a phishing website that mocks the real one and that when clicked gathers the users' information. Phishing can be further classified as general phishing and spear phishing. Both differ in their method and targets. General phishing makes a large-scale attack without targeting any individual, while spear phishing targets an individual or organization [30].

8.11 ADVANCEMENTS IN SECURE ML TECHNIQUES

The research and advancement of artificial intelligence (AI) and the Internet of Things (IoT) has led to unmatched revolutions across the globe. It has also led to unparalleled automation of devices and data collection, making systems autonomous and making all the devices smart on which we depend in our daily lives. Further the advancements in machine learning has increased the self-analyzing and decision-making power of the smart devices. We can see these self-analyzing devices like driverless cars getting large acceptance in the human community worldwide. With the improvement in technology, however, smart devices bring with them the threat of theft of data, cyberattacks, and so forth. The security for the IoT devices against theft and cyberattacks are of utmost requirement in today's world. For this, we can make use of the ML techniques as follows:

i) Detection of misuse of the devices using ML Algorithms: In this technique the current attack will be compared with the large number of attacks that have happened earlier. For this technique, different types of ML algorithms are used. One among them is using the ANN for intrusion detection, where the technique uses supervised and unsupervised learning procedures, where the model is trained with the labeled dataset in the case of supervised and unlabeled datasets in the case of unsupervised learning.
ii) Detection of anomalies: Anomaly detection is the technique where the attack is identified based on the unusual pattern of browsing or the unusual act that doesn't abide to a particular norm. This kind of detection is done to identify any intrusions in the network and any fraudulence. Certain deep learning techniques like long short-term memory (LSTM) are used to detect unusual behavior in the connected network environment. Basically, studies show creating the model based on the normal dataset and the dataset with anomaly behavior.
iii) Early detection of malwares: Devices like smartphones and laptops or any smart devices are liable to cyberattacks as they have apps, which can possibly collect huge personal data. To secure smart devices, many deep learning models have been proposed that can detect malwares in android devices. Again, the supervised and unsupervised techniques for model training are used [31].

8.12 CONCLUSION

As the world moves toward AI and IoT, which involve self-analyzing and self-decision-making devices, the security of these devices cannot be overlooked. For large organizations or an individual, protection of their devices against cyberattack is an overhead. This overhead can be reduced with the involvement of ML techniques, which can be used for the early detection of attacks, intrusions, and anomalies. ML techniques enable proactive systems for defending cyberattacks. They also enable to find the vulnerabilities in networks that could not be found by any other frameworks. ML techniques allow models to learn from the previous experience of different attacks and hence further similar attacks can be prevented. ML allows a device to identify malwares by scanning large amounts of data, which prevents the invasion of malware in the device. ML techniques provide a level of security by means of facial recognitions, fingerprint recognition, and so on, which makes it hard for cybercriminals to steal the data. The ML algorithms reduce the human workloads and also reduce human errors. By including ML algorithms in the business, people can maintain a level of trust with their stakeholders on securing their data. Involving ML frameworks with cyber security makes a business ecosystem more trustworthy.

REFERENCES

1. Sarker, I. H. (2023). Machine Learning for Intelligent Data Analysis and Automation in Cybersecurity: Current and Future Prospects. *Annals of Data Science*, 10, 1473–1498. https://doi.org/10.1007/s40745-022-00444-2
2. Steck, H., Baltrunas, L., Elahi, E., Liang, D., Raimond, Y., & Basilico, J. (2021). Deep Learning for Recommender Systems: A Netflix Case Study. *AI Magazine*, 42(3), 7–18. https://doi.org/10.1609/aimag.v42i3.18140
3. Gong, J., et al. (2019). Hybrid Deep Neural Networks for Friend Recommendations in Edge Computing Environment. *IEEE Access*, 8, 10693–10706.
4. IntelliArts. (n.d.). Machine Learning Business Applications. *IntelliArts*. Retrieved September 29, 2024, from https://intelliarts.com/blog/machine-learning-business-applications/
5. Bose, I., & Mahapatra, R. K. (2001). Business Data Mining – A Machine Learning Perspective. *Technological Forecasting and Social Change*, 68(1), 1–16.
6. Davenport, T. H. (2018). Artificial Intelligence for the Real World. *Harvard Business Review*, 96(1), 108–116.
7. Friedman, J. H., Hastie, T., & Tibshirani, R. (2001). The Elements of Statistical Learning. Springer Series in Statistics. Springer.
8. Choudhury, A. S., & Tabrizi, B. (2014). *The New Digital Age: Reshaping Business and Society*. Harvard Business Review.
9. Kumar, V., & Reinartz, W. (2016). Creating Enduring Customer Value. *Journal of Marketing*, 80(6), 36–68.
10. NextGen Invent. (2021). *6 Reasons Why Data Management Solutions Are Important for Businesses*. https://nextgeninvent.medium.com/6-reasons-why-data-management-solutions-are-important-for-businesses-85744121c294.
11. Goodfellow, I. J., Shlens, J., & Szegedy, C. (2014). Explaining and Harnessing Adversarial Examples. *arXiv preprint arXiv:1412.6572*.
12. Buolamwini, J., & Gebru, T. (2018). Gender Shades: Intersectional Accuracy Disparities in Commercial Gender Classification. In *Proceedings of the 1st Conference on Fairness, Accountability, and Transparency*.
13. Steinhardt, J., et al. (2017). Certified Defenses for Data Poisoning Attacks. In *Proceedings of the 34th International Conference on Machine Learning*.
14. He, D., et al. (2019). *Challenges of Machine Learning in Cybersecurity*. ACM Transactions on Intelligent Systems and Technology.
15. Doshi-Velez, F., & Kim, P. (2017). Towards a Rigorous Science of Interpretable Machine Learning. In *Proceedings of the 34th International Conference on Machine Learning*.
16. Vermeulen, A. F. (2018). *Practical Data Science: A Guide to Building the Technology Stack for Turning Data Lakes into Busnisse Assets*. Apress. https://doi.org/10.1007/978-1-4842-3054-1
17. Dari, Sukhvinder Singh, Dhabliya, Dharmesh, Govindaraju, K., & Mahalle, Parikshit N. (2024, February). *E3S Web of Conferences*, 491. https://doi.org/10.1051/e3sconf/202449102024

18. Mehrabi, N., Morstatter, F., Saxena, N., Lerman, K., & Galstyan, A. (2021). A Survey on Bias and Fairness in Machine Learning. ACM Computing Surveys (CSUR), 54(6), 1–35, Article 115. https://doi.org/10.1145/3457607
19. Barocas, S., & Selbst, A. D. (2016). Big Data's Disparate Impact. California Law Review, 104(3), 671–732. https://doi.org/10.2139/ssrn.2477899
20. Carlini, N., & Wagner, D. (2017). Towards Evaluating the Robustness of Neural Networks. In *2017 IEEE Symposium on Security and Privacy* (pp. 39–57). IEEE. https://doi.org/10.1109/SP.2017.49
21. Tramèr, F., et al. (2017). Ensemble Adversarial Training: Attacks and Defenses. *arXiv preprint arXiv:1705.07204.*
22. Liu, Y., Dolgov, D., & Wei, W. (2017). Adversarial Examples for Deep Learning. *arXiv preprint arXiv:1705.07288.*
23. O'Neil, C. (2016). *Weapons of Math Destruction: How Big Data Increases Inequality and Threatens Democracy.* Crown Publishing Group.
24. Lipton, Z. C. (2016). *The Mythos of Model Interpretability.* Cornell University. *arXiv preprint arXiv:1606.03490.* https://arxiv.org/abs/1606.03490
25. Zhou, Shuai, Liu, Chi, Ye, Dayong, Zhu, Tianqing, Zhou, Wanlei, & Yu, Philip S. (2022/2023, August). Adversarial Attacks and Defenses in Deep Learning: From a Perspective of Cybersecurity. *ACM Computing Surveys*, 55(8), 39, Article 163. https://doi.org/10.1145/3547330
26. Szegedy, C., Zaremba, W., Sutskever, I., Bruna, J., Erhan, D., Goodfellow, I., & Fergus, R. (2014). Intriguing Properties of Neural Networks. In *Proceedings of the 2nd International Conference on Learning Representations (ICLR 2014).*
27. Kumar, S., Guerrero, A., & Navarro, C. (2023). Cyber Security Flood Attacks and Risk Assessment for Internet of Things (IoT) Distributed Systems. In *2023 IEEE World AI IoT Congress (AIIoT)*, Seattle, WA, USA, pp. 392–397. https://doi.org/10.1109/AIIoT58121.2023.10174553.
28. Conti, M., Dragoni, N., & Lesyk, V. (2016, thirdquarter). A Survey of Man in the Middle Attacks. *IEEE Communications Surveys & Tutorials*, 18(3), 2027–2051. https://doi.org/10.1109/COMST.2016.2548426.
29. Coscia, A., Dentamaro, V., Galantucci, S., Maci, A., & Pirlo, G. (2024). PROGESI: A PROxy Grammar to Enhance Web Application Firewall for SQL Injection Prevention. *IEEE Access*, 12, 107689–107703. https://doi.org/10.1109/ACCESS.2024.3438092.
30. Li, W., Manickam, S., Laghari, S. U. A., & Chong, Y.-W. (2023). Uncovering the Cloak: A Systematic Review of Techniques Used to Conceal Phishing Websites. *IEEE Access*, 11, 71925–71939. https://doi.org/10.1109/ACCESS.2023.3293063.
31. Liang, F., Hatcher, W. G., Liao, W., Gao, W., & Yu, W. (2019). Machine Learning for Security and the Internet of Things: The Good, the Bad, and the Ugly. *IEEE Access*, 7, 158126–158147. https://doi.org/10.1109/ACCESS.2019.2948912

9 Privacy-Preserving Deep Learning Techniques for Business Big Data

Spoorthi M, Priyanka Mohan, Gururaj H L, and Jaroslav Frnda

9.1 INTRODUCTION

Massive and diverse datasets that grow rapidly and contain immense amounts of information are known as big data. These datasets are employed in advanced analytical techniques, including predictive modeling and machine learning, to solve business challenges and facilitate informed decision-making. Online and startup businesses were the first to adopt big data when it initially emerged in the first ten years of the 21st century. Big data may have been the foundation upon which companies such as Google, eBay, LinkedIn, and Facebook were constructed early on. Important data and insights are necessary for any size of business organization. Big data plays a critical part in comprehending your target audience and customers' preferences [1]. You can even use it to anticipate their requirements. Proper analysis and presentation of the appropriate data are necessary. It can aid a commercial organization in achieving several objectives. The concept of big data emerged from the necessity to understand trends, preferences, and patterns within the vast information generated by user interactions with various systems and with each other. Like many other emerging information technologies, big data has the capacity to substantially reduce expenses, dramatically decrease computation time, and create opportunities for new products and services. It offers the same potential as conventional analytics in supporting internal corporate decision-making. While big data's underlying technology and principles enable firms to accomplish a wide range of goals, most of the organizations we spoke with were concentrated on just one or two. The selected goals affect not just the result and monetary gains from big data, but also the procedure: who spearheads the effort, where it fits in the company, and what project management techniques will be followed [2].

In order to optimize operations, enhance consumer experiences, and drive decision-making, businesses collect, store, and analyze a vast amount of data known as business big data (Figure 9.1). The emergence of digital technologies has enabled businesses to generate and access data on an unprecedented scale. This data is sourced from a variety of sources, including consumer transactions, social media interactions, website traffic, IoT devices, and supply chain systems (see Figure 9.1). Organizations can leverage big data analytics to pinpoint their most valuable customers [3]. This

DOI: 10.1201/9781003540045-9

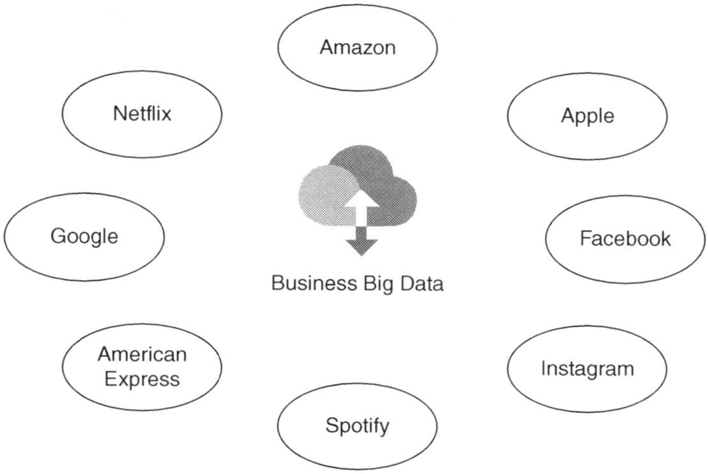

FIGURE 9.1 Business Big Data.

technology also enables companies to create innovative experiences, products, and services. Before the advent of big data platforms and technologies, many firms could only utilize a small fraction of their data for operational and analytical purposes. The remaining information was often disregarded and categorized as "dark data," which was processed and stored but never utilized again. By implementing effective big data management strategies, companies can extract more value from their data assets [4, 5]. This expands the scope of data analytics that businesses can perform and the benefits they can derive for their operations. The enhanced opportunities provided by big data contribute to various data science and advanced analytics fields, including machine learning, predictive analytics, data mining, streaming analytics, and text mining. Big data analytics applications utilize these disciplines to assist businesses in numerous ways, such as managing supply chains, detecting fraud, identifying operational issues, and understanding consumers. Well-executed business operations can lead to effective marketing and advertising campaigns, improved business processes, increased revenue, reduced costs, and more robust strategic planning. These outcomes can provide a competitive edge in the marketplace and superior financial results. Additionally, big data supports advancements in science, law enforcement, smart city initiatives, medical diagnosis and treatment, and other governmental activities.

Big data finds applications across various sectors, including healthcare and information technology. In the medical field, data experts are analyzing pharmaceutical outcomes. Companies are focusing on uncovering risks and benefits that were not apparent during the initial phases of clinical research. The use of big data can enhance trial evaluation and assist in predicting outcomes. Some early adopters of this concept have begun utilizing sensor data from diverse products, ranging from children's playthings to industrial machinery. This helps companies understand how their products are being used, facilitating the development of future items and new services. According to experts, big data has the potential to create numerous business opportunities. It might even spawn an entirely new category of companies, such as those specializing in gathering and examining industry information. Many of these firms will likely position themselves at the center of extensive data streams concerning products and services, suppliers and consumers, customer intentions and preferences, and more [6]. Companies across all industries should prioritize developing their big data capabilities. Big data enables businesses to create detailed customer profiles, allowing for personalized, real-time communication with clients. The ultimate goal is to provide customers with what they truly desire.

9.2 IMPORTANCE OF DATA PRIVACY

In an increasingly data-driven society, data privacy is critical because it protects individual rights, fosters confidence in digital interactions, and preserves personal integrity. Using big data techniques, you may map the company's whole data landscape. This enables you to examine various internal risks. You can protect critical information with the help of these techniques. Big data is stored in accordance with legal standards and is safeguarded appropriately.

Businesses are rapidly gathering information on their users. The last two years have produced 90% of the data that are currently in use. Data privacy is the privilege of individuals to control the way companies collect and manage their personal data. Users also have the right to be informed if their information is shared with third parties and to have a say in the matter.

It is distinct from data security in that the latter is concerned with safeguarding data from unauthorized access, loss, corruption, and theft [7].

Businesses are discovering new ways to add value and gaining deeper insights into their customers. People are getting better search results, and important industries like healthcare are seeing improvements in patient outcomes. But in the midst of all the enthusiasm surrounding the potential of data, data privacy laws are being discussed. Companies are confronted with the difficulty of adhering to legislation in several jurisdictions where customers access their web and mobile applications. Information that is necessary for the business to function is also a matter of data privacy. This may include confidential research, development data, or financial data, among other things. As a result, in order to guarantee data security and protection, most industries have been concentrating on big data. In businesses that handle financial data, credit and debit card information, and other similar activities, it's even more crucial [8].

Data privacy is crucial for the following main reasons (see Figure 9.2):

1. Protection of personal information: Data privacy keeps sensitive information like Social Security numbers, bank account details, and medical records safe by preventing unwanted access to personal information about individuals. People can reduce their risk of fraud, identity theft, and other bad things by keeping control over their personal data.
2. Trust and confidence: Building trust between people and organizations depends on data privacy. Businesses establish credibility and dependability

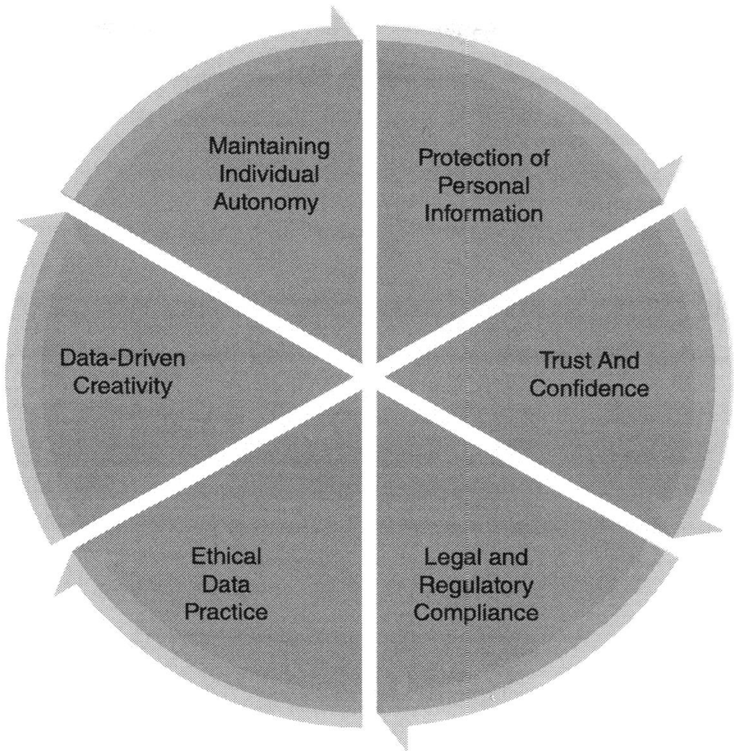

FIGURE 9.2 Importance of Data Privacy.

when they put data protection first and show that they are committed to safeguarding personal data. Customers become more confident as a result, strengthening bonds and fostering enduring loyalty.

3. Legal and regulatory compliance: Organizations must put policies in place to safeguard individuals' data privacy rights in order to comply with a number of data protection laws and regulations, including the California Consumer Privacy Act (CCPA) and the General Data Protection Regulation (GDPR). Adherence to these regulations assists enterprises in evading legal consequences, substantial penalties, and harm to their image.
4. Ethical data practices: It is morally required to protect personal information. Data-handling organizations need to make sure they have the right kind of consent for gathering, using, and sharing data Businesses demonstrate their commitment to upholding individual rights and fostering openness in their operations by following ethical data practices.
5. Data-driven creativity: Data privacy fosters creativity in addition to providing protection. People are more inclined to voluntarily disclose information when they have confidence that it will be handled appropriately. In turn, these data can be utilized to provide tailored experiences, gain

insightful knowledge, and promote research and development in a number of industries.

6. Maintaining individual autonomy: People are empowered to keep control over their personal data thanks to data privacy. They can choose how their data are gathered, put to use, and distributed thanks to it. Data privacy guarantees that personal information is not utilized improperly or exploited without permission by upholding individuals' autonomy.

To sum up, data privacy is critical for safeguarding private information, building trust, adhering to rules, upholding moral standards, spurring innovation, and preserving individual liberty. Setting data privacy as a top priority promotes a responsible and safe data ecosystem that is advantageous to both individuals and enterprises [9]. It is critical to protect sensitive and confidential data. Access to data such as bank account information, medical records, and other private consumer or user data by those unauthorized and malicious can lead to dire consequences. The absence of access control measures pertaining to personal information may expose persons to fraudulent activities and identity theft. Data privacy is not merely a legal obligation in the realm of business big data; it is a foundational business practice that develops trust, safeguards consumers, and improves overall operational efficiency. Businesses are able to protect the sensitive information of their customers and promote long-term development and success by emphasizing data privacy [10].

9.3 ROLE OF ML AND DL

ML and DL are essential for maximizing the potential of business big data, allowing companies to derive actionable insights, improve decision-making, and optimize operational efficiency. Artificial intelligence (AI) includes both ML and DL as subcategories. DL is a more advanced type of ML, while ML refers to algorithms that learn from data and provide predictions. The following is an explanation of their contribution to the field of commercial big data:

1. Generation of Insights and Data Analysis:
   ML algorithms are deployed extensively to analyze extensive datasets, recognize patterns, and produce insights. Forecasting, market trend analysis, customer segmentation, and risk assessment are all potential applications of these insights. Businesses can make data-driven decisions more precisely and quickly by utilizing ML models to process vast amounts of structured and unstructured data.

   DL models are particularly adept at analyzing unstructured data, including images, videos, and text, which are becoming an increasingly significant component of business big data. For instance, sentiment analysis in social media, image recognition in retail, and customer feedback analysis using natural language processing (NLP) are all applications of DL models.
2. Customer Personalization:
   Personalized consumer experiences are significantly influenced by ML. ML algorithms can forecast individual preferences and customize product

recommendations or marketing strategies by analyzing customer data, including browsing history, past purchases, and demographic information.

Deep learning further enhances personalization by comprehending more intricate data, such as a customer's visual interactions with online products or the tone of voice they use in chatbots. This enhances consumer engagement and satisfaction by enabling businesses to provide highly personalized experiences.

3. Forecasting and Predictive Analytics:
By utilizing historical data to predict future trends, behaviors, or hazards, ML enables businesses to perform predictive analytics. For instance, ML models can anticipate stock price fluctuations, customer attrition, equipment malfunctions, or sales trends. These predictions assist businesses in optimizing inventory, resource allocation, or marketing strategies and preparing for future demands.

   In complex prediction tasks, such as financial forecasting, demand planning, or fraud detection, where the relationships between variables are nonlinear and intricate, DL is employed to enhance accuracy.
4. Process Optimization and Automation:
By learning from patterns and behaviors, ML automates routine business processes. For instance, ML can enhance inventory management, demand forecasting, and delivery routes in supply chain management. In the realm of customer service, chatbots and virtual assistants that are powered by ML are capable of effectively addressing common inquiries.

   In areas such as computer vision and NLP, DL elevates automation to a new level. Businesses have the ability to automate a variety of duties, including document processing (e.g., scanning and reading handwritten text), visual inspections in manufacturing, and advanced language translation services.
5. Security and Fraud Detection:
In order to identify anomalies in transactional data that may suggest fraudulent activities, ML algorithms are implemented. These models enhance their capacity to detect fraud in real time by continuously learning from historical data. This is especially beneficial in sectors such as finance, insurance, and e-commerce, where fraudulent activities can result in substantial losses.

   DL improves fraud detection by analyzing more intricate data features, such as identifying anomalies in network behavior, user interactions, or biometric data. This enables businesses to identify even the most intricate or inconspicuous fraud patterns that conventional systems may overlook.
6. Market Research and Sentiment Analysis:
Sentiment analysis employs ML to evaluate feedback, social media posts, and consumer reviews. It enables businesses to monitor brand sentiment, gauge market reactions, and comprehend consumer opinions in real time. This can be beneficial in the provision of guidance for marketing strategies, product development, and customer service.

   Advanced sentiment analysis can be performed by DL, particularly through NLP models, which can extract a more profound emotional and contextual understanding from text or voice data. This allows companies to analyze a broader variety of unstructured data sources, including social media content, voice conversations, and chat logs.

7. The Use of Big Data to Improve Decision-Making:
   By unearthing trends and insights that are not apparent through conventional data analysis methods, ML systems assist businesses in transforming big data into actionable intelligence. These insights empower managers and administrators to make more informed decisions that are based on data rather than intuition.

   By continuously processing and learning from live data streams, DL enables real-time decision-making. This can be essential in situations such as real-time customer service adjustments, automated marketing campaigns, or stock trading.
8. Enhancing Product Development:
   Companies can guide product development and refinement by analyzing large datasets related to user feedback, market trends, and performance metrics through the use of ML. ML models have the capacity to anticipate potential issues, identify the features that consumers use the most, and suggest changes or improvements to products and services.

   In industries such as healthcare and automotive, DL is particularly beneficial because it necessitates the comprehension of high-dimensional data in order to engage in advanced modeling of physical processes, such as disease detection through medical images or self-driving vehicle systems [11, 12].
9. Resource Efficiency and Cost Reduction:
   By optimizing resource utilization and automating processes, both DL and ML assist businesses in minimizing operational expenses. For instance, ML can enhance supply chains by more accurately predicting demand, while DL can automate quality control processes in manufacturing by utilizing image recognition systems.

   The manner in which businesses manage large data has been significantly influenced by ML and DL. By utilizing these technologies, businesses can maintain their competitiveness in a rapidly evolving digital landscape while maximizing the value of big data, personalizing customer experiences, automating processes, and improving decision-making across various industries. Additionally, they enable companies to uncover hidden insights and predict trends.

9.4 PRIVACY CONCERNS IN BUSINESS BIG DATA

Big data privacy concerns are related to the risks and hazards associated with collecting, storing, processing, and using vast amounts of personal data in an era where decisions are made based on data. In recent years, there has been an abundance of news on social media concerning privacy issues and data breaches. Businesses are becoming more susceptible to privacy issues, data breaches, and insufficient consumer privacy laws as a result of handling large amounts of sensitive data [13]. Your clients have valid privacy concerns about their personal information in this digital

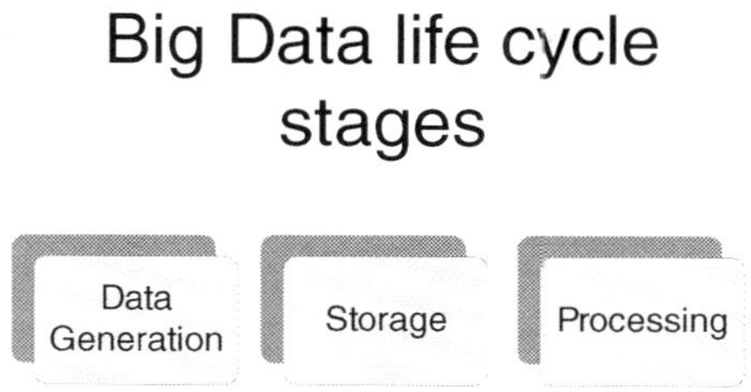

FIGURE 9.3 Life Cycle of Big Data.

age. Big data invariably poses a risk to data security, but the data itself are not the issue. Poor data handling is. Inadequate data management cannot be made up for by any privacy legislation.

1. Privacy of big data at the data generation stage:
   (see Figure 9.3) Active data generation and passive data creation are the two types of data generation. Active data creation refers to situations where the data owner will give the data to a third party, as opposed to passive data generation, which describes circumstances where the data are created by the data owner's online actions and the data owner may not be aware that the data are being collected by a third party. There is a decrease in the potential for privacy infractions by access controls or data falsification during data collecting [14].
   a) Accessibility restrictions: If the data owner feels that such data would reveal private information that shouldn't be shared, they won't provide it. If the data owner is giving the information voluntarily, there are a number of ways to preserve privacy, such as using script or ad blockers, encryption software, and anti-tracking extensions.
   b) Data fabrication: It is not always possible to prevent access to private information. In that case, a third party can manipulate data using specific tools before obtaining it. Skewed data makes it difficult to uncover genuine information [15].
2. Big data privacy in data storage phase:
   The emergence of cloud computing and other advancements in data storage technology have made it unnecessary to worry about storing massive amounts of data. However, should a breach occur in the big data storage system, the exposure of an individual's personal data could be disastrous. A privacy protection issue may arise when an application needs several datasets from various data centers in a distributed environment. Traditional security techniques for data protection come in four varieties. These include encryption systems at the application level, and security mechanisms at the media level, database level, and file level. The storage infrastructure must to be adaptable to the three Vs of big data analytics—volume, velocity, and variety. It should be able to change its configuration on the fly to accommodate various uses. Storage virtualization is a possible method to address

these demands, driven by the evolving cloud computing paradigm. Storage virtualization is a technique that combines numerous network storage devices into what seems to be a single storage unit. Data storage and cloud compute audit security are both considered in the SecCloud cloud data security paradigm. Consequently, there is a lack of discussion on the subject of data privacy while stored on cloud servers [16].

3. Big data privacy preserving in data processing:
   Systems are divided into batch, stream, graph, and ML processing categories by the big data processing paradigm. To safeguard privacy, we can divide the data processing part into two stages. The goal of the first phase is to safeguard information against unauthorized disclosure because the collected data may include sensitive information that belongs to the data owner. Finding useful information in the data while protecting privacy is the aim of the second stage. Effective data management is essential for any firm handling large amounts of sensitive data. Businesses that prioritize data protection are better able to retain customers by respecting their right to privacy. In the long run, it protects their brand and cultivates a corporate culture that prioritizes privacy protection and well-informed decision-making. Big data can be advantageous in the digital age, but if not managed appropriately, it can also pose a privacy danger. It turns into a tremendous advantage rather than a significant obstacle when your company places a high priority on cyber security. Making effective use of big data helps companies like yours create marketing and retention plans, enhance customer comprehension, and promote prudent decision-making in general. However, big data security is difficult because of the sheer amount of data it manages, as well as the constant flow, variety, and storage of data on cloud servers. The following are a few of the main obstacles to big data security:
   1. Safe computations: To handle massive volumes of data, big data technologies employ distributed programming frameworks. The security safeguards for these distributed frameworks, such as MapReduce, are inadequate. In MapReduce, the data are divided, a mapper processes the data, and storage is assigned. Since the mapper lacks an extra security layer, it is possible for someone to alter the settings and alter the data that are processed. Furthermore, it is quite challenging to identify these unreliable mappers. To guarantee that data integrity is preserved, it is crucial to safeguard the computations carried out in these distributed programming frameworks.
   2. Safeguarding transaction logs and data: Transaction logs and data are kept in multitiered storage environments with auto-tiering capabilities due to their size. The location of the data is not tracked by auto-tiering. Because of unknown physical data locations and untrusted storage devices, auto-tiering systems may reveal new vulnerabilities that cause businesses to lose control over their data. Information about user actions and data attributes that might be exploited by attackers can also be obtained through data transfer across tiers. To preserve data's

availability, confidentiality, and integrity, data and transaction logs must be safeguarded [17, 18].

3. Validation of endpoint inputs: Big data gathers information from a range of sources, including endpoints. It might be gathering logs from a sizable number of apps and devices. Rogue data transmitted by an untrusted endpoint may be present in the data that big data is receiving. The organization's analytical outputs may be impacted by this. Verifying all of the inputs that big data is receiving to make sure they are coming from reliable sources presents a difficulty.
4. Safe non-relational data stores: Big data technologies are quickly utilizing non-relational data stores, such as No Structured Query Language (NoSQL). Currently, these data repositories are not developed and safe enough. They contain numerous security flaws, such as unencrypted data at rest that poses a privacy risk, poor authentication between the client and server, and no encryption support for the data files.
5. Data analytics that protect privacy: When using big data technology for analytics, privacy is a crucial concern. As more and more data are gathered, user privacy may be violated through data analytics and data aggregation. An employee of an unreliable third party may be able to deduce personal information about users if the data analytics is outsourced. While using big data analytics techniques to improve consumer happiness, enterprises must make sure that user privacy is protected.
6. Access control: Sensitive data, including user protected health information (PHI), is handled by big data, which manages a wide range of data. To protect those data, numerous legal and compliance standards must be met. Policies for granular access control should be put in place to ensure that only individuals with permission can access sensitive user data and analytics performed on certain sets of data. To guarantee data confidentiality, this is required.
7. Real-time security monitoring: Big data infrastructure and the analytics it processes require real-time security monitoring. This has never been an easy undertaking because of how many alerts gadgets create. There are also a lot of false positives associated with these notifications. This is why businesses frequently find it difficult to track real-time data.

9.5 PRIVACY-PRESERVING TECHNIQUES IN ML

The goal of privacy-preserving machine learning (PPML) is to close the gap between protecting privacy and enjoying the advantages of ML. Upholding data privacy regulations and enabling the monetization of gathered data depend on it. Stopping data leaks in ML systems is the essence of the systematic PPML strategy. With the help of PPML's array of privacy-enhancing approaches, numerous input sources can work together to train ML models without disclosing their private information in its original version (see Figure 9.4). These are the techniques employed to guarantee that a

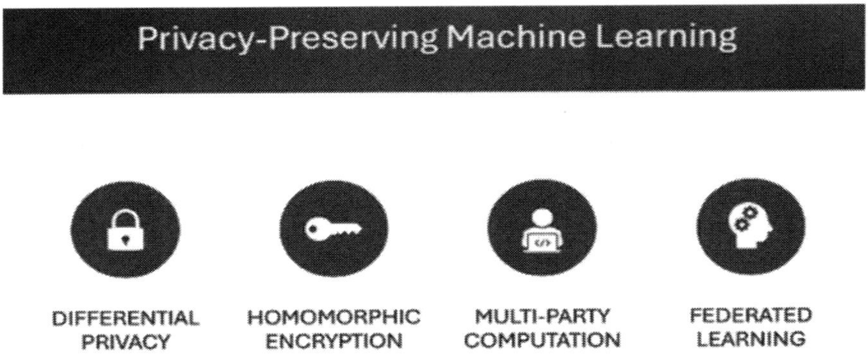

FIGURE 9.4 Privacy-Preserving Techniques in Machine Learning.

third party cannot steal the data. As a result, different types of attacks are prevented with the following techniques:

1. Differential privacy: The sort of privacy known as differential privacy enables you to provide pertinent details about a dataset without disclosing any personal data about it. This technique prevents the outcome of a differentially private operation from being used to connect a particular record to an individual, even in the event that an attacker gains access to every entry in a dataset. Put otherwise, the existence of a person's record in the dataset does not (significantly) affect the analysis's conclusion. Therefore, whether a person uses the dataset, the privacy risk is essentially the same. Adding random noise to the output is the process that achieves differential privacy. Differentially private processes like the Laplace, exponential, and randomized response techniques can be used to accomplish this [18].
2. Homomorphic encryption: A cryptographic technique known as homomorphic encryption (HE) produces an encrypted output that is the same as the original, unencrypted input. Here's an example of applying the strategy in practice:
   a. The third party computes the encrypted data using the encrypted input data.
      and generates the output that has been encrypted.
   b. The data owner encrypts the data and provides the result using a homomorphic function. A calculation must be done by a third party.
   c. Following output decryption, the data owner obtains the outcome of the calculation using the original data in plain text. The system cannot access the third party's unencrypted input or output at any stage of this procedure.
3. Multiparty Computation: A method called Multiparty Computation (MPC) enables numerous users to calculate a function without sharing any of their own inputs. The parties are suspicious of one another and self-contained. The essential idea is to maintain data privacy while enabling calculation on private information. MPC makes sure that every participant gains as much

knowledge from the final product as they can from their own effort. While MPC and homomorphic encryption are both good methods for maintaining privacy, they have significant processing and communication costs.

4. Federated learning: Federated learning makes it possible for ML procedures to be decentralized, which minimizes the quantity of data that is made public from contributor datasets and lessens the risk of identity and data privacy being violated. Federated learning works on the basic principle of letting each contributor train locally with its dataset and then updating the central ML model M (i.e., updating the model's parameter) on new private datasets from data contributors. The central authority (e.g., a company) owns the ML model M. Specifically, federated learning functions as follows:
   - The core model M is given to a set of *n* participants (data contributors);
   - Using their own local dataset Zl for training, each participant changes the model M locally, producing a new Local parameter l.
   - Every participant provides an update to the central authority.
   - To update the central model, the central authority integrates the local parameters of each participant to create a new parameter. You can keep going through this process until the main model is thoroughly trained.

The preservation of privacy has become a crucial priority as businesses and organizations depend more and more on ML for insights. To sum it up, effective methods for safeguarding sensitive data while enabling the use of ML capabilities include adversarial learning, federated learning, homomorphic encryption, and differential privacy. In the big data and AI era, organizations may preserve user privacy, adhere to legal requirements, and foster trust by incorporating these techniques [19].

9.6 DL TECHNIQUES FOR PRIVACY PRESERVATION

To reduce the possibility of private information about the training data being disclosed, DL models are equipped with Differential Privacy (DP). Every access to the data during the training phase results in a certain loss of privacy. This enables the model's developer to evaluate the model's overall privacy loss prior to release. Conversely, the model's author can stop training the model as soon as it goes over a predetermined budget for privacy. But this can make the model less precise.

Privacy-preserving (PP) models are those that have been trained with the use of PP approaches. Non-private trainers are those who don't use any specific methods to reduce the loss throughout training. Minimizing the privacy loss for each access to the training data is essential for creating a suitable model under privacy limitations. The training protocol has a major role in this loss. DP is frequently used by reducing the impact of a single data item by adding random noise perturbations to the model on the optimization of the network. There are various methods for adding random noise to the prototype. Three kinds of ways to release PP models were created by Boulemtafes et al. [1] based on how the noise is added to the model: (i) differentially private model parameters, (ii) differentially private input information, and (iii) differentially private mimic learning. Furthermore, the writers recommend three performance metrics for evaluating the efficacy of a privacy-preserving model. These

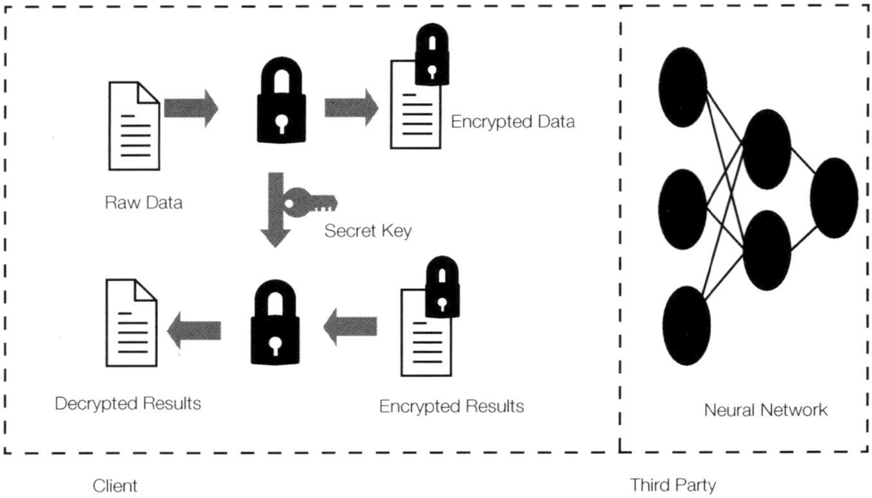

FIGURE 9.5 Secure Computation Process Between a Client and a Third-Party Service.

three factors include a model's effectiveness (also known as prediction accuracy), training efficiency, and privacy.

Figure 9.5 shows an analysis of the working process. Client-Side: The client possesses raw data intended for processing via a third-party neural network but seeks to guarantee the security of the data. The unprocessed data are encrypted with a confidential key, yielding encrypted data.

External Entity (Neural Network): The encrypted data are transmitted to the third-party service, which does computations (e.g., utilizing the neural network) on this encrypted data without decryption.

The neural network generates encrypted outcomes derived from the encrypted data.

Client-Side (Postprocessing): The customer obtains the encrypted outcomes from the third party. The client utilizes the identical secret key to decrypt the results and derive the final output. This configuration is used in PPML models, wherein sensitive data are encrypted prior to transmission to a third-party service for processing, thereby assuring that the service cannot access the unprocessed data or the final outcomes. Methods such as homomorphic encryption are frequently employed to facilitate this form of secure computation.

Techniques for privacy-preserving deep learning (PPDL) are essential for enterprises managing substantial volumes of sensitive information. These methodologies enable enterprises to leverage DL while safeguarding data privacy. The following is a comparison of various PPDL methodologies:

(i) Differential private model parameters:
There are two main approaches that can be used to generate differential private model parameters that safeguard the original training data: (i) directly

TABLE 9.1
Various Privacy-Preserving Deep Learning Methodologies

Technique	Description	Advantages	Challenges	Examples of Use in Business
Differential Privacy (DP)	Adds random noise to the data or model gradients to ensure individual data points can't be distinguished	– Strong privacy guarantees – Can be combined with other techniques	– May reduce model accuracy – Difficult to tune the noise for optimal privacy-utility trade-off	– Customer feedback analysis without revealing individual responses
Federated Learning (FL)	Data remains on local devices, and only model updates (not raw data) are shared with a central server	– Data never leaves the device – Reduces risks of central data breaches	– Communication overhead – Requires coordination of multiple devices	– Collaborative model training across multiple business departments
Homomorphic Encryption (HE)	Data are encrypted before training, and computations are performed on encrypted data without decryption	– Data privacy is fully preserved – High security due to encryption	– High computational cost – Slower training times	– Secure financial data processing
Secure Multiparty Computation (SMPC)	Allows multiple parties to compute a function over their data without revealing the data to each other	– Data remains private to each party – No need for a trusted third party	– Complex setup – High communication costs and slower computations	Joint analysis of confidential business data across departments
Split Learning	A deep learning model is split between the client and server, and only partial model information is shared	– Reduces the amount of information shared – Can be more efficient than federated learning	– Requires careful partitioning of the model – Sensitive data could still leak through gradients	Collaborative AI development between business partners
Encrypted Deep Learning (EDL)	Combines encryption techniques with deep learning to perform operations on encrypted data	– High security – Ensures confidentiality during the entire learning process	– High computational complexity – Needs specialized encryption algorithms	Secure predictive modeling for customer trends
Private Aggregation of Teacher Ensembles (PATE)	Uses an ensemble of teacher models to aggregate knowledge without revealing individual training examples	– High privacy with ensemble learning – Good for privacy in semi-supervised settings	May require multiple teacher models – Can be computationally expensive	Anonymized customer behavior prediction

perturbing model parameters and (ii) perturbing objective functions rather than results, which can also be combined with affine transformation perturbation. The goal is to increase accuracy by combining layer-wise relevance propagation (LRP) with differential privacy. LRP is used to categorize neurons into high and low relevance categories. After that, neurons are given Laplace noise using a proportional privacy budget based on the relevance category of each neuron. The amount of noise produced increases with decreasing privacy budget. Additionally, the loss function perturbs the target value at each batch, protecting each data access point and providing a dependable PP model. For this, the Maclaurin series is used to polynomially approximate the loss function, and the Laplace method is used to perturb it. The solution's evaluation findings demonstrated that, even with significant noise injection, the resulting accuracy was comparable to the non-privacy-preserving version. In the worst scenario—which featured extremely dense noise—there was an accuracy loss of less than 5%. Furthermore, the authors noted that the total budget is only derived from the two privacy budgets that correspond to the high and low relevance categories because neuron relevancy is not taken into account in the loss function perturbation [15].

(ii) Differential private input data:
Here the concept of "Anonymizing First" entails first anonymizing the source dataset to meet ε-differential privacy requirements, and then using the anonymized data to apply the model. The authors also suggested introducing noise to each set of records rather than to each record in order to lessen the influence of noise. The evaluation's findings demonstrated that the suggested strategy may produce highly accurate estimations. The accuracy and f-measure of the "Anonymizing First" strategy are greater than those of the "Learning First" technique that was previously described for a small privacy budget, while "Learning First" performs better than both "Anonymizing First" and "Anonymized Learning" with a big privacy budget. In terms of privacy, differential privacy makes sure that there is less chance that a certain level of sensitive information leaks out.

(iii) Differential private mimic learning:
Here it permits the preservation of the initial training set after the release of a deep model. Training a first effective model, known as the instructor model, on the initial training set of data is the general concept of mimic learning. Next, an important unlabeled dataset is annotated by the teacher and used to train the student model, a different model. In some instances, the student model was able to anticipate outcomes that were comparable to or higher to those of the teacher in terms of performance. Teachers are employed as an ensemble to annotate unlabeled non-sensitive data after being trained on various subsets of the original sensitive data. Next, the pupil will pick up the skill of faithfully imitating the instructor's group. The teachers who are deployed as an ensemble combine their individual forecasts into a single prediction in order to protect privacy during annotation. Laplace noise is then added to the vote counts to create uncertainty. The annotation of student training data using noisy aggregation suggests that the quantity of

questions students ask professors determines how well they are trained. The quality of the student's model is thus traded off. Semi-supervised knowledge transfer, which is regarded as the most effective method among others and allows for a reduction in the privacy budget, is used to address this trade-off.

As companies and sectors continue to integrate AI and big data in their business processes, deep learning solutions for privacy preservation are essential. Organizations can take advantage of the potential of DL while lowering the risk of privacy violations by using strategies like federated learning, DP, homomorphic encryption, and synthetic data generation. These techniques help companies to reconcile innovation with protecting people's data in accordance with ethical standards and privacy laws.

9.7 METRICS FOR PRIVACY PRESERVATION

The effectiveness of PP methods in data processing, DL, and ML is evaluated using metrics for privacy preservation. These measures assist in putting a number on the degree of privacy protection offered while guaranteeing that the data or model's usefulness is maintained. The most used metrics for privacy preservation are as follows:

1. Differential Privacy (ε-Differential Privacy):
   Definition: This concept quantifies the amount that an algorithm's output alters when a single person's data is added or deleted. One of the measures that is most frequently employed in privacy preservation is this one.
   Metric: The degree of privacy is measured by the privacy parameter ε (epsilon). Stronger privacy is indicated by a smaller ε value, which reduces the impact of any one person's data on the model's results.
   Privacy level: Generally speaking, $\varepsilon = 0.01$ to 1 is regarded as a robust privacy assurance.
   Trade-off: Stronger privacy is achieved with smaller ε, but the additional noise usually leads to lower model accuracy.
2. Differential Privacy Loss (δ (ε, δ))-Privacy
   Description: The parameter δ permits a tiny chance that privacy protection may fail beyond the bound defined by ε in the relaxed form of differential privacy known as (ε, δ)-differential privacy.
   Metric: The likelihood of privacy failure is represented by δ. Reduced values of δ (for example, 10^{-6}) indicate a decreased likelihood of privacy violations. The parameter δ is usually set at a small value.
   Privacy level: For strong guarantees, $\delta = 10^{-6}$ or smaller is typically selected.
3. Mutual Information
   Definition: The quantity of information shared by two variables, such as input data and model output, is measured by mutual information. It is used in privacy preservation to ascertain the extent to which the model's output discloses private data.
   Metric: Stronger privacy protection is indicated by lower mutual information between the model's output and the input data.

Privacy level: A mutual information value near zero indicates very little personal data leaking.

4. Attack Accuracy (Adversarial Metrics):
   Membership inference, model inversion, and attribute inference assaults are examples of privacy attacks that are used to evaluate privacy hazards. Attack accuracy quantifies the degree to which enemies are able to obtain personal data.
   Metric: One measure of privacy attacks' effectiveness is their success rate. Improved privacy protection is implied by lower attack accuracy [19].
   Privacy level: An attack success rate of roughly 50% for a binary attack is ideal, as is approaching random guesswork.
5. Loss of Data Utility
   Definition: The term "data utility loss" refers to the amount of meaningful information that is lost because of PP modifications (such as noise addition, encryption, or anonymization).
   Metric: The model's performance on the original data compared to the converted (PP) data is measured. The model's performance is less affected by privacy preservation when the utility loss is smaller.
   Privacy level: It is ideal to lose as little utility as possible, but doing so frequently results in less privacy.

In ML and DL systems, these measures offer a means of striking a compromise between privacy and usefulness. These measures can be used to assess PP methods, like federated learning, homomorphic encryption, and DP, to make sure they maintain model performance while adhering to privacy rules. Different aspects of privacy are evaluated by each metric, ranging from the direct measurement of privacy protection to the assessment of trade-offs between privacy and utility.

9.8 DATA PRIVACY CONCERNS IN BUSINESS ML APPLICATIONS

Data are essential to the functioning of any organization. A secure database is the least a corporation can provide for itself and its clientele. Data breaches present substantial risks to organizations, encompassing reputational harm and legal repercussions. A 2023 IBM analysis indicated that the average cost of a data breach is $4.45 million. Moreover, this price is 15% elevated compared to its 2020 level. Multiple factors have contributed to the increase in data breaches. AI, an emerging technology aimed at delivering a more efficient and accessible datasets for personal and organizational utilization, has faced significant criticism. This arises from concerns around user data protection and copyright violations, as seen by recent litigation initiated by non-fungible token (NFT) artists and the UMG music company. In the face of significant obstacles, AI and ML have discovered unexpected applications: data protection. This chapter examines the importance of AI and ML in protecting personal and corporate data [20].

Currently, enterprises must manage many kinds of data to maintain relevance. Despite ongoing expansion, inadequate security procedures perpetuate organizational apprehension around data breaches. A recent analysis from a public tracking organization that assesses the breach-level index indicated that there were around 9,198,580,293 breaches over a decade. These violations entail significant repercussions, which are as follows:

a. Tarnished brand image and customer loss: Data breaches undermine an organization's reputation, resulting in diminished customer trust. In a very competitive market, clients are inclined to transition to a rival that provides superior data security [21].
b. Loss of crucial business data: Breaches frequently lead to the acquisition of sensitive information, encompassing trade secrets, intellectual property, and internal records. The loss of this data can jeopardize a company's competitive advantage.
c. Loss of privacy and identity theft: Breaches render people susceptible to identity theft, which can lead to financial losses, reputational harm, and psychological distress.
d. Hidden costs: In addition to immediate damages, there are enduring expenditures, including forensic investigations, customer notifications, litigation, and compensation disbursements, which may not be immediately apparent.
e. Legal implication: Data breaches may result in legal repercussions if a business is deemed noncompliant with data protection rules, such as GDPR or Health Insurance Portability and Accountability Act (HIPAA), potentially incurring fines or sanctions.
f. Bankruptcy: The aggregate effect of these repercussions can lead a company into financial turmoil, potentially culminating in bankruptcy, particularly for smaller firms that lack adequate resources for recovery.

To mitigate these threats, organizations must implement stringent cyber security measures, such as encryption, routine security audits, and rigorous access controls.

9.9 VULNERABILITIES IN ML PIPELINES

The revolutionary potential of ML pipelines is indisputable. Automated workflows such as data intake, model training, and data preprocessing are transforming businesses by optimizing logistics in the supply chain and customizing healthcare advice. In the supply chain, machine learning may evaluate extensive data to forecast demand variations, enhance shipping routes, and refine warehouse operations, resulting in substantial cost reductions and efficiency improvements. A recent study indicates that 49% of firms are assessing the implementation of machine learning, while 51% of companies assert that they are early adopters of this technology. Nonetheless, this swift adoption has revealed a concealed risk: flaws in the ML pipeline security. The intricate, multiphase procedures that acquire, process, and train ML models frequently become oversight areas for security teams [22]. This establishes a novel attack channel for cybercriminals, who may exploit vulnerabilities in the pipeline to obtain unauthorized access to important information, alter outputs, or interrupt entire operations. The repercussions can be extensive, resulting in monetary losses, reputational harm, and potential safety risks. This chapter seeks to elucidate the security threats inherent in ML pipelines (machine learning vulnerabilities) and provide you with practical techniques for safeguarding AI models and the entire pipeline.

9.9.1 The Emergence of a Novel Threat

Historically, security protocols concentrated on safeguarding fundamental assets such as data and information technology (IT) infrastructure. This methodology benefited enterprises for an extended period, safeguarding the confidentiality, integrity, and availability of essential information systems. Nonetheless, the increasing implementation of ML has created a novel attack surface: ML pipelines. These intricate, multifaceted procedures frequently harbor vulnerabilities that fraudsters may exploit. The intricate structure of ML pipelines, comprising multiple stages with diverse tools, scripts, and settings, engenders security vulnerabilities that are challenging to detect and control, listed as follows:

Access to Sensitive Data: Pipelines frequently manage vast quantities of sensitive information, like client details, financial records, or medical data. A data breach in the pipeline may compromise this sensitive information.

Advancing Attack Strategies: Cybercriminals are formulating novel techniques specifically aimed at exploiting machine learning vulnerabilities.

Data Poisoning Attacks: This attack involves the injection of altered data into the training dataset by malicious actors. This may lead the model to acquire erroneous patterns and generate imprecise or biased results. A data poisoning attack on a loan approval model could result in the unjust denial of loans to qualified applicants.

Model Hijacking: In this scenario, adversaries seize control of a trained model and alter its functionality to fulfil their objectives. This may entail supplying the model with hostile inputs intended to elicit unanticipated responses. Envision a facial recognition technology employed for security being compromised to provide illicit access [23].

(a) Threat Model Definition

Define the threat model, where T represents all potential adversaries or threats that might attack the machine learning system. This can include:

$$T=\{t_1, t_2,\ldots,t_n\}$$

where t_i represents specific types of threats, such as data poisoning, adversarial attacks, model inversion, and eavesdropping.

A Hypothetical Illustration of Vulnerability in an ML Pipeline: A healthcare institution employs an ML pipeline to evaluate medical images and aid physicians in disease diagnosis. The pipeline has multiple phases: data ingestion and preprocessing, model training, and model deployment.

- *Vulnerability*: Malicious entities infiltrate the system during the data import phase. They subsequently incorporate a series of altered medical photos into the training dataset. These edited photos may depict healthy tissue modified to resemble malignant cells. The contaminated training data results in bias

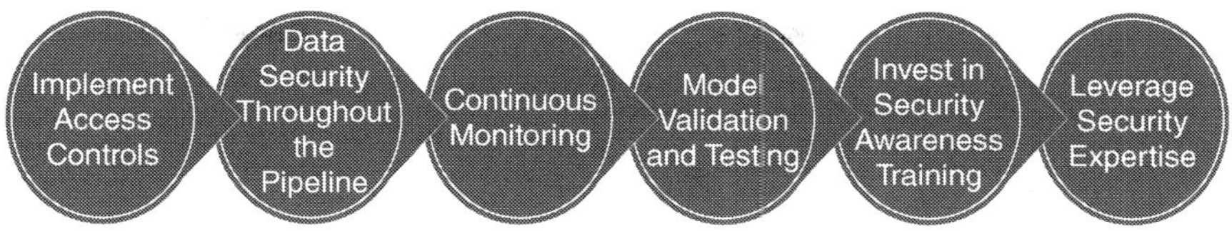

FIGURE 9.6 Securing Your ML Pipelines.

within the ML model. Thus, when the model evaluates actual patient photos during deployment, it may erroneously classify healthy individuals as having cancer, resulting in superfluous interventions and psychological discomfort.

- *Protection*: Establish stringent protocols to maintain the integrity and validity of data along the pipeline. Additionally, rigorously validate the training data to detect and eliminate anomalies or biases.

1. **Implement Access Controls**: (see Figure 9.6) Limit access to the pipeline and its components according to the concept of least privilege. This guarantees that only authorized individuals can alter or access confidential information [24].
2. **Secure the Entire Pipeline**: Implement stringent data security protocols across the full pipeline life cycle, encompassing data collection through to model deployment. This encompasses encryption, anonymization, and data lineage monitoring.
3. **Continuous Monitoring**: Persistently oversee the pipeline for anomalous behavior and possible weaknesses. Employ instruments for anomaly detection and threat intelligence to recognize potential assaults in real time.
4. **Model Validation and Testing**: Conduct thorough testing and validation of your ML models prior to deployment. This entails measuring the model's efficacy on novel data and evaluating its resilience to adversarial assaults.
5. **Invest in Security Awareness Training**: Educate people engaged in the development and deployment of the ML pipeline on security best practices. This promotes a culture of security awareness throughout your organization.
6. **Leverage Security Expertise**: Consider collaborating with a cyber security services provider to perform thorough vulnerability assessments and penetration testing (VAPT) on your machine learning pipelines. Furthermore, a Security Operations Center (SOC) service can offer ongoing surveillance and threat identification functionalities.

(b) **Business Data Representation**

Let D represent the business data used in machine learning. Typically, business data are structured as a collection of features and labels:

$$D=\{(x_1,y_1),(x_2,y_2),\ldots\ldots.,(x_m,y_m)\}$$

where *xi* is the feature vector for a data point and *yi* denotes the matching label.

(c) **Machine Learning Model**
The machine learning model M is a function that maps input features x_i to predicted outputs $\hat{y}_i$. Mathematically, this can be defined as

$$M:X \rightarrow \hat{Y}, \hat{y}_i = M(x_i)$$

The goal of the model is to minimize the loss function L, typically representing the error between the predicted and actual output:

$$L = \frac{1}{m}\sum_{i=1}^{m} l(y_i, \hat{y}_i)$$

(d) **Adversarial Attacks**
Adversarial attacks seek to modify input data x by introducing a minor perturbation δ, resulting in the model misclassifying the input. The adversarial example is presented as follows:

$$x' = x + \delta$$

An adversarial attack seeks to maximize the loss function by manipulating δ,

$$\delta = \arg\max_{\delta} L(M(x+\delta), y)$$

where δ must satisfy certain constraints, like $||\delta||_p \leq_{\in}$, where p is the norm and $\in$ is a small value representing the attack strength.

This mathematical model incorporates many cyber security dangers and countermeasures alongside ML algorithms in company data. It assists in identifying potential vulnerabilities and quantifying the impact of various assaults while providing solutions such as adversarial training, differential privacy, and encryption to protect company data.

9.10 DATA BREACHES IN BUSINESS CONTEXT

The last couple of years have demonstrated that data security breaches are not merely approaching; they are intruding. The severity of this issue has become increasingly evident. Breaches are not only occurring more frequently but also becoming more costly, detrimental, intricate, and challenging to avert. The financial repercussions of a breach are no longer a trivial matter; they can determine the success or failure of a firm. Investing in robust cyber security technology and performing regular data risk assessments to uncover vulnerabilities before to prevent their exploitation by attackers is essential [23]. Notwithstanding the dismal cost trends, there is optimism: AI and automation are demonstrating their potential as transformative solutions for alleviating the consequences of a breach. The analysis indicates that firms employing comprehensive AI and automation for security prevention saved approximately $2.22 million in breach expenses relative to those lacking such measures. AI-powered data security protocols can swiftly identify threats, prioritize issues, and autonomously implement remediation strategies, thereby minimizing breach duration and overall impact.

Insider threats will persist as a significant worry for enterprises, resulting in data breaches, money laundering, intellectual property theft, and many issues. The potential hazards, either from malicious insider intent or, more frequently, from unintended activities, can significantly endanger sensitive data, affect financial performance, and harm reputations. Businesses must take proactive efforts and establish appropriate controls and protective protocols for sensitive data to mitigate the risk of unauthorized disclosure and utilization across all data assets [24, 25].

Assessing the subject of "Privacy-Preserving Deep Learning Techniques for Business Big Data" requires an understanding of the difficulties associated with safeguarding sensitive information and the sophisticated methodologies employed to uphold data privacy while using DL models on extensive business datasets. Business data frequently include sensitive and secret information such as client profiles, transaction records, and financial details. Safeguarding the confidentiality of sensitive data is crucial, both for ethical considerations and regulatory compliance (e.g., GDPR, CCPA). Inadequate data protection may lead to monetary fines, erosion of confidence, and harm to reputation. PP methodologies enable enterprises to utilize big data analytics and ML insights while maintaining data protection. For instance, models can continue to forecast consumer behavior, enhance supply chains, or identify fraud without revealing sensitive customer or firm data. Organizations that use these strategies can achieve a competitive advantage by fostering customer trust and adhering to privacy regulations, all while deriving significant insights from their data. A trade-off frequently exists between privacy and model efficacy. For example, whereas federated learning and DP provide security, they may result in increased latency or diminished prediction accuracy. Organizations must evaluate these trade-offs considering the significance of accuracy relative to privacy in their particular application. In highly sensitive operations, privacy may be prioritized, whereas other scenarios may emphasize performance.

9.11 CONCLUSION

In summary, this chapter provides critical solutions for tackling the increasing issues of security and confidentiality of data in the contemporary digital landscape. As business organizations increasingly depend on big data for decision-making and operational efficiency, the necessity to protect sensitive information while harnessing its potential becomes critical. Methods such Differential Privacy, Federated Learning, Homomorphic Encryption, and Secure Multiparty Computation allow businesses to build DL models while safeguarding individual data points from privacy threats. By using these strategies, enterprises may cultivate trust and openness, guaranteeing adherence to international data protection laws such as GDPR and CCPA, while simultaneously deriving useful insights through their datasets. The future of DL in commercial data depends on harmonizing the capabilities of AI with stringent privacy protections. Ongoing innovation and research in this domain will facilitate the development of more efficient, scalable, and secure systems, allowing enterprises to prosper in a progressively data-driven economy while safeguarding the privacy of their users and customers.

As rules advance and the quantity of company data increases, PPDL is expected to become a fundamental component of AI strategy in enterprises. Advancements such as quantum computing and enhanced encryption techniques may resolve existing compromises between privacy and performance.

REFERENCES

1. Boulemtafes, Amine, Abdelouahid Derhab, and Yacine Challal. "A Review of Privacy-Preserving Techniques for Deep Learning." *Neurocomputing* 384 (2020): 21–45.
2. Fan, Yongkai, Wanyu Zhang, Jianrong Bai, Xia Lei, and Kuanching Li. "Privacy-Preserving Deep Learning on Big Data in Cloud." *China Communications* 20, no. 11 (2023): 176–186.
3. Vasa, Jalpesh, and Amit Thakkar. "Deep Learning: Differential Privacy Preservation in the Era of Big Data." *Journal of Computer Information Systems* 63, no. 3 (2023): 608–631.
4. Gupta, Rishabh, Ishu Gupta, Deepika Saxena, and Ashutosh Kumar Singh. "A Differential Approach and Deep Neural Network Based Data Privacy-Preserving Model in Cloud Environment." *Journal of Ambient Intelligence and Humanized Computing* 14, no. 5 (2023): 4659–4674.
5. Naresh, Vankamamidi S., Muthusamy Thamarai, and V. V. L. Divakar Allavarpu. "Privacy-Preserving Deep Learning in Medical Informatics: Applications, Challenges, and Solutions." *Artificial Intelligence Review* 56, no. Suppl. 1 (2023): 1199–1241.
6. Chang, J. Morris, Di Zhuang, G. Samaraweera, and G. Dumindu Samaraweera. *Privacy-Preserving Machine Learning*. Simon and Schuster, 2023.
7. Amaithi Rajan, Arun, and V. Vetriselvi. "Systematic Survey: Secure and Privacy-Preserving Big Data Analytics in Cloud." *Journal of Computer Information Systems* 64, no. 1 (2024): 136–156.
8. Basha, M. John, T. Satyanarayana Murthy, A. S. Valarmathy, Ahmed Radie Abbas, Djuraeva Gavhar, R. Rajavarman, and N. Parkunam. "Privacy-Preserving Data Mining and Analytics in Big Data." In *E3S Web of Conferences*, vol. 399, p. 04033. EDP Sciences, 2023.
9. El Mestari, Soumia Zohra, Gabriele Lenzini, and Huseyin Demirci. "Preserving Data Privacy in Machine Learning Systems." *Computers & Security* 137 (2024): 103605.
10. Nair, Akarsh K., Jayakrushna Sahoo, and Ebin Deni Raj. "Privacy Preserving Federated Learning Framework for IoMT Based Big Data Analysis Using Edge Computing." *Computer Standards & Interfaces* 86 (2023): 103720.
11. Han, Qiwei, Carolina Lucas, Emila Aguiar, Patrícia Macedo, and Zhenze Wu. "Towards Privacy-Preserving Digital Marketing: An Integrated Framework for User Modeling Using Deep Learning on a Data Monetization Platform." *Electronic Commerce Research* 23, no. 3 (2023): 1701–1730.
12. Panzade, Prajwal, Daniel Takabi, and Zhipeng Cai. "Privacy-Preserving Machine Learning Using Functional Encryption: Opportunities and Challenges." *IEEE Internet of Things Journal* 11, no. 5 (2024): 7436–7446. https://doi.org/10.1109/JIOT.2023.3338220
13. Terziyan, Vagan, Bohdan Bilokon, and Mariia Gavriushenko. "Deep Homeomorphic Data Encryption for Privacy Preserving Machine Learning." *Procedia Computer Science* 232 (2024): 2201–2212.

14. Lee, Hankang, Daniel Finke, and Hui Yang. "Privacy-Preserving Neural Networks for Smart Manufacturing." *Journal of Computing and Information Science in Engineering* 24, no. 7 (2024): 071002.
15. Chopra, Bhuvi, and Vinayak Raja. "Towards Improved Privacy in Digital Marketing: A Unified Approach to User Modeling with Deep Learning on a Data Monetization Platform." *Journal of Artificial Intelligence General Science (JAIGS)* 4, no. 1 (2024): 163–178. ISSN: 3006-4023.
16. Safaei Yaraziz, Mahdi, Ahmad Jalili, Mehdi Gheisari, and Yang Liu. "Recent Trends Towards Privacy-Preservation in Internet of Things, Its Challenges and Future Directions." *IET Circuits, Devices & Systems* 17, no. 2 (2023): 53–61.
17. Boopathi, Mythili, Sachin Gupta, A. N. Mohammed Zabeeulla, Rupal Gupta, Vipul Vekriya, and Arvind Kumar Pandey. "Optimization Algorithms in Security and Privacy-Preserving Data Disturbance for Collaborative Edge Computing Social IoT Deep Learning Architectures." *Soft Computing* (2023): 1–13.
18. Gururaj, H. L., M. Spoorthi, Vinayakumar Ravi, J. Shreyas, and Kumar Sekhar Roy. *Securing the Future: Introduction to Zero Trust in Cybersecurity*. Springer, 2024. https://doi.org/10.1007/978-3-031-63781-0_1
19. Spoorthi, M., and H. L. Gururaj. "Federated Learning and Its Classifications." In *Federated Learning Techniques and Its Application in the Healthcare Industry*, pp. 27–53. 2024. https://doi.org/10.1142/13722
20. Spoorthi, M., and H. L. Gururaj. "Federated Learning and Its." *Federated Learning Techniques and Its Application in the Healthcare Industry* (2024): 27. https://doi.org/10.1142/13722
21. Sanu, Kumar, and Peter Egeghy. "Next-Gen Education Security: Blockchain, AI, and Quantum Cryptography Solutions." DOI: 10.13140/RG.2.2.17306.45767
22. Kirubha, D., S. Deekshitha, and Spoorthi Netra. "Suspicious Activity Recognize Implementing Deep Learning Approach." *International Journal of Multidisciplinary Research in Science, Engineering and Technology* 7, no. 8 (2024): 2024.
23. Dasi, Ugandhar, Nikhil Singla, Rajkumar Balasubramanian, Siddhant Benadikar, and Rishabh Rajesh Shanbhag. "Analyzing the Security and Privacy Challenges in Implementing Ai and Ml Models in Multi-Tenant Cloud Environments." *International Journal of Multidisciplinary Innovation and Research Methodology* 3, no. 2 (2024): 262–270. ISSN: 2960-2068.
24. Gupta, Rajesh, Sudeep Tanwar, Sudhanshu Tyagi, and Neeraj Kumar. "Machine Learning Models for Secure Data Analytics: A Taxonomy and Threat Model." *Computer Communications* 153 (2020): 406–440.
25. Dasgupta, Dipankar, Zahid Akhtar, and Sajib Sen. "Machine Learning in Cybersecurity: A Comprehensive Survey." *The Journal of Defense Modeling and Simulation* 19, no. 1 (2022): 57–106.

10 Navigating Cyber Security Tools

A Comprehensive Guide from Entry to Expert Level

Ashitha V Naik, Nalini H C, Anupama K, Yu-Chen Hu, and Shrikanth N G

10.1 INTRODUCTION

Cyber security is today more critical than ever in the connected world. Cyber threats, ranging from simple attacks to intricate multilayered breaches, are relentless and pose a barrage of challenges to organizations and individuals alike [1, 2]. The very heart of this concept of safeguarding against these risks lies in the effective usage of cyber security tools, which turn out to be the first line of defense in order to detect, mitigate, and address vulnerabilities and assaults. This chapter presents an in-depth analysis of these tools, functionalities, applications, and varying levels of effectiveness from beginner to advanced levels.

We begin with basics tools that are the foundation in cyber security practice. These tools, for novices to those trying to consolidate their cyber security, are for basic security operations such as scanning for vulnerabilities, detecting threats, and monitoring networks; they offer critical functionality that guides users in understanding the conceptual and practical ideas behind cyber security. For instance, basic antivirus and firewall functions are at least some guarantee of minimal security, whereas more specific instruments, like intrusion detection systems (IDS) or basic encryption utilities, are just some of the more subtle security measures [3]. It is important to master the fundamental tools for any journey into cyber security, because all of them are precursors to more complex ideas and approaches [4].

As we move forward, we discuss tools for the intermediate user, one who is familiar with the basics but wants more features to improve their capability. These tools have a lot of functionality and are applied in projects such as advanced threat hunting, penetration testing, and comprehensive vulnerability management. For instance, the users may be able to carry out a more sophisticated analysis and pinpoint the weaknesses in the system with the help of advanced threat intelligence platforms, vulnerability assessment tools, and advanced network analyzers [5, 6]. In this process, the tools are employed to gain an in-depth understanding of the concepts concerning cyber security that may then be interpreted and acted upon on the basis of the obtained information. This section of the chapter examines how to use such tools

DOI: 10.1201/9781003540045-10

to maximize the overall security posture and to adequately respond to new emerging threats.

At the advanced level, we investigate tools designed for the use of expert users and cyber security professionals requiring management and security of complex systems and networks. They include highly specialized features and capabilities like advanced forensic analysis, real-time incident response, and extensive security information and event management (SIEM) systems [7]. Typically advanced tools require substantial expertise to operate effectively and the users are often involved with critical processes such as in-depth forensic investigations, complex attacks, or extensive security monitoring. Thus, this chapter informs and clarifies the use of high-level tools in high-stakes situations where the stakes could become even higher if any inappropriate management of security incidents should happen quickly and accurately.

10.2 TOOL DOCUMENTATION

10.2.1 Nmap

Nmap, or Network Mapper, is a free and powerful network scanning tool. It was developed by Gordon Lyon, who is also known as Fyodor. This tool is widely used in network discovery and security auditing. Nmap can determine the live hosts on the network, scan for open ports, identify services running on those ports along with their versions, and even the operating system and hardware characteristics of network devices. Its capabilities go further with the Nmap Scripting Engine (NSE), which enables advanced service detection, vulnerability scanning, and much more through custom scripts [8]. Nmap can be installed on Windows, Linux, and macOS platforms. It is a network administrator's, security expert's, and ethical hacker's best friend, not to mention the malicious attacker's favorite tool. Its versatility and depth make it an indispensable tool in network security.

- **Basic Scan:** A simple and quick scan to check for open ports on a target host.
- Cmd – **nmap 192.168.1.1**

1. This is a very fast and straightforward scan.
2. It does a simple scan, identifying which hosts are up and which ports are open on the target IP address (192.168.1.1).
3. It has a default set of 1,000 common transmission control protocol (TCP) ports.

10.2.2 Wireshark

Wireshark is a highly recognized network protocol analyzer and widely used in network troubleshooting, analysis, software and protocol development, and education. With this tool, the users are able to observe real-time data traffic at detailed levels on their networks. Thus, this proves to be one of the critical diagnostic tools for network-related issues. The tool supports the deep inspection of hundreds of protocols, providing both live capture and offline analysis capabilities. Its standard three-pane packet browser and powerful display filters make it easy to dissect and understand complex network communications.

10.2.2.1 Basic Level

Understanding Wireshark Interface:

Wireshark is a powerful network protocol analyzer that allows users to capture and inspect data packets in real time.

- **Capture Interfaces**: Learn how to select the correct network interface to capture traffic (e.g., Ethernet, Wi-Fi).
- **Start and Stop Capture**: Know how to start and stop packet capture using the "Start" and "Stop" buttons.
- **Packet List Pane**: Recognize the list of captured packets and basic information such as source, destination, protocol, length, and info.
- **Packet Details Pane**: View detailed information about a selected packet, including its protocol tree.
- **Packet Bytes Pane**: Understand the raw data of the selected packet in both hexadecimal and American Standard Code for Information Interchange (ASCII) formats.

Basic Filters and Navigation:

- **Display Filters**: Apply simple display filters (e.g., internet protocol, transmission control protocol, hypertext transfer protocol) to focus on specific types of traffic.
- **Saving Captures**: Learn how to save captured packets to a file for later analysis.
- **Color Coding**: Understand the default color coding used to highlight different types of packets.

10.2.2.2 Intermediate Level

Advanced Filtering and Analysis:

- **Capture Filters**: Use capture filters (e.g., tcp port 80) to limit the packets captured based on specific criteria.
- **Complex Display Filters**: Create more complex display filters using logical operators (e.g., ip.src == 192.168.1.1 && tcp).
- **Following Streams**: Use the "Follow TCP/UDP Stream" feature to view the full conversation between two endpoints.
- **Statistics**: Utilize built-in statistics tools like "Protocol Hierarchy," "Conversations," and "Endpoint Statistics" to analyze network traffic patterns.

Network Troubleshooting:

- **Identifying Latency and Packet Loss**: Spot issues like high latency or packet loss by examining packet details and timing.
- **Resolving DNS Issues**: Analyze DNS traffic to troubleshoot domain resolution problems.

- **Diagnosing Application Layer Problems**: Look at HTTP, FTP, SMTP, and other application layer protocols to identify issues affecting application performance.

10.2.3 Metasploit Framework

The Metasploit Framework is an open-source penetration testing platform designed by Rapid7 to provide a comprehensive set of tools used to discover, exploit, and validate vulnerabilities on various systems for security professionals and ethical hackers.

Basic Level

- **Command**: msfconsole (see Figures 10.1 and 10.2)

Command:

```
msfconsole
search samba
use exploit/multi/samba/usermap_script
set RHOSTS <target_ip>
run
```

FIGURE 10.1 msf console

10.2.3.1 Intermediate Level

Advanced information of msfconsole command and Techniques:

- **Using Auxiliary Modules**: Utilize auxiliary modules for tasks such as scanning, fuzzing, and gathering information about targets.

```
msfconsole
search portscan
use auxiliary/scanner/portscan/tcp
set RHOSTS <target_ip>
set  PORTS 1-1000
run
```

FIGURE 10.2 Usage of Auxiliary Modules.

- **Meterpreter Payloads**: Employ Meterpreter payloads for advanced post-exploitation tasks, such as system reconnaissance and data exfiltration.
- **Exploitation Workflow**: Implement a typical exploitation workflow, including reconnaissance, vulnerability identification, exploitation, and post-exploitation.

10.2.4 Autopsy

Autopsy is an open-source digital forensics platform used by law enforcement, military, and corporate examiners to conduct thorough investigations on digital devices [9]. Developed as a graphical interface to the Sleuth Kit, Autopsy simplifies the process of analyzing hard drives, mobile devices, and other storage media to recover evidence such as deleted files, emails, browser history, and more. Its user-friendly interface and robust set of features make it a powerful tool for forensic analysis, enabling investigators to efficiently examine large volumes of data, create detailed reports, and ensure the integrity of their findings.

10.2.4.1 Basic Level

Getting Started with Autopsy:

- **Installation**: Install Autopsy on your system.
  - **Command**: Download the installer from the official website and follow the installation instructions.
- **Creating a New Case**: Start a new case to begin an investigation.
  - **Command**:
    - Open Autopsy.
    - Click "Create New Case".
    - Enter the case details and click "Finish".
- **Adding a Data Source**
- **Command**:
    - Click "Add Data Source".
    - Select the type of data source (e.g., Disk Image).
    - Follow the prompts to add the data source.
- **Basic File Analysis**: Browse and analyze files in the data source.
  - **Command**: Use the "File Browser" module to navigate through the file system and view file contents.

10.2.4.2 Intermediate Level

Advanced Forensic Analysis:

- **Keyword Search**: Perform keyword searches to locate specific terms within the data.
  - **Command**:
    - Go to the "Keyword Search" module.
    - Enter the keywords and click "Search".
- **Extracting Deleted Files**: Recover deleted files from the data source.
  - **Command**:
    - Use the "Data Artifacts" module.
    - Select "Deleted Files" and view the recoverable files.
- **Analyzing Web Activity**: Examine browser history, cookies, and cache files.
  - **Command**:
    - Go to the "Web History" module.
    - Select the browser and view the history, cookies, and cache files.

- **Email Analysis**: Analyze email data from the data source.
  - **Command**:
    - Use the "Email Parser" module.
    - Select the email client and view the extracted emails.

10.2.5 Social Engineering Toolkit

The Social Engineering Toolkit (SET) is an open-source framework for social engineering attacks, available to penetration testers, security professionals, and ethical hackers [10]. The firm TrustedSec developed it, and SET automates many techniques in the realm of social engineering to conduct real-world attacks. It is mostly used to test the human element in cyber security by designing convincing phishing emails, creating malicious websites, and delivering payloads via social engineering vectors. SET is the best available attack vector variety, offering high customization, and hence, a must-have tool for assessing and improving an organization's social engineering attack defense mechanisms and security awareness [11].

10.2.5.1 Basic Level

Getting Started with Social Engineering Tool:

- **Installation**: Install SET on your system.
- **Launching SET**: Start the Social Engineering Toolkit.
  - sudo setoolki
- **Simple Phishing Attack**: Create a basic phishing email using SET.
  - **Command**:
    - Select "1) Social-Engineering Attacks".
    - Select "2) Website Attack Vectors".
    - Select "3) Credential Harvester Attack Method".
    - Select "2) Site Cloner".
    - Enter the URL to clone and your IP address for the POST back.
- **Cloning a Website**: Clone a website to use as part of a phishing attack.
  - **Command**:
    - Select "1) Social-Engineering Attacks".
    - Select "2) Website Attack Vectors".
    - Select "3) Credential Harvester Attack Method".
    - Select "2) Site Cloner".
    - Enter the URL to clone and your IP address for the POST back.

10.2.5.2 Intermediate Level

Advanced Social Engineering Attacks:

- **Spear Phishing Attack**: Create a more targeted phishing email campaign.
  - **Command**:
    - Select "1) Social-Engineering Attacks".
    - Select "1) Spear-Phishing Attack Vectors".
    - Select "1) Perform a Mass Email Attack".
    - Choose the template or create a new email template.
    - Enter the target email addresses and send the phishing emails.

- **Java Applet Attack**: Deliver payloads using a malicious Java applet.
  - **Command**:
    - Select "1) Social-Engineering Attacks".
    - Select "2) Website Attack Vectors".
    - Select "4) Java Applet Attack Method".
    - Follow the prompts to configure and launch the attack.
- **Infectious Media Generator**: Create a malicious Universal Serial Bus (USB) or Compact Disc/Digital Versatile Disc (CD/DVD) to infect systems.
  - **Command**:
    - Select "1) Social-Engineering Attacks".
    - Select "5) Infectious Media Generator".
    - Select "2) Standard Metasploit Executable".
    - Follow the prompts to generate the media.

10.2.6 WAFW00F

- This package identifies and fingerprints Web Application Firewall (WAF) products using the following logic:
- Sends a normal HTTP request and analyzes the response; this identifies a number of WAF solutions.
- If that is not successful, it sends a number of (potentially malicious) HTTP requests and uses simple logic to deduce which WAF it is.
- If that is also not successful, it analyzes the responses previously returned and uses another simple algorithm to guess if a WAF or security solution is actively responding to the attacks.
- Installed size: 240 KB
- How to install: sudo apt install wafw00f

10.2.6.1 Basic Scan

A simple scan to check if a WAF is present on the target web application.

Command:- ***wafw00f http://example.com***

- **Usage:** This command is used to check if a WAF is present on the target web application.
- **Purpose:** It provides a quick assessment to determine whether further investigation or bypass techniques are needed.

10.2.6.2 Intermediate Scan

The intermediate scan is a more detailed scan that attempts to fingerprint the WAF and gather more information.

Command: *wafw00f -a http://example.com*

- Usage: This command includes the -a (aggressive) option to perform a more thorough scan.
- Purpose: It attempts to fingerprint the WAF, providing information about the specific type and possibly the version.

- Benefit: It helps in understanding the WAF technology in use, which is crucial for planning bypass strategies or penetration tests.

10.2.7 Dirb

Dirb is an online content scanner that has capabilities to search for existing web objects, possibly hidden behind server-side technologies. It usually allows penetration testers to determine non-linked directories and files at a web server site as they are not accessed and linked in the visible website contents. Dirb uses a word list to perform brute-force attacks as well.

Key Features of Dirb:

- **Wordlist-Based Scanning:** It uses a predefined list of words to find directories and files.
- **Recursive Scanning:** It can recursively search through directories.
- **Customizable:** It allows users to specify their own wordlists and extensions.
- **Reports:** It generates detailed reports of the findings.

10.2.7.1 Dirb Scans

The following are the three types of scans (basic, intermediate, and advanced) with corresponding commands:

1. Basic Scan
   A simple scan to discover directories and files using the default wordlist.
   Command: *dirb http://example.com*

   - **Usage:** This command uses Dirb's default wordlist to scan the target URL for common directories and files.
   - **Purpose:** It provides a quick overview of potentially interesting web objects on the target server.

2. Intermediate Scan
   A more detailed scan that uses a custom wordlist for a more thorough search.
   Command:- *dirb http://example.com/path/to/custom/wordlist.txt*

   - **Usage:** This command uses a specified custom wordlist to scan the target URL.
   - **Purpose:** It performs a more detailed search by using a wordlist tailored to specific needs or target characteristics.
   - **Benefit:** Using this increases the chances of discovering less common or custom directories and files.

3. Advanced Scan
   A comprehensive scan that includes recursive directory scanning and searches for multiple file extensions.

Command: *dirb http://example.com/path/to/custom/wordlist.txt -X .php,.html,.txt -R*

- **Usage:** This command uses a custom wordlist, checks for specified file extensions (.php, .html, .txt), and enables recursive scanning.
- **Purpose:** It provides the most thorough scan by exploring multiple file types and recursively scanning through all directories found.
- **Benefit:** It offers a comprehensive view of the web server's directory structure and content, identifying deeply nested and various file types.

10.2.8 WPScan

WPScan is, in essence, a specialized security scanner tailored solely for WordPress sites. WPScan finds vulnerabilities hidden behind the face of WordPress installations, themes, and plugins. It is an indispensable tool for security professionals and website administrators to review and strengthen the security layer of WordPress sites.

Key Features of WPScan:

- **Core Vulnerability Detection:** Identifies vulnerabilities in the WordPress core.
- **Plugin and Theme Detection:** Detects and checks vulnerabilities in installed plugins and themes.
- **User Enumeration:** Enumerates WordPress users.
- **Brute Force Attack:** Performs password attack-forcing for WordPress accounts.
- **Database Updates:** Regularly updated vulnerability database.

10.2.8.1 WPScan Scans

The following are the three types of scans (basic, intermediate) with corresponding commands:

1 BasicScan
This is a simple scan to check for basic information about the WordPress site, including version detection.
Command: *wpscan – url http://example.com*

2 Intermediate Scan
This is a more detailed scan that includes plugin enumeration and checks for known vulnerabilities.
Command: *wpscan – url http://example.com – enumerate p*

- **Usage:** This command enumerates installed plugins and checks for known vulnerabilities.
- **Purpose:** Detects vulnerabilities in plugins, which are common vectors for attacks on WordPress sites.
- **Benefit:** Helps in identifying potential security risks associated with plugins.

10.2.9 Maltego

Maltego is a powerful open-source intelligence (OSINT) and forensic tool. This tool comes with an interactive graphical interface that helps in the analysis as well as data mining of information. This makes it quite good at finding relationships that exist between information on the internet. It is often used within cyber security for mapping infrastructure, tracing connections between entities, or gathering information from different sources.

Key Features of Maltego:

- **Data Mining:** Collects data from numerous public sources.
- **Graphical Link Analysis:** Visualizes relationships between entities like domains, IP addresses, social media profiles, and more.
- **Transforms:** Uses various transforms (automated scripts) to fetch related data.
- **Customization:** Supports creating custom transforms and datasets.
- **Collaboration:** Allows sharing of graphs and findings with team members.

10.2.9.1 Maltego Scans

The following are the three types of scans (basic, intermediate, and advanced) with corresponding use cases:

1 Basic Scan
This is a simple scan to identify basic information about a domain, such as associated IP addresses and DNS records.

Use Case:

- Open Maltego, create a new graph.
- Drag and drop a "Domain" entity onto the graph.
- Enter the domain name (e.g., example.com).
- Right-click the domain entity and select Run All Transforms.

2 Intermediate Scan
A more detailed scan that includes discovering linked email addresses, social media profiles, and associated websites.

10.2.10 Subfinder

Subfinder is an assistant for finding subdomains. The tool gets them from a variety of sources, including search engines, passive DNS data, and web archives. It is a simple, fast tool. Its speed and simplicity help security researchers and penetration testers keep an eye on the vulnerable aspects of a target domain.

Key Features of Subfinder:

- Multiple data sources: Gathers subdomains from a variety of sources.
- Speed: Designed to be fast, efficient.

- Extensible: It is very extensible as it easily works with other tools and custom settings.
- JSON output: Its output file format makes results easily reusable with other tools and tasks.
- Active enumeration: It can make use of active techniques to identify subdomains.

10.2.10.1 Subfinder Scans

The following are the three types of scans (basic, intermediate, and advanced) with corresponding commands:

1 Basic Scan
This is A simple scan to quickly gather subdomains using default data sources.
Command: *subfinder -d example.com*

- **Usage:** This command uses Subfinder's default settings to find subdomains for the specified domain.
- **Purpose:** It provides a quick overview of subdomains associated with the target domain.

2 Intermediate Scan
A more detailed scan involves verbose output and additional data sources for a more comprehensive subdomain list.
Command: *subfinder -d example.com -v*

- **Usage:** This command uses verbose mode to show more detailed output during the subdomain discovery process.
- **Purpose:** It offers a more comprehensive list of subdomains, including additional details about the sources and progress of the scan.

10.2.11 Wifite

Wifite is an automated wireless attack tool designed for auditing wireless fidelity (Wi-Fi) networks. It simplifies the procedure of launching attacks on a wireless network by automating usage of several popular tools including aircrack-ng, reaver, and many others. Wifite allows performing de-authentication attacks, capturing handshakes, and attempting to crack passwords for WEP, WPA, and WPS.

Key Features of Wifite:

- **Automated Attacks:** Simplifies the process of launching various wireless attacks.
- **Multiple Attack Types:** Supports WEP, WPA, WPA2, and WPS attacks.
- **Integration:** Uses other popular tools for different stages of the attack.
- **User-Friendly:** Designed to be easy to use with minimal configuration.
- **Customization:** Allows users to specify targets, attack types, and other parameters.

10.2.11.1 Wifite Scans

The following are the three types of scans (basic and intermediate) with corresponding commands:

1 Basic Scan
A simple scan to discover nearby wireless networks. Command:- Wifite – Scan

- **Usage:** This command scans for available wireless networks within range.
- **Purpose:** It provides a quick overview of the wireless networks in the vicinity.

2 Intermediate Scan
This is a more detailed scan that captures handshakes from WPA/WPA2 networks.
Command:- wifite – handshake

- **Usage:** This command captures handshakes from WPA/WPA2 networks for offline password cracking.
- **Purpose:** Allows for the collection of data necessary to attempt cracking WPA/WPA2 passwords offline.

10.3 CONCLUSION

In short, using cyber security tools is very important in keeping businesses safe from the changing cyber threats. This chapter takes a closer look at the various types of cyber security solutions that are utilized in companies—from the basic options such as firewalls and antivirus software to the more advanced technologies like IDS and threat intelligence platforms. We have demonstrated that applying practical insight to select, adopt, and integrate such tools is crucial. A multilayered security approach that uses multiple defensive mechanisms against various types of threats is necessary.

In the end, it helps the organization stay strong and keeps business running smoothly by giving business leaders and IT professionals a clear understanding of these tools and what they do. Adding strong cyber security steps to their IT systems can help organizations protect important information, keep operations going, and maintain trust from stakeholders in a world that is becoming more digital. This chapter informs the reader about information and methods that create a strong base to build a strong cyber security framework that can handle today's complex cyber threats.

REFERENCES

1. Brooks, C. J., & Cole, L. K. (2020). *Cybersecurity essentials*. CRC Press.
2. Sanford, A. (2022). *Cybersecurity for beginners*. Apress.
3. Stallings, W. (2018). *Network security essentials: Applications and standards* (6th ed.). Pearson.
4. Ahmed, M., Hu, J., & Roberts, M. L. (2021). A survey of intrusion detection systems. *Computer Networks*, 184, 107749. https://doi.org/10.1016/j.comnet.2020.107749
5. Chien, D. K. (2022). Threat intelligence: A review of current research and future directions. *Journal of Cybersecurity*, 10(1), 1–15. https://doi.org/10.1093/cybersec/tyac010

6. Forrester Research. (2023). The Forrester Wave™: Endpoint security suites, Q3 2023. *Forrester*. https://go.forrester.com/research/
7. Gartner. (2023). Gartner Magic Quadrant for network firewalls. *Gartner*. www.gartner.com/en/doc/4576160
8. SANS Institute. (n.d.). *Resources*. www.sans.org/resources/
9. CISO Magazine. (n.d.). *Articles and White Papers*. https://cisomag.eccouncil.org
10. National Institute of Standards and Technology (NIST). (2020). NIST special publication 800-53: Security and privacy controls for information systems and organizations. *NIST*. https://doi.org/10.6028/NIST.SP.800-53r5
11. International Organization for Standardization (ISO). (2022). ISO/IEC 27001: Information security management systems. *ISO*. www.iso.org/isoiec-27001-information-security.html

11 Improving Cyber Security Measures in Business Analytics for E-Commerce Platforms in Africa

Cyber Laws, Challenges, and Solutions

Rose Oluwaseun Adetunji, Olaniyi Felix Olayinka, and Praise Aanuoluwa Bobola

11.1 INTRODUCTION

In recent years, the business sector in Africa has experienced substantial expansion, particularly in the realm of electronic commerce (e-commerce) [1]. Over the last ten years, the African e-commerce industry has consistently grown, propelled by enhanced internet connectivity and an expanding population of online consumers [2]. Furthermore, the Covid-19 epidemic has expedited the implementation of e-commerce platforms throughout Africa [3]. Africa's e-commerce industry had a valuation of $16.5 billion in 2017 and is projected to surpass $75 billion by 2025 [4]. Nevertheless, the expansion of the e-commerce sector may face obstacles such as data breaches, payment fraud, and identity theft, which have the potential to negatively impact consumer confidence and retail demand [5]. Ensuring the security of business analytics is crucial for safeguarding intellectual property, customer data, and other information that is utilized to improve management decisions and operational effectiveness [6]. Indeed, apart from the possibility of severe financial damage, violations of business analytics can also undermine the competitive edge of the organization. Hence, it is crucial to prioritize the improvement of cyber security protocols in business analytics for e-commerce platforms in order to safeguard customer and company data [7].

Analytics is being employed in the field of e-commerce for crucial operational domains such as market-basket analysis, dynamic pricing, customer segmentation, fraud detection, social network analysis, and recommendations derived from social

DOI: 10.1201/9781003540045-11

tags [8]. However, the use of analytics amplifies the vulnerability to attacks and jeopardizes the safeguarding of privacy and confidentiality within the organization [9]. The current implementation of privacy measures is inadequate in terms of addressing the data used for business analytics and the threat models that pose a risk to data privacy. Securing business analytics presents several challenges, including the current state of data accessibility, the vulnerability of emerging technologies (such as middleware, big data, and cloud computing), the level of security of new analytics techniques [such as online analytical processing (OLAP) and machine learning (ML)], and the trade-off between security performance and the needs of business analytics on e-commerce platforms [10]. Various approaches, such as novel cryptographic methods, suitable privacy layer techniques, security by design in emerging technologies, and privacy-specific protocols and measures aligned with analytical techniques and attack patterns, have been suggested to tackle the difficulties of securing business analytics [10].

11.1.1 Background and Significance

The advent of digitalization is facilitating significant changes in the worldwide commercial business operations [11]. The pursuit of interests in the digital realm is becoming more prevalent among both organizations and consumers [12]. Within this global context, business analytics can be regarded as a crucial method to access the manageable aspects of customer interest domains, provide cost-effective services, and restore customer compliance and satisfaction [13]. This approach is highly lucrative for easily accessible service providers, whether it be for intangible assets such as music and movies or tangible goods and system services in the contemporary digital e-commerce industry [13]. As the advancements facilitated by open and widely available global networks, technologies, platforms, systems, and tools have provided organizations with completely new opportunities to offer their products and services, they have also brought about significantly new risks and challenges for the stakeholders in these ecosystems [14]. Under hazardous conditions, various service providers have the ability to provide a wide range of services to both commercial enterprises and individuals [15].

In addition to this transparency, various types of fraudulent, malicious, and profitable activities seem to prevail, manifesting in the design, development, and dissemination of fraudulent and questionable applications, infrastructure resources, and software development tools, training and enabling individuals to implement false and questionable things and exploit different platform resources for illicit impromptu profit [16]. Although some of these dangerous attempts can be recognized and identified by the returned services in the digital realm, such as spam, advertising/hoax organizations, and phishing emails, others are notoriously difficult to recognize and identify [17]. These include various algorithms and technical tools designed to detect fraudulent analysis surfaces due to their false service character and classifications [18]. The present review delineates a range of potential strategies and mechanisms to augment the security of analytics procedures for e-commerce platforms. This chapter presents an overview of the most common fraudulent and malicious activities carried out against business analytics. It also explores both non-technical and technical mitigation strategies. This chapter examines and outlines the feasibility, difficulties in implementation, and suitability of both types of controls. The global improvement in security, achieved through the implementation of these measures and controls, also mitigates the risks associated with other forms of fraud and malicious activities.

11.1.2 Research Objectives

The rapid adoption of mobile and internet technologies in Africa presents a promising opportunity for emerging economies to implement sophisticated business analytics in a secure manner [19]. These developments are fostering the emergence of novel services and business models, stimulating entrepreneurial activities and economic expansion, and generating job opportunities [20]. Data is increasingly recognized as a valuable corporate resource [21]. Nevertheless, it is being actively pursued and manipulated for illicit intentions [21]. Data breaches and cyberattacks that result in the loss, unauthorized access, and misuse of data assets jeopardize the integrity of analytics [22]. The competitive landscape for African enterprises is frequently concealed, as predators remain hidden, and attacks can originate from any part of the globe. Certain attackers possess substantial financial resources and have access to sophisticated capabilities. Therefore, e-commerce platforms are progressively required to provide strong business analytics safeguards. However, each new response is inherently susceptible to being targeted or can frequently be rendered ineffective by attackers who adopt novel techniques. The development of algorithms capable of detecting and mitigating adversarial attacks, frequently facilitated by artificial intelligence (AI), is imperative [23]. Nevertheless, the task of creating novel business analytic safeguards overcoming the inherent incompatibility with existing systems is quite difficult [24]. Emerging economies face a disproportionate level of risk, as they lack the ability to protect themselves and are constrained to depend on business analytical solutions developed in other countries, typically affluent democracies, which may not be optimal or appropriate for their own governance [25].

The primary objective of this chapter is to comprehensively investigate the obstacles and remedies associated with improving cyber security protocols particularly for business analytics on e-commerce platforms in Africa. This investigation aims to enhance comprehension of the risks present in the e-commerce ecosystem. The presentation will address relevant concerns related to current or proposed safeguarding measures, evaluating the effectiveness and appropriateness of current business analytics protective measures, the resilience of algorithms against adversarial attacks, and developing frameworks to aid in detecting, quantifying, mitigating, and warning about vulnerabilities, in direct response to the increasing types of attacks on business analytics. The analysis will also indicate potential prospects and the necessity for additional investigation.

11.2 LITERATURE REVIEW OF CYBER SECURITY IN AFRICA

Previous studies show that there are countless benefits if a country is equipped with a crime-free cyber system, as it boosts investment, job creation, and faster economic growth, to name a few. For example, cyber capability and capacity building for cyber security emergencies potentially save lives and respond post emergencies by rebuilding confidence in the associated critical infrastructure services [26]. Africa is regrettably wide in governance strategies and other aspects, and many initiatives remain at the expert and civil society level, such as Cyber Security Knowledge Management (CKSM) and Information Sharing Analysis Centre (AISA) [27]. Yet, many cyber security awareness and knowledge initiatives do not necessarily address all of the cyber security risks and outcomes that are publicly argued for in global and truly primary national cyber security strategies and policies [28]. Critical, without a doubt, are the efforts in addressing cyber capabilities and capacities in responding to cyber security crises that play into foreign, criminal, and other acts or consequences associated with a weak cyber security environment [27, 29].

Communication ministers and the African Union (AU) have committed to ratify the Malabo and other AU treaties in the area of cyber security, especially to address cybercrime. The challenges to a cybercrime-enabled secure environment are common, and in some African states, various legislation on cybercrime are misused to suppress independent media and other digital freedom actors [30]. The development of information and communication technologies (ICTs) and the increasing use of cyberspace have given birth to sophisticated criminal activities, such as cybercrimes, with a particular focus on crimes committed against or over the internet. Despite the increasing misuse of cyberspace, and the AU and respective governments taking various steps to address and mitigate cyber-related risks and threats, many African countries do not have cyber security policies, and some do not have the necessary legislation or national structures to manage and protect the national cyber infrastructure [31].

11.2.1 Cyber Security Threats in E-Commerce Platforms

With the global expansion of e-commerce platforms, there is greater increase of cyber security risks, which exert substantial influence on both corporate activities and customer confidence [32]. This chapter highlights and categorizes many common threats, such as phishing attacks, malware, Structured Query Language (SQL) injection attacks, distributed denial of service (DDoS) attacks, and credential stuffing [33]. Each of these threats presents distinct hazards to e-commerce platforms, including unauthorized access to data, interruptions in operations, and financial inefficiencies. Phishing and malware attacks frequently focus on confidential user data, while SQL injections take advantage of weaknesses in databases to undermine the integrity of data content [34].

The ramifications of these cyber security threats go beyond immediate monetary damages. Such actions have the potential to greatly harm the reputation of a company, undermine customer confidence, and result in possible legal consequences [35]. Financial losses encompass the expenses incurred from direct theft, ransom payments, and recovery efforts, while harm to reputation can undermine customer confidence and result in reduced market sales. Furthermore, failure to adhere to data protection laws can lead to substantial civil fines for e-commerce enterprises [36]. Research has found that to reduce these risks, e-commerce platforms should adopt strong security measures such as firewalls, rigorous coding practices, and frequent updates. Furthermore, it is essential to improve user awareness by means of education and training, which will effectively prevent attacks, in addition to performing routine security audits to detect and resolve vulnerabilities [37]. An integral aspect of efficiently handling and recovering from cyberattacks is the development of a thorough incident response plan. The implementation of these strategies can enhance the operational security of e-commerce enterprises and uphold customer confidence in the face of ever-changing cyber threats [38].

11.2.2 Common Cyberattacks in Africa

Africa's swift digitalization has rendered it rather vulnerable to a range of cyberattacks [39]. Phishing, ransomware, and DDoS attacks are common. Cybercriminals frequently use phishing to steal sensitive data from individuals and organizations [40]. An increase in ransomware attacks has been observed, specifically affecting industries such as healthcare and finance through the encryption of data and subsequent demand for payment. DDoS attacks inundate government services, financial institutions, and e-commerce platforms with an overwhelming volume of traffic, resulting in disruptions. Furthermore, the prevalence of mobile malware and identity theft is increasing, exploiting the use of mobile devices to unlawfully acquire personal information [41]. The impact of cyberattacks on Africa's economic situation, public confidence, and digital progress is substantial. Businesses incur financial losses and reputational damage, while individuals suffer privacy breaches and financial detriment [42]. National security threats and service disruptions pose a significant risk to governments and public institutions. The escalating occurrence and intricacy of these attacks emphasize the pressing necessity for strong cyber security protocols to protect both individuals and organizations [42]. From researchers' perspectives of addressing these risks, Africa should strengthen its cyber security infrastructure by advocating for public awareness, implementing sophisticated security technologies, and establishing reliable national policies [43]. Effective exchange of threat intelligence and prompt incident response require collaborative efforts among governments, private sectors, and international organizations. Implementing these measures will enable Africa to establish a more robust digital infrastructure, enhance its ability to protect against increasing cyber risks, and guarantee a secure future for its digital economy [43].

11.2.3 Cyber Security Enhances Economic Growth

Africa is rich in natural resources, yet it faces significant challenges with poverty and underdevelopment. Despite decades of progress, Africa still struggles to achieve sustainable and inclusive economic growth. This chapter discusses demographics, technology, and policy reforms that can boost African economic growth. African countries can accelerate economic transformation and improve citizen well-being by identifying opportunities and addressing challenges.

Opportunities for economic growth: Africa has strong economic potentials due to its abundant natural resources, young population, and urbanization. Mineral, oil, and gas reserves on the continent offer export-led growth and industrialization.

Africa's young and growing population provides a demographic dividend of a large, dynamic workforce that drives innovation, entrepreneurship, and consumer demand [44]. Rural-to-urban migration creates infrastructure, housing, and service investment opportunities, which boosts African economies. Rapid mobile technology and digital innovation are also changing business models, increasing productivity, and opening up financial services and markets across the continent [45]. Africa faces many obstacles to economic growth despite its potential. Infrastructure deficiencies like poor transportation, power, water, and sanitation limit productivity and investment. Corruption, weak governance, and political instability hurt investor confidence and private sector growth. Poverty, unemployment, and gender inequality also hinder inclusive growth and social cohesion [46].

Pro-growth facilitation strategies: Policy reforms, infrastructure and human capital investment, and business facilitation are needed to solve Africa's economic problems. To boost trade, lower transaction costs, and unlock the continent's economic potentials, governments must invest in roads, ports, and energy. Building investor confidence and attracting foreign direct investment requires strengthening governance institutions, promoting transparency, and fighting corruption [47].

Research study has stated that to prepare workers for the global economy, education, skills development, and healthcare must be prioritized. Expanding access to basic services, promoting gender equality, and supporting vulnerable populations are needed to promote inclusive growth and address poverty, inequality, and social exclusion [48]. Technology and innovation must be harnessed to boost African productivity, competitiveness, and growth. Governments can promote digital infrastructure, entrepreneurship, and innovation ecosystems and use emerging technologies like AI, blockchain, and renewable energy to solve development problems and create new economic opportunities [49]. Africa faces a critical moment in its economic development. The continent could become a global economic powerhouse in the 21st century by using its abundant resources, youthful population, and technological innovation [28]. Jameaba [50] mentioned in a research that to address infrastructure deficits, governance issues, and socioeconomic inequalities, governments, the private sector, civil society, and the international community must work together. Strategic reforms, investing in human capital and infrastructure, and creating a business-friendly environment can help Africa reach its full economic potential and achieve sustainable and inclusive growth for all its citizens [50].

11.2.4 Safeguarding Africa's Connectivity: Securing Telecommunications Networks and Critical Infrastructure

Telecommunications networks have connected millions of Africans, businesses, and governments, changing the continent's socioeconomic landscape [51]. Telecommunications infrastructure—from mobile networks and internet service providers to satellite communications and fiber-optic cables—drives economic growth, digital inclusion, and innovation. These networks are increasingly vulnerable to cyberattacks, physical sabotage, and natural disasters due to their interconnectedness. To ensure Africa's connectivity and information and service flow, telecommunications networks and critical infrastructure must be secured [51].

Telecommunications Network Security Challenges: Cyber security and physical vulnerabilities make securing African telecommunications networks difficult. DDoS attacks, malware infections, and phishing scams threaten network integrity and data confidentiality. Lack of cyber security awareness and skilled staff makes it hard for organizations to detect and respond to cyber threats. Telecommunications network towers, cables, and data centers are vulnerable to natural disasters, vandalism, and theft, reducing network reliability and resilience [52].

Telecom Network Security Strategies: Technical, organizational, and regulatory measures are needed to secure telecommunications networks [53]. First, organizations must use firewalls, intrusion detection systems, and encryption to defend against cyberattacks. Regular security audits can identify vulnerabilities and ensure industry standards and best practices compliance. Investing in cyber security training and awareness programs helps create a cyber security-conscious culture and empower employees to identify and mitigate cyber risks. Telecommunications networks need physical security and resilience as well as cyber security. Surveillance cameras, access controls, and perimeter fencing can prevent unauthorized entry and physical sabotage. If infrastructure fails, redundancy and backup systems like alternative power sources and geographically dispersed data centers are essential for service continuity [54].

Information Sharing and Collaboration: Telecommunications cyber security relies on collaboration and information sharing. Industry partnerships, government agencies, and international organizations can share threat intelligence, best practices, and cyber incident responses [55]. Public–private partnerships create a collaborative ecosystem where stakeholders solve cyber security issues. Regional and international initiatives like the African Union Convention on Cyber Security and Personal Data Protection (AUCC) and the Budapest Convention on Cybercrime provide cyber security cooperation and capacity-building frameworks [56].

African connectivity requires a comprehensive and collaborative approach to telecommunications network and critical infrastructure security. African countries can reduce cyber threats and physical disruptions by improving cyber security, physical security, and collaboration and information sharing. Building a secure and resilient telecommunications sector that supports Africa's socioeconomic development and digital transformation requires investing in cyber security capacity building, raising awareness, and strengthening regulatory frameworks [56].

11.2.5 Strengthening National Security in Africa: Advancements in Cyber Defense Capabilities

The rise of cyber threats and digital interconnectedness have made cyber security a global priority for governments. Critical infrastructure and sensitive data must be protected from cyberattacks in Africa, where rapid technological advancements are changing economies and societies. African nations are strengthening their cyber defenses to reduce risks, protect national interests, and maintain sovereignty in cyberspace.

Cyber Defense Strategy Evolution: Cyber defense strategies in Africa began to evolve in the early 2000s when governments recognized the potential threat of cyberattacks to national security. Awareness, basic cyber security policies, and computer emergency response teams (CERTs) to respond to cyber incidents were initially prioritized [57]. The focus shifted to stronger cyber security frameworks, legislative and regulatory reforms, and technology and human capital development. The creation of national cyber security agencies or authorities to coordinate cyber security efforts, develop cyber strategies, and promote public–private partnerships is notable. Kenya, Nigeria, South Africa, and Mauritius have actively strengthened their cyber defense [58].

Effective cyber defense requires institutional capacity building. African nations are investing in cyber security training and capacity building to create a skilled workforce. Academic institutions, technical schools, and specialized training centers offer a range of courses and certifications to meet the demand for cyber security professionals [58]. International collaborations with the AU, Economic Community of West African States (ECOWAS), and Southern African Development Community (SADC) are strengthening regional cyber resilience through the facilitation of knowledge sharing, provision of technical assistance, and promotion of cooperative endeavors [59].

Promoting International Cooperation: The global nature of cyber threats requires intensive international cooperation to ensure efficient defense. African nations are collaborating with regional and international counterparts to exchange information on potential threats, develop and implement effective strategies, and synchronize their actions in response to cyber events [60]. The AUCC, the Budapest Convention on Cybercrime, and the International Criminal Police Organization (INTERPOL)'s Global Complex for Innovation (IGCI) facilitate collaboration and the development of necessary skills in the field of cyber security [61].

Best Practices and Case Studies: African nations have become frontrunners in the field of cyber security by embracing cutting-edge methodologies and exemplary strategies to strengthen their cyber defenses [62]. Moroccan authorities have established the National Cyber Security Authority (ANRC) and enacted comprehensive cyber security legislation to effectively combat cyber threats and protect vital infrastructure. Likewise, Rwanda prioritized the promotion of cyber security awareness and innovation through the establishment of the Rwanda National Cyber Security Authority (RNCA) and the Cyber Security Innovation Hub [63].

Notwithstanding all the advancements, African nations encounter substantial obstacles in enhancing their cyber defense capabilities, such as constrained resources, capacity weaknesses, and deficiencies in awareness and coordination. Efficient resolution of these challenges requires unwavering dedication from political authorities, heightened allocation of resources toward cyber security, and improved collaboration among regional actors [65]. Notwithstanding these shortcomings, African countries have significant prospects to utilize technology, innovation, and international collaborations in order to enhance their ability to withstand cyber threats. The implementation of a comprehensive and cooperative strategy toward cyber security enables African nations to effectively mitigate cyber threats, protect their national security, and fully exploit the opportunities presented by the digital economy [63]. Enhancing cyber defense capabilities, strengthening institutional capacity, and fostering international cooperation are crucial for augmenting national security in Africa. The development of cyber defense strategies in the region demonstrates an increasing acknowledgment of the significance of cyber security in protecting national interests and promoting socioeconomic progress. Through the resolution of obstacles, exploitation of favorable circumstances, and adoption of innovative approaches, African nations possess the capacity to assume a leading position in the field of cyber security on a global scale [66].

11.2.6 Increasing Security through International Cooperation: Sharing Information and Joint Operations in Africa

Africa faces a multitude of security issues that endanger peace, stability, and development throughout the continent. The transboundary character of challenges such as violent extremism, insurgency, organized crime, and illegal trafficking underscores the necessity for cooperation at both regional and global levels. This chapter analyzes the significance of exchanging information and conducting joint operations to promote increased collaboration between African nations and their international counterparts in tackling common security objectives [67].

The significance of information sharing in efficient security cooperation resides in its capacity to enable the interchange of intelligence, scrutinize threats, and synchronize reactions to emerging challenges [68]. Within Africa, the Peace and Security Architecture (APSA) of the AU and regional organizations like the ECOWAS and the East African Community (EAC) function as forums for member states to share pertinent information and collaborate [69]. Collaborations with global institutions such as INTERPOL, the United Nations Office on Drugs and Crime (UNODC), and the Global Counterterrorism Forum (GCTF) are crucial for exchanging knowledge and enhancing operational capacities in vital domains such as counterterrorism, border security, and law enforcement [70].

The joint operations and task forces play a vital role in strengthening security cooperation in Africa. These programs consolidate military, law enforcement, and peacekeeping endeavors to address particular threats by combining resources, knowledge, and operational capacities. Specifically, the Multinational Joint Task Force (MNJTF) focuses on combating Boko Haram in the Lake Chad Basin, while the AU Mission to Somalia (AMISOM) aims to establish stability in Somalia. Moreover, the Djibouti Code of Conduct and the Yaoundé Architecture for Maritime Security enable collaborative patrols, exchange of information, and enhancement of capabilities to address maritime piracy, illegal fishing, and other breaches of maritime law [71, 72].

International collaboration in Africa improves situational awareness, interoperability, and security threat response [63]. Not only that, developing countries can anticipate and mitigate risks by sharing intelligence, leveraging resources, and coordinating responses, promoting regional peace and stability. However, information sensitivities, sovereignty concerns, and divergent national interests can hinder international collaboration. Trust-building, diplomatic engagement, clear information sharing, and joint operation protocols are needed to overcome these challenges. Notwithstanding the difficulties, collaboration on an international scale in Africa has considerable potential for tackling security concerns. Through the implementation of a cohesive security vision, strengthening institutional capabilities and regional cooperation mechanisms, African countries and their international allies can enhance safety throughout the continent [73].

The effective resolution of Africa's intricate and ever-changing security challenges requires the imperative of international information exchange and collaborative military actions. Through international cooperation and the maximization of combined capacities, nations can strengthen their capacity to proactively address, identify, and counteract security threats. Securing a safer and more resilient Africa requires enhanced collaboration and coordination among all parties involved in addressing the continent's security environment [73].

11.3 CYBER SECURITY SOLUTIONS BASED ON AFRICAN INDIGENOUS TECHNOLOGIES FOR E-COMMERCE

11.3.1 Introduction to African Indigenous Technology in Cyber Security

African Indigenous Technology (AIT) is a progressively employed methodology on which Africans have depended for an extended period to address diverse challenges. This approach emphasizes the cultural flexibility of African societies in surmounting obstacles associated with restricted availability or deployment of Western technology. African Indigenous Knowledge Systems (AIKS) are derived from the cultural, environmental, scientific, and technological traditions that have been generated by the indigenous people of Africa [74]. This approach presents an alternative strategy for tackling the difficulties encountered by underdeveloped nations by utilizing indigenous expertise and innovative solutions. The concept encompasses the application of Artificial Intelligence Technologies (AIT) and AIKS in several domains including education, sustainable development, internet and web technologies, ecology, and healthcare platforms. The primary purpose of cyber security tools is to safeguard computer and network systems against unauthorized access, hijacking, or damage, thereby guaranteeing the security of equipment and digital data [74].

11.3.2 The Importance of Cyber Security in E-commerce

E-commerce needs cyber security to safeguard customer data. E-commerce platforms handle a lot of personal and financial data, making them attractive targets for cybercriminals. Security measures like encryption, secure payment gateways, and security audits are crucial. These measures prevent unauthorized access, identity theft, and financial fraud, protecting customer trust and data protection compliance [7]. Cyber security protects against data breaches and ensures business continuity. Cyberattacks disrupt operations, costing money and customer loyalty. Intrusion detection systems and robust backup procedures reduce these risks, allowing businesses to maintain service and customer confidence during and after an incident [75]. Cyber security best practices are essential for e-commerce regulatory compliance. Business must comply with data protection laws and standards to avoid legal issues and maintain operations. Effective risk management and long-term success in the digital marketplace require vigilantly monitoring evolving cyber threats and updating security strategies. Thus, cyber security investments protect against financial losses and reputational damage, build customer trust, and strengthen business resilience [75].

11.4 IMPORTANCE OF BUSINESS ANALYTICS IN CYBER SECURITY

According to research, organizations must take sophisticated measures to protect their digital assets from changing cyber threats. Business analytics, traditionally used to improve operational efficiency and decision-making, is now essential to cyber security. This chapter discusses how business analytics can help cyber security by identifying vulnerabilities, anomalies, and risks. Analytics help organizations move from reactive to proactive defense strategies, improving their cyber incident prevention and management.

11.4.1 Role of Business Analytics in Cyber Security

Business analytics is essential for threat detection and analysis, allowing organizations to scrutinize extensive datasets for anomalous patterns and possible security weaknesses [76]. Sophisticated analytical instruments, such as machine learning (ML) algorithms and predictive analytics, evaluate network traffic, user behaviors, and system logs to detect anomalies that could signify cyber threats. By utilizing these technologies, organizations can improve their capacity to identify and react to threats in real time, consequently diminishing the probability of successful attacks [77]. Besides threat detection, business analytics facilitates efficient risk management and vulnerability assessment by offering insights into the potential consequences of diverse cyber threats. Analytical methods can assess the probability of various attack types, evaluate the efficacy of current security measures, and prioritize remedial actions based on potential risks. This data-centric methodology enables organizations to enhance resource distribution and concentrate on significant vulnerabilities, thereby fortifying their overall cyber security framework. Moreover, business analytics enhances incident response and recovery by providing a comprehensive understanding of the extent and consequences of a cyberattack, assisting organizations in identifying impacted systems, assessing their responses, and refining future readiness [78].

11.4.2 Role of Data Analytics in Identifying Threats

As cyber threats become more complex and widespread, organizations are using data analytics to strengthen their cyber security infrastructure. Methodical data analysis yields valuable insights that can be used to identify and mitigate security risks. The following section discusses how data analytics improves threat detection and response. This shows how advanced analytical methods can turn unprocessed data into digital asset protection insights [79]. Security threats like unusual network traffic or unauthorized access attempts are detected by anomaly detection algorithms. ML methods like clustering and classification improve accuracy and reduce false positives. Behavioral analytics helps organizations detect insider threats and account compromises by examining user and system behaviors for abnormalities. Threat intelligence and predictive analytics analyze past incidents and emerging attack vectors to predict future cyber threats using historical data and threat feeds. This proactive approach helps organizations prevent and mitigate risks, strengthening their defenses against sophisticated attacks [80]. Data-driven insights prioritize threats by impact and probability, improving risk management. Data analytics provides insights from past incidents to improve security. Organizations can prevent cyberattacks with real-time data monitoring and analysis [81].

11.5 CYBER SECURITY, CHALLENGES, AND SOLUTIONS

11.5.1 Cyber Security Laws in Africa for Business Analytics in African E-commerce

African cyber security laws affect e-commerce, business analytics, e-commerce platform data protection, compliance, and risk management. E-commerce in Africa raises cyber security concerns, requiring a comprehensive legal framework to protect businesses and consumers. The state has a duty to provide legislation and state policies to give a conducive environment for economic activities. Legal provisions are made by the legislative arm of government to regulate business activities. There are also international and domestic instruments to complement the domestic laws of a nation [82]. Consequently, Goal 16 of the United Nations Sustainable Development Goals 2030, on peace, justice, and strong institutions, promotes peaceful and inclusive societies for sustainable development.

At the state level, however, the set of laws afford the courts working documents to make interpretations and decisions. Failing the above, a nation cannot enjoy the benefit of having such legal provisions. In response to cyber security concerns, African nations have gradually passed data protection and privacy laws. The Protection of Personal Information Act (POPIA) in South Africa regulates data processing, storage, and management, which impacts how e-commerce platforms handle customer data [83]. The Data Protection Regulation of Nigeria (NDPR) provides detailed instructions for data processing and breach reporting. These regulations require enterprises to implement strict security protocols and ensure data transparency, affecting e-commerce business analytics [84]. Many African nations have extensive cybercrime and security regulations in addition to data protection laws. The Computer Misuse and Cybercrimes Act in Kenya and the Cyber Security Act in Ghana address unauthorized access, data breaches, and cyberattacks. Legal frameworks govern how e-commerce platforms and their business analytics teams handle security threats and incidents [85].

The right to obtain effective remedy upon violation of fundamental rights and freedom is recognized under Articles 7 and 8 of Universal Declaration of Human Rights (UDHR) as well as under Article 14 of ICCPR [86]. On compliance and enforcement of cyber security laws, African cyber security laws mandate data breach notification, security, and audit compliance. Government agencies monitor compliance and handle infractions in some countries. The Nigerian National Information Technology Development Agency (NITDA) and South African Information Regulator must protect data. Working with regulatory bodies to align analytics processes with legal requirements can reduce noncompliance risks for e-commerce companies [87].

More importantly, the courts have the authority to adjudicate and to interpret all laws with the powers to provide appropriate relief for every violation of right.

A major problem in this regard is access to court. The formal justice system is not user-friendly, most times. It proves to be very technical, causing undue delay, is costly, and with the consequent effect of denied access to justice. The law courts sometimes do not have the desired independence that can afford them the status of impartiality on cases they handle [88]. There is communication gap and inadequate publicity and enlightenment by government on laws that are made. Moreover, there are major challenges in the enforcement of the rule of law in a state as the data herein establish.

11.5.1.1 Data Analysis/Presentation/Results and Discussions

11.5.1.1.1 Preliminary Survey Details

For this study, the online questionnaire was filled out by 100 respondents using Google Forms. The response rate from the respondents was quite impressive. The responses were downloaded and imported into the Statistical Package for Social Science (SPSS) for descriptive analysis.

Research Objective 1: Discuss legal strategies for combating cybercrime in Africa, precisely in Nigeria

Table 11.1 presents data on individuals' awareness of laws against cybercrime, their ability to name specific laws, and their perception of the effectiveness of current laws in combating cybercrime. In terms of awareness of laws aimed explicitly against cybercrimes, 30% of respondents indicated that they knew of such laws, while 60% stated they did not, and 10% couldn't recall. This suggests a significant portion of the surveyed population lacks awareness of legislation targeting cyber offences.

TABLE 11.1
Awareness of Laws against Cybercrime

Awareness of Laws against Cybercrime		Frequency	(%)
Do you know any laws specifically enacted to combat cybercrimes	Yes	30	30
	No	60	60
	Can't remember	10	10
	Total	**100**	**100.0**
Can you name any of these laws?	Cybercrimes Act 2015	25	25
	Criminal Code	6	6
	Lack of Knowledge (NIL/Don't Know)	57	57
	Data Protection Act 2024	8	8
	Other Cyber Security Laws and Regulations	4	4
	Total	**100**	**100.0**
Do you believe the current laws are effective in combating cybercrime	Yes	49	49
	No	39	39
	Not adequate	12	12
	Total	**100**	**100**

Among those aware of cybercrime laws, 25% could name the Cybercrimes Act 2015, 6% mentioned the Criminal Code (including Section 419), and 8% cited the Data Protection Act 2024. However, the majority (57%) responded with "Lack of Knowledge" or "Don't Know," indicating a widespread gap in the understanding of specific legal frameworks addressing cybercrime. When asked about their perception of the effectiveness of current laws in combating cybercrime, 49% of respondents expressed belief in their efficacy, while 39% disagreed, and 12% considered them inadequate. This suggests a mixed sentiment regarding the effectiveness of existing legislation in addressing the challenges posed by cybercrime. The citizens are not able to take advantage of laws made to protect them when they are not even aware of the same.

Research objective 2: Examine the provisions of the Cybercrime Act of Nigeria, 2015 and other legal provisions.

Table 11.2 delineates respondents' perspectives on the provisions of the Cybercrime Act of 2015 and other legal provisions, along with their corresponding frequencies and percentages. First, a significant majority, comprising 84% of respondents, assert the necessity for an amendment to the Cybercrime Act of 2015, suggesting a widespread sentiment for legislative revisions to address evolving cyber threats. Conversely, 16% of respondents believe that no amendment is required, indicating a

TABLE 11.2
Respondents' Opinion on the Provisions of the Cybercrime Act of 2015 and Other Legal Provisions.

		Frequency	(%)
I think there is any need for an amendment	Yes	84	84
	No	16	16
	Total	**100**	**100**
I think there is enough public awareness about cybercrime laws in Nigeria.	Yes	30	30
	No	53	53
	Not adequate	7	7
	Total	**100**	**100.0**
I believe penalties for cybercrimes in Nigeria are sufficient punishments	No response at all	55	55
	Slow and ineffective	24	24
	Immediate and effective	21	21
	Total	**100**	**100**
There should be specific legislation targeting cybercrimes against vulnerable groups such as children and the elderly	Yes	34	34
	No	66	66
	Total	**100**	**100**
I think there are no government initiatives to educate the public about cybercrime prevention	Yes	20	20
	No	80	80
	Total	**100**	**100**

minority viewpoint. Regarding public awareness about cybercrime laws in Nigeria, only 30% of respondents perceive existing awareness as adequate, while a substantial majority of 53% express concerns over insufficient awareness. Additionally, 7% of respondents consider public awareness to be inadequate, highlighting the need for enhanced educational efforts. Furthermore, opinions on the sufficiency of penalties for cybercrimes vary, with 24% perceiving them as slow and ineffective, while 21% deem them immediate and effective. There is a divided perspective on the necessity of specific legislation targeting cybercrimes against vulnerable groups, with 34% advocating for such measures and 66% opposing them. Finally, while 80% of respondents believe there are government initiatives to educate the public about cybercrime prevention, 20% perceive a lack of such initiatives, indicating discrepancies in perceptions of governmental efforts in this regard. It is important, however, that where there are amendments to the cyber security laws, and there should be enough publicity and enlightenment on laws and on government's general activities.

11.5.2 Challenges in Executing Cyber Security Processes for E-commerce in Africa

The swift proliferation of e-commerce platforms across Africa underscores the increasing significance of robust cyber security measures. However, the execution of effective security measures encounters multiple challenges due to technical limitations, resource constraints, and regulatory requirements. This section provides a thorough analysis of these issues, focusing specifically on the distinct challenges faced by African e-commerce businesses and their implications for cyber security systems.

Technological challenges: E-commerce companies in several African countries struggle to adopt advanced cyber security measures due to poor technological infrastructure. Lack of high-quality hardware, software, and internet connections can hinder security system implementation. This infrastructure gap creates vulnerabilities that are difficult to mitigate with existing resources [89]. The lack of cyber security experts in e-commerce further makes many companies in several African countries struggle to adopt advanced cyber security measures due to poor technological infrastructure. Lack of high-quality hardware, software, and internet connections can hinder security system implementation. This infrastructure gap creates vulnerabilities that are difficult to mitigate with existing resources [90, 91].

Organizational challenges: Limitations on resources affect African e-commerce small and medium-sized enterprises (SMEs) that lack the funds to invest in advanced cyber security technologies. Budget constraints often lead to insufficient security, putting businesses at risk. Smaller companies may also struggle to update and maintain security systems to meet changing risks [92]. Lack of cognitive ability and education impact organizations, which makes them struggle with cyber security best practices training [93]. E-commerce companies and their employees often don't understand cyber security and how to protect digital assets [94]. Insufficient knowledge can lead to poor security practices, such as weak passwords and data protection, making cyberattacks more likely [95].

Regulatory challenges: African nations often have different cyber security laws and standards. Regional e-commerce companies may have compliance issues due to this inconsistency. Companies may struggle to comply with complex regulations and standardize security across jurisdictions [96, 97]. The implementation of and conformity to regional cyber security laws can be inconsistently applied [98]. Regulatory agencies may lack the resources or jurisdiction to oversee and implement cyber security standards. This can lead to legal loopholes and inconsistent security measures among enterprises, compromising cyber security strategies [98, 99].

11.6 SOLUTIONS AND BEST PRACTICES OF IMPLEMENTING CYBER SECURITY IN E-COMMERCE IN AFRICA

The rapid growth of electronic commerce in Africa offers digital businesses both opportunities and challenges. It boosts economic growth but makes firms more vulnerable to data breaches, fraud, and cyberattacks. Establishing strong cyber security protocols protects digital assets, customer confidence, and regulatory compliance. This section examines methodology and best practices for improving cyber security in the African e-commerce industry, focusing on pragmatic approaches that businesses can use to protect their online activities.

Strengthening technical infrastructure: E-commerce platform security requires strong technical infrastructure [100]. These include advanced firewalls, intrusion detection systems (IDS), and secure network architectures to prevent unauthorized access and cyberattacks. Encrypting data during storage and transmission protects sensitive information from interception and misuse [101]. To fix vulnerabilities and deter cybercriminals, software and systems must be updated regularly [34]. To overcome technical obstacles, companies must invest in technological infrastructure and training. Enhancing secure and reliable technology and cyber security education and training can close the skills gap and improve e-commerce security [34, 102].

Implementing multifactor authentication (MFA): MFA mandates multiple valid verifications before allowing access, improving online transaction and account security [103]. MFA like SMS or email one-time passwords (OTPs), biometric verification, or hardware tokens prevent unauthorized access [104]. This prevents account breaches and ensures only authorized users can access confidential data.

Conducting regular security audits and penetration testing: Routine security audits and penetration testing are needed to find and fix e-commerce system vulnerabilities [105]. Security audits check security policies, procedures, and technologies for compliance with industry standards and regulations [106]. Penetration testing simulates cyberattacks to evaluate security measures and identify vulnerabilities, according to research. These methods help organizations identify security vulnerabilities and strengthen defenses [107].

Harmonizing regulations and strengthening enforcement: Uniform cyber security regulations across Africa can improve compliance and unify e-commerce law [108]. Implementing stronger enforcement mechanisms and helping enterprises comply with regulations can boost cyber security efficiency [109]. Additionally, implementing cyber security in African e-commerce faces technical, organizational, and regulatory challenges. Businesses can improve cyber security resilience by upgrading infrastructure, expanding training, and complying with regulations [110]. Despite the growth of the e-commerce industry, these issues must be addressed to secure digital transactions and sensitive data in Africa's digital economy [110].

Best practices for cyber security implementation: Promoting cyber security awareness and training for cyber security best practices must be adopted across employees and stakeholders to reduce human error and improve security. Phishing detection, strong passwords, and data security should be covered in structured training and awareness campaigns. Organizations can reduce internal threats and improve security by promoting cyber security awareness [111, 112].

Designing incident response and recovery plans: Comprehensive incident response and recovery plans are needed to manage and mitigate cyber incidents. Security breach incident response plans outline protocols for identifying, responding to, and recovering from security breaches, while recovery plans focus on restoring operations and reducing downtime. These plans are tested and updated regularly to ensure cyberattack readiness [113, 114].

Ensuring regulatory compliance: Maintaining legal and ethical standards requires strict compliance with regional and global cyber security regulations [115]. Organizations should stay abreast of data protection and privacy laws and ensure their operations comply. Compliance measures prevent legal penalties, build customer trust, and demonstrate a commitment to data security [116].

11.7 CHALLENGES AND FUTURE DIRECTIONS

Notwithstanding the existence of efficient solutions and optimal methods, the implementation of cyber security in e-commerce in Africa encounters several obstacles, such as constrained resources, diverse regulatory landscapes, and ever-changing cyber risks [39]. Future endeavors should prioritize enhancing regional cooperation, allocating resources to cyber security infrastructure, and progressing research and development in next-generation security technologies [117]. By effectively tackling these obstacles and adopting sophisticated strategies, enterprises can strengthen their ability to withstand cyber threats and facilitate the ongoing expansion of the retail industry in Africa.

Research evidence suggests that implementing strong cyber security protocols is crucial for ensuring the security of digital transactions and safeguarding confidential data in the African e-commerce industry [118]. In bolstering their security stance, organizations can fortify their technical infrastructure, deploy multifactor authentication, and conduct routine security evaluations [117]. Moreover, it is advisable to develop emergency response plans, establish cyber security awareness programs, and guarantee regulatory compliance as measures to enhance the overall capacity for resilience [119]. The sustained expansion of e-commerce necessitates the strategic resolution of obstacles and the implementation of optimal methods to uphold a secure and reliable digital marketplace [120].

11.8 CONCLUSION

The rapid expansion of electronic commerce in Africa underscores the pressing requirement for strong cyber security protocols, particularly to protect business analytics. This chapter has examined the significance of cyber security legislation, described primary obstacles, and put forth efficacious recommendations to enhance security protocols. While existing regulations provide a fundamental legal structure, they often fail to address the full spectrum of cyber security challenges faced by businesses in the present day.

The recognized issues, including resource constraints, inadequate technological infrastructure, and inconsistent regulatory frameworks, emphasize the need for adopting a comprehensive strategy to ensure cyber security. In order to mitigate risks and ensure the security of e-commerce platforms, it is imperative to embrace cutting-edge technologies, improve cyber security training, and advocate for regulatory changes. By incorporating these solutions and optimal methodologies, enterprises can enhance their capacity to withstand cyber threats, attain superior adherence to regulations, and establish a more robust digital marketplace.

In conjunction with the ongoing growth of e-commerce in Africa, it is imperative to adapt strategies aimed at safeguarding business analytics. The implementation of the aforementioned measures will enhance the security of e-commerce platforms and foster increased confidence in the digital economy. The adoption of this proactive approach is essential for promoting continuous development and innovation while effectively addressing the difficulties posed by an ever more digital environment.

REFERENCES

1. Ezennia, C.S. and M. Marimuthu, Factors that positively influence e-commerce adoption among professionals in Surulere, Lagos, Nigeria. *African Journal of Science, Technology, Innovation and Development*, 2022. 14(2): p. 405–417.
2. Okolie, U.C. and A.H. Ojomo, E-commerce in Nigeria: Benefits and challenges. *Humanities & Social Sciences Latvia*, 2020. 28(2).
3. Johnston, L.A., World trade, e-commerce, and COVID-19. *China Review*, 2021. 21(2): p. 65–86.
4. AfricaBusinessPages, *Africa Business Page*. 2020. Article. [cited 9-9-2024]. https://news.africa-business.com/post/ecommerce-in-africa.
5. Jibril, A.B., et al., The impact of online identity theft on customers' willingness to engage in e-banking transaction in Ghana: A technology threat avoidance theory. *Cogent Business & Management*, 2020. 7(1): p. 1832825.
6. Ogborigbo, J.C., et al., Strategic integration of cyber security in business intelligence systems for data protection and competitive advantage. *World Journal of Advanced Research and Reviews*, 2024. 23(1): p. 81–96.
7. Bhatia, N.L., et al. Growing aspects of cyber security in e-commerce, in *2021 International conference on communication information and computing technology (ICCICT)*. 2021. IEEE.
8. Fatunmbi, T.O., Impact of data science and cybersecurity in e-commerce using machine learning techniques. *World Journal of Advanced Research and Reviews*, 2022. 13(1): p. 832–846.
9. Ngesa, J., Tackling security and privacy challenges in the realm of big data analytics. *World Journal of Advanced Research and Reviews*, 2024. 21(2): p. 552–576.
10. Gupta, R., et al., Machine learning models for secure data analytics: A taxonomy and threat model. *Computer Communications*, 2020. 153: p. 406–440.
11. Luo, Y., A general framework of digitization risks in international business. *Journal of International Business Studies*, 2022. 53(2): p. 344.
12. Morgan-Thomas, A., L. Dessart, and C. Veloutsou, Digital ecosystem and consumer engagement: A socio-technical perspective. *Journal of Business Research*, 2020. 121: p. 713–723.

13. Sullimada Biddappa, R.D., *The impact of business analytics on strategic decision making*. 2021. Politecnico di Torino.
14. Marion, T.J. and S.K. Fixson, The transformation of the innovation process: How digital tools are changing work, collaboration, and organizations in new product development. *Journal of Product Innovation Management*, 2021. 38(1): p. 192–215.
15. Beverungen, D., D. Kundisch, and N. Wünderlich, Transforming into a platform provider: Strategic options for industrial smart service providers. *Journal of Service Management*, 2021. 32(4): p. 507–532.
16. Almalki, K., *Factors engendering corporate fraud and mechanisms for enhancing the detection and prevention of fraudulent financial practices in the UK retail industry*. 2022. University of Sheffield.
17. Fadeyi, I.O., et al., Impact of unsolicited SMS on Covid-19 non-pharmaceutical protocol awareness among civil servants. *Nigerian Journal of Communication Review (NJCR)*, 2024. 3(1).
18. Jha, B.K., G. Sivasankari, and K. Venugopal, Fraud detection and prevention by using big data analytics, in *2020 Fourth international conference on computing methodologies and communication (ICCMC)*. 2020. IEEE.
19. Bello, O.A., The role of data analytics in enhancing financial inclusion in emerging economies. *International Journal of Developing and Emerging Economies*, 2024. 11(3): p. 90–112.
20. Shkabatur, J., R. Bar-El, and D. Schwartz, Innovation and entrepreneurship for sustainable development: Lessons from Ethiopia. *Progress in Planning*, 2022. 160: p. 100599.
21. Ranjan, J. and C. Foropon, Big data analytics in building the competitive intelligence of organizations. *International Journal of Information Management*, 2021. 56: p. 102231.
22. Shukla, S., et al., Data security, in *Data ethics and challenges*. 2022. Springer. p. 41–59.
23. Hashmi, E., M.M. Yamin, and S.Y. Yayilgan, Securing tomorrow: A comprehensive survey on the synergy of Artificial Intelligence and information security. *AI and Ethics*, 2024. p. 1–19.
24. Liu, J., T.W. Tong, and J.V. Sinfield, Toward a resilient complex adaptive system view of business models. *Long Range Planning*, 2021. 54(3): p. 102030.
25. Ufere, N. and J. Gaskin, Evasive entrepreneurship: Circumventing and exploiting institutional impediments for new profit opportunity in an emerging market. *PLoS One*, 2021. 16(2): p. e0247012.
26. Świątkowska, J., Tackling cybercrime to unleash developing countries' digital potential. *Pathways for Prosperity Commission Background Paper Series*, 2020. 33: p. 2020-01.
27. Lebogang, V., O. Tabona, and T. Maupong, Evaluating cybersecurity strategies in Africa, in *Cybersecurity capabilities in developing nations and its impact on global security*. 2022. IGI Global, p. 1–19.
28. Mwangi, T., T. Asava, and I. Akerele, Cybersecurity threats in Africa, in *The Palgrave handbook of sustainable peace and security in Africa*. 2022. Springer, p. 159–180.
29. Dagada, R. and M. Eloff, Integration of policy aspects into information security issues in South African organisations. *African Journal of Business Management*, 2013. 7(31): p. 3069.
30. Ifeanyi-Ajufo, N., Cyber governance in Africa: At the crossroads of politics, sovereignty and cooperation. *Policy Design and Practice*, 2023. 6(2): p. 146–159.
31. Awosusi, O.E., The imperative of cyber diplomacy and cybersecurity in Africa: A new means to a'borderless' regional end? *Journal of African Foreign Affairs*, 2022. 9(3).
32. Mishra, A., et al., Attributes impacting cybersecurity policy development: An evidence from seven nations. *Computers & Security*, 2022. 120: p. 102820.
33. Mallick, M.A.I. and R. Nath, Navigating the cyber security landscape: A comprehensive review of cyber-attacks, emerging trends, and recent developments. *World Scientific News*, 2024. 190(1): p. 1–69.
34. Aslan, Ö., et al., A comprehensive review of cyber security vulnerabilities, threats, attacks, and solutions. *Electronics*, 2023. 12(6): p. 1333.

35. Uddin, M.H., M.H. Ali, and M.K. Hassan, Cybersecurity hazards and financial system vulnerability: A synthesis of literature. *Risk Management*, 2020. 22(4): p. 239–309.
36. George, A.S., T. Baskar, and P.B. Srikaanth, Cyber threats to critical infrastructure: Assessing vulnerabilities across key sectors. *Partners Universal International Innovation Journal*, 2024. 2(1): p. 51–75.
37. Al Naim, A.F. and A.M. Ghouri, Exploring the role of cyber security measures (encryption, firewalls, and authentication protocols) in preventing cyber-attacks on e-commerce platforms. *International Journal of eBusiness and eGovernment Studies*, 2023. 15(1): p. 444–469.
38. Staves, A., et al., A cyber incident response and recovery framework to support operators of industrial control systems. *International Journal of Critical Infrastructure Protection*, 2022. 37: p. 100505.
39. Abbey, E.D., *Impact of digital transformation on cybersecurity in African businesses*. 2024. St. Thomas University.
40. Alkhalil, Z., et al., Phishing attacks: A recent comprehensive study and a new anatomy. *Frontiers in Computer Science*, 2021. 3: p. 563060.
41. Verma, A. and C. Shri, Cyber security: A review of cyber crimes, security challenges and measures to control. *Vision*, 2022. p. 09722629221074760.
42. Dagada, R., The advancement of 4IR technologies and increasing cyberattacks in South Africa. *Southern African Journal of Security*, 2024. p. 27.
43. Eboibi, F.E., Concerns of cyber criminality in South Africa, Ghana, Ethiopia and Nigeria: Rethinking cybercrime policy implementation and institutional accountability. *Commonwealth Law Bulletin*, 2020. 46(1): p. 78–109.
44. Sarma, M., T. Matheus, and C. Senaratne, Artificial intelligence and cyber security: A new pathway for growth in emerging economies via the knowledge economy?, in *Business practices, growth and economic policy in emerging markets*. 2021. World Scientific, p. 51–67.
45. Okoye, C.C., et al., Accelerating SME growth in the African context: Harnessing FinTech, AI, and cybersecurity for economic prosperity. *International Journal of Science and Research Archive*, 2024. 11(1): p. 2477–2486.
46. Teoh, C.S. and A.K. Mahmood, National cyber security strategies for digital economy, in *2017 International conference on research and innovation in information systems (ICRIIS)*. 2017. IEEE.
47. Mpofu, F.Y., Industry 4.0 in finance, digital financial services and digital financial inclusion in developing countries: Opportunities, challenges, and possible policy responses. *International Journal of Economics and Financial Issues*, 2024. 14(2): p. 120–135.
48. Nthangeni, N.W., *The potential of rural growth centers in fostering local economic development: Case study of Makhado Biaba*. 2020. South Africa: University of Johannesburg.
49. Jameaba, M.-S., Digitalization, emerging technologies, and financial stability: challenges and opportunities for the Indonesian banking sector and beyond, in *Emerging Technologies, and Financial Stability: Challenges and Opportunities for the Indonesian Banking Sector and Beyond (April 26, 2024)*. 2024.
50. Jameaba, M.-S., Digitalization, emerging technologies, and financial stability: Challenges and opportunities for the Indonesian banking industry and beyond. 2022. https://doi.org/10.32388/CSTTYQ
51. Anwar, M.A. and M. Graham, *The digital continent: Placing Africa in planetary networks of work*. 2022. Oxford University Press.
52. Riggs, H., et al., Impact, vulnerabilities, and mitigation strategies for cyber-secure critical infrastructure. *Sensors*, 2023. 23(8): p. 4060.
53. Gunduz, M.Z. and R. Das, Cyber-security on smart grid: Threats and potential solutions. *Computer Networks*, 2020. 169: p. 107094.
54. Sicari, S., A. Rizzardi, and A. Coen-Porisini, 5G in the internet of things era: An overview on security and privacy challenges. *Computer Networks*, 2020. 179: p. 107345.

55. Oriola, O., et al., A collaborative approach for national cybersecurity incident management. *Information & Computer Security*, 2021. 29(3): p. 457–484.
56. Nweze-Iloekwe, N., The legal and regulatory aspect of international cybercrime and cybersecurity: Limits and challenges, 2022.
57. Solar, C., Cybersecurity and cyber defence in the emerging democracies. *Journal of Cyber Policy*, 2020. 5(3): p. 392–412.
58. Tropina, T. and C. Callanan. *Self-and co-regulation in cybercrime, cybersecurity and national security*. 2015. Springer.
59. Calandro, E. and N. Berglund, Unpacking cyber-capacity building in shaping cyberspace governance: The SADC case, in *GIGAnet annual symposium*. 2019.
60. Mutemwa, M., J. Mtsweni, and N. Mkhonto, Developing a cyber threat intelligence sharing platform for South African organisations, in *2017 Conference on information communication technology and society (ICTAS)*. 2017. IEEE.
61. Ball, K.M., African union convention on cyber security and personal data protection. *International Legal Materials*, 2017. 56(1): p. 164–192.
62. Tambo, E. and K. Adama, Promoting cybersecurity awareness and resilience approaches, capabilities and actions plans against cybercrimes and frauds in Africa. *International Journal of Cyber-Security and Digital Forensics*, 2017. 6(3): p. 126–138.
63. Ngwu, F., O. Nwuke, and E. Agu, Opportunities, challenges, and risks: The African business environment, in *Sustainable and Responsible Business in Africa: Studies in Ethical Leadership*, 2023. p. 11–39.
64. Eleshin, F., A. D. Hoggar, F. E. Ayite, N. A. Atombo-Sackey, A. Ayekor, I. A. Ituze, I. Ingabire, and E. M. Nzivugira. Emerging trends in information security policy regulation and their potential impact on organizations in Rwanda, in *2023 31st Telecommunications Forum (TELFOR)*. 2023. IEEE, p. 1–4.
65. Kayode-Ajala, O., Establishing cyber resilience in developing countries: An exploratory investigation into institutional, legal, financial, and social challenges. *International Journal of Sustainable Infrastructure for Cities and Societies*, 2023. 8(9): p. 1–10.
66. Bada, M., B. Von Solms, and I. Agrafiotis, Reviewing national cybersecurity awareness for users and executives in Africa. 2019. *arXiv preprint arXiv:1910.01005*.
67. Rein, C., Enhancing peace and security in Africa through institutional cooperation. *Contemporary Security Policy*, 2015. 36(2): p. 267–295.
68. Yang, A., Y.J. Kwon, and S.-Y.T. Lee, The impact of information sharing legislation on cybersecurity industry. *Industrial Management & Data Systems*, 2020. 120(9): p. 1777–1794.
69. African Union. African Union convention on cyber security and personal data protection. 2014. p. 27.
70. World Health Organization. United Nations Office on Drugs and Crime. *International standards for the treatment of drug use disorders: Revised edition incorporating results of field-testing*. 2020. License: CC BY-NC-SA 3.0 IGO. 2024.
71. Eruaga, O.O.A., Towards effective maritime security cooperation in addressing the threat of piracy and armed robbery against ships in the Gulf of Guinea: A review of extant issues and challenges. *Ajayi Crowther University Law Journal*, 2023. 4(1).
72. Brits, P. and M. Nel, African maritime security and the Lomé Charter: Reality or dream? *African Security Review*, 2018. 27(3–4): p. 226–244.
73. Ali, M.L., K. Thakur, and B. Atobatele, Challenges of cyber security and the emerging trends, in *Proceedings of the 2019 ACM international symposium on blockchain and secure critical infrastructure*. 2019.
74. Oguamanam, C., From science, technology and innovation to Fourth Industrial Revolution strategies in Africa: The case for indigenous knowledge systems, in *Leap 4.0. African perspectives on the fourth industrial revolution*. 2021. A Mistra Publication.
75. Sharma, P., D. Gupta, and A. Khanna, e-Commerce security: Threats, issues, and methods. in *Cyber security in parallel and distributed computing: Concepts, techniques, applications and case studies*, 2019. p. 61–77. Willey.

76. Yuan, S. and X. Wu, Deep learning for insider threat detection: Review, challenges and opportunities. *Computers & Security*, 2021. 104: p. 102221.
77. Shaukat, K., et al., Cyber threat detection using machine learning techniques: A performance evaluation perspective, in *2020 International conference on cyber warfare and security (ICCWS)*. 2020. IEEE.
78. Isakov, A., et al., Enhancing cybersecurity: Protecting data in the digital age. *Innovations in Science and Technologies*, 2024. 1(1): p. 40–49.
79. Pang, G., et al., Deep learning for anomaly detection: A review. *ACM Computing Surveys (CSUR)*, 2021. 54(2): p. 1–38.
80. Maalem Lahcen, R.A., et al., Review and insight on the behavioral aspects of cybersecurity. *Cybersecurity*, 2020. 3: p. 1–18; Khan, M., Exploring the dynamic landscape: Applications of AI in cybersecurity. 2023. EasyChair.
81. Yeboah-Ofori, A., et al., Cyber threat predictive analytics for improving cyber supply chain security. *IEEE Access*, 2021. 9: p. 94318–94337.
82. Olayinka, O.F., 'University students' right to fair trial: How adequate is legal protection? *International Journal of Human Rights and Constitutional Studies*, 2020. 7(3): p. 249.
83. Montasari, R., et al., Application of artificial intelligence and machine learning in producing actionable cyber threat intelligence, in *Digital forensic investigation of internet of things (IoT) devices*, 2021. Springer, p. 47–64; Olayinka, O.F., Implementing the socio-economic and cultural rights in Nigeria and South Africa: Justiciability of economic rights. *African Journal of International and Comparative Law*, 2019. 27(4): p. 569.
84. Malapane, T.A. and N.K. Ndlovu, Towards a policy framework for e-commerce risk management: A case of South African online shopping, in *2024 Systems and information engineering design symposium (SIEDS)*. 2024. IEEE.
85. Ralarala, S., *The impact of cyber crime on e-commerce and regulation in Kenya, South Africa and the United Kingdom*. 2020. Strathmore University; Pervaiz, H.S. and S.H. Bhatti, Analyses of cybercrime regulations falling behind new technologies. *Journal of Social Sciences Review*, 2023. 3(1): p. 460–469.
86. Olayinka, O.F., 'University students' right to fair trial: How adequate is legal protection? *International Journal of Human Rights and Constitutional Studies*, 2020. 7(3): p. 249.
87. Tropina, T., Cybercrime: Setting international standards, in *Routledge handbook of international cybersecurity*. 2020. Routledge, p. 148–160; Väyrynen, R., Norms, compliance and enforcement of global governance, in *Raimo Väyrynen: A pioneer in international relations, scholarship and policy-making: With a foreword by Olli Rehn and a preface by Allan Rosas*. 2023. Springer, p. 433–454.
88. Olayinka, O.F., Towards the sustenance of democracy in Nigeria: The role of an independent judiciary in elections, in Adeola, R. and A.O. Jegede (eds), *Governance in Nigeria post-1999: Revisiting the democratic "new dawn" of the Fourth Republic*. 2019. Pretoria University Law Press, p. 142; Olayinka, O.F., H. Nwaechefu, and A.A. Adepoju, The concept of equality under the indigenous and western legal systems: Issues and challenges on sustainable development of Africa. *Scholars International Journal of Law Crime Justice*, 2024. 7(3): p. 114.
89. Sharma, V., International human rights law: Enforcement mechanisms and challenges in a globalized world. *Indian Journal of Law*, 2024. 2(3): p. 1–6.
90. Degli Antoni, G. and C. Franco, The effect of technological behaviour and beliefs on subjective well-being: The role of technological infrastructure. *Journal of Evolutionary Economics*, 2022. 32(2): p. 553–590.
91. Furnell, S., The cybersecurity workforce and skills. *Computers & Security*, 2021. 100: p. 102080.
92. Francois, G., P. Laskov, I. Pekaric, M. Felderer, A. Dürr, and F. Thiesse, Towards understanding the skill gap in cybersecurity, in *Proceedings of the 27th ACM conference on innovation and technology in computer science education*, vol. 1. 2022. p. 477–483.

93. Adomako, S. and M. Ahsan, Entrepreneurial passion and SMEs' performance: Moderating effects of financial resource availability and resource flexibility. *Journal of Business Research*, 2022. 144: p. 122–135.
94. Ioannou, M., E. Stavrou, and M. Bada, Cybersecurity culture in computer security incident response teams: Investigating difficulties in communication and coordination, in *2019 International conference on cyber security and protection of digital services (cyber security)*. 2019. IEEE.
95. Khan, D.S.W., Cyber security issues and challenges in e-commerce, in *Proceedings of 10th international conference on digital strategies for organizational success*. 2019.
96. Djenna, A., S. Harous, and D.E. Saidouni, Internet of things meet internet of threats: New concern cyber security issues of critical cyber infrastructure. *Applied Sciences*, 2021. 11(10): p. 4580.
97. Ratner, S.R., Regulatory takings in institutional context: Beyond the fear of fragmented international law. *American Journal of International Law*, 2008. 102(3): p. 475–528.
98. Marcos, H., From fragmented legal order to globalised legal system: Towards a framework of general principles for the consistency of international law. *Athena: Critical Inquiries Law Philosophy & Globalization*, 2023. 3: p. 90.
99. Harris, M.A. and R. Martin, Promoting cybersecurity compliance, in *Cybersecurity education for awareness and compliance*. 2019. IGI Global, p. 54–71.
100. Uzougbo, N.S., C.G. Ikegwu, and A.O. Adewusi, Cybersecurity compliance in financial institutions: A comparative analysis of global standards and regulations. *International Journal of Science and Research Archive*, 2024. 12(1): p. 533–548.
101. Alazzam, F.A.F., et al., Formation of an innovative model for the development of e-commerce as part of ensuring business economic security. *Business: Theory and Practice*, 2023. 24(2): p. 594–603.
102. Omotunde, H. and M. Ahmed, A comprehensive review of security measures in database systems: Assessing authentication, access control, and beyond. *Mesopotamian Journal of CyberSecurity*, 2023. 2023: p. 115–133.
103. Thakur, M., Cyber security threats and countermeasures in digital age. *Journal of Applied Science and Education (JASE)*, 2024. 4(1): p. 1–20.
104. Das, S., et al., MFA is a necessary chore!: Exploring user mental models of multi-factor authentication technologies, in *HICSS*. 2020.
105. Suleski, T., et al., A review of multi-factor authentication in the internet of healthcare things. *Digital Health*, 2023. 9: p. 20552076231177144.
106. Al-Matari, O.M., et al., Integrated framework for cybersecurity auditing. *Information Security Journal: A Global Perspective*, 2021. 30(4): p. 189–204.
107. Saxena, N., et al., Impact and key challenges of insider threats on organizations and critical businesses. *Electronics*, 2020. 9(9): p. 1460.
108. Thiébaut, R., Advancing regional cooperation within AfCFTA through an integrated cross border e-commerce system. *South African Journal of International Affairs*, 2024. p. 1–24.
109. Wong, L.-W., et al., The role of cybersecurity and policy awareness in shifting employee compliance attitudes: Building supply chain capabilities. *International Journal of Information Management*, 2022. 66: p. 102520.
110. Marotta, A. and S. Madnick, Convergence and divergence of regulatory compliance and cybersecurity. *Issues in Information Systems*, 2021. 22(1).
111. Popoola, O.A., et al., Exploring theoretical constructs of cybersecurity awareness and training programs: Comparative analysis of African and US Initiatives. *International Journal of Applied Research in Social Sciences*, 2024. 6(5): p. 819–827.
112. Alahmari, S., K. Renaud, and I. Omoronyia, Moving beyond cyber security awareness and training to engendering security knowledge sharing. *Information Systems and e-Business Management*, 2023. 21(1): p. 123–158.

113. Ahmad, A., et al., How can organizations develop situation awareness for incident response: A case study of management practice. *Computers & Security*, 2021. 101: p. 102122.
114. Khang, A., et al., Cyber-physical-social system and incident management, in *AI-centric smart city ecosystems*. 2022. CRC Press, p. 21–35.
115. Hendricks, S. and S.D. Mwapwele, A systematic literature review on the factors influencing e-commerce adoption in developing countries. *Data and Information Management*, 2024. 8(1): p. 100045.
116. Yanamala, A.K.Y., S. Suryadevara, and V.D.R. Kalli, Evaluating the impact of data protection regulations on AI development and deployment. *International Journal of Advanced Engineering Technologies and Innovations*, 2023. 1(1): p. 319–353.
117. Takahashi, K., et al., *Building cooperation: Cyber, critical technology and national security. Quad tech network series*. 2021. Australian National University.
118. Vitus, E.N., Cybercrime and online safety: Addressing the challenges and solutions related to cybercrime, online fraud, and ensuring a safe digital environment for all users – a case of African states. *Tijer-International Research Journal*, 2023. 10(9): p. 975–989.
119. Chisty, N.M.A., P.R. Baddam, and R. Amin, Strategic approaches to safeguarding the digital future: Insights into next-generation cybersecurity. *Engineering International*, 2022. 10(2): p. 69–84.
120. Santos, V., T. Augusto, J. Vieira, L. Bacalhau, B.M. Sousa, and D. Pontes, E-commerce: Issues, opportunities, challenges, and trends, in *Promoting organizational performance through 5G and agile marketing*. 2023. p. 224–244.

12 Optimizing User Engagement with Personalized Recommendations and Targeted Advertising

Anusha K S, Pranav Koushik R, Pradyumna V N, and Yu-Chen Hu

12.1 INTRODUCTION

We have two ways of shopping in real time, online shopping and offline or manual shopping. The main objective of any business is to generate good profits, but customer satisfaction is also crucial. It is vital for all businesses to provide services tailored to customer needs. If a business caters to customer preferences and needs, profits will surely follow. Both manual and online shopping must attract and impress customers by offering promotions like discounts and coupons in order for clients to feel more drawn to and pleased with the business, ultimately driving profits. Advertisements provide a way to reach consumers. We can advertise via platforms like television, social media, newspapers, and company websites. When placing advertisements, it's important to identify the target audience for the business. Currently, advertisements are posted universally so all customer types see the posts in both online and manual shopping. Advertisements play a key role in attracting suitable customers and bettering the business.

In real time, customer tastes differ and vary individually. So it's very important to determine customer wants. Identifying customer interests is a challenging undertaking, and in the current state of business, both online and offline shopping must predict customer areas of interest or buying behavior. Many existing e-commerce sites offer customer-focused features like product suggestions made using browsing history, related product suggestions, frequently bought together products, and purchased product ratings. However, these recommendations are generic and shown to all customer categories.

DOI: 10.1201/9781003540045-12

12.2 LITERATURE SURVEY

The following are some examples from the literature of how organizations approach optimizing user engagement.

1. Saikat Raj et.al., "Mall Customer Segmentation Using Machine Learning" [1]:

In our hypothetical firm, we employ clustering techniques like K-means, Fuzzy C-means, and Mean Shift to segment clients according to market behaviour for a deeper understanding of product performance [2]. By analysing factors such as gender, age, interests, and spending habits, we aim to identify distinct client segments [3]. This segmentation approach prioritizes market perspective over advertising or recommendation concepts, focusing solely on grouping similar customers to gauge product viability. As a result, the process involves considerable data processing time due to the complexity of the segmentation criteria [4]. Specifically, we impose constraints based on gender and age to refine our segmentation, ensuring a more targeted analysis [5]. Through this approach, we aim to gain insights into how different customer groups are likely to respond to our product offerings, facilitating more effective marketing strategies tailored to specific segments [1].

2. V. Lakshman Narayana et.al., "Recommender Systems for E-commerce in online video advertising: Survey" [6]:

In recent years, recommendation systems (RS) have gained widespread usage, aiding clients in decision-making by providing data-driven suggestions, particularly when faced with unfamiliar choices [7]. These systems assist in efficient information organization, filtering vast datasets to offer tailored recommendations aligned with user preferences [8]. By accurately identifying user likes and preferences, RS ensures the delivery of relevant suggestions from extensive data repositories [9]. In the context of online video advertising, RS plays a pivotal role in introducing new products to the market by leveraging content-based filtering techniques. The system primarily focuses on recommending new products based on customer tastes, omitting advertising recommendations grounded in consumer perception. Currently, the system operates solely based on survey data, lacking real-time implementation [10]. Despite this, its reliance on content-based filtering signifies a proactive approach to suggesting items tailored to individual preferences, enhancing user experience and engagement.

3. Heba Adnan Raheem et.al., "Customer Segmentation Using Machine Learning" [11]:

In the dynamic business landscape, where customer numbers surge daily, personalized attention to each customer becomes challenging [12]. Analyzing past transactions becomes imperative for sellers to meet customer demands and attract new ones [13]. Segmentation strategies enable companies to maximize profits and boost sales by understanding customer data. Leveraging unsupervised learning techniques like K-means clustering and hierarchical clustering, companies identify similarities and differences in customer needs effectively [14]. Focusing on the K-means algorithm, this system aims at sales forecasting based on customer preferences, albeit with limited datasets. Notably, it excludes advertising recommendations based on consumer perception and lacks real-time implementations [15]. However, its emphasis on clustering techniques signifies a proactive apprcach to understanding and meeting diverse customer needs, potentially enhancing sales performance and customer satisfaction.

4. S. Sivapalan et.al., "Data Mining Application in Segmenting Customers with Clustering" [16]:

In the fiercely competitive landscape of customer retention, organizations are turning to data mining as a crucial tool for maintaining dominance in e-business and related fields [17]. Data mining offers efficient assistance by analyzing vast, multidimensional datasets and transforming them into actionable insights. However, managing such extensive databases, particularly in online shops, poses significant challenges [18]. To address this, a two-phase clustering technique is employed, leveraging both modified k-means algorithm and agglomerative clustering to enhance customer retention strategies [19]. The first phase involves adapting the k-means algorithm using a heuristic approach, while the second phase detects outliers through agglomerative clustering [20]. This process yields effective data analysis tailored to the e-commerce sector, mitigating the risk of customer churn. Although data mining algorithms necessitate substantial datasets, the primary objective remains customer retention, with no emphasis on advertising recommendations or real-time implementations.

12.2.1 Observations

In the very competitive e-commerce market, websites like Amazon, Flipkart, eBay, Snapdeal, and Shop Clues strive to captivate customers and maximize profits by offering a plethora of features. These include personalized product recommendations based on customer history, suggestions for similar items, universal advertising for new products, discounts, and reviews with rating options. Despite these offerings, existing e-commerce applications often fall short in catering to individual customer tastes and preferences in real time. The needs of customers change over time and differ greatly from person to another, necessitating the identification of target customers for tailored advertisements to boost business profits. The current challenges include reliance on universal product recommendations and a lack of customer-centric services. Identifying target customers for precise advertising remains elusive, resulting in the dissemination of generic advertisements to a broad audience. This approach leads to unwanted ads and recommendations, contributing to customer dissatisfaction. Moreover, the process is time consuming and costly, further hindering effective targeting and personalization efforts. To overcome these hurdles, e-commerce platforms need to pivot toward customer-centric strategies, leveraging data analytics and machine learning to provide individualized experiences that suit each person's tastes, which will ultimately increase customer happiness and drive business growth.

12.3 PROPOSED SYSTEM

The easiest and most well-known data science technique is most likely association (or relation). To find patterns, we simply correlate two or more items—often of the same type—here. For instance, using market-basket analysis, which tracks consumer

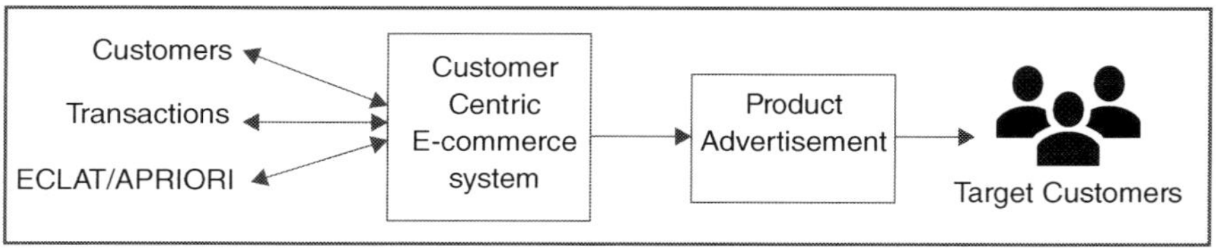

FIGURE 12.1 Proposed System Architecture.

behavior, we may discover that a client consistently purchases cream when they purchase strawberries. Based on this information, we could advise the customer to consider purchasing cream the next time they buy strawberries.

The proposed system uses algorithms such as the Apriori algorithm and Equivalence Class Clustering and bottom-up Lattice Traversal (ECLAT) algorithm to find the target customers for advertisements. Figure 12.1 shows the proposed system architecture.

The objectives and scope of the proposed system are as follows:

a) **Objectives**
   - The proposed system is a new e-commerce application that provides services according to customer needs.
   - It is a graphical user interface (GUI)-based application where customers can browser products, add products into a cart, and buy products.
   - The gadget's predominant goal is to predict the target clients primarily based on their transactions for advertisements.
   - This system is an Ads-based Recommendation system for customers using machine learning algorithms.
   - It uses unsupervised learning algorithms to process the customer transactions datasets and predicts the customer's area of interest and taste.
   - It uses algorithms such as the FP-growth algorithm, Apriori algorithm, ECLAT algorithm, or SFIT algorithm to identify target clients for advertisements.
   - The proposed system is a browser-based software which can be accessed using browsers.
   - In real time, we require internet connection to access it.

b) **Scope**
   - Actual time application beneficial for the public;
   - To build a system that gives better and faster decisions, which helps the business sector;
   - The challenge is a primarily browser-based software that can be accessed with the usage of browsers like Google Chrome, Opera, and Mozilla Firefox;
   - The project is a UI-based application that requires internet to access in real time.

12.3.1 The Architecture Design

The proposed structure focuses on identifying a system as a combination of multiple distinct components and understanding how they interact to produce the desired outcome. The emphasis lies in recognizing key components or subsystems and analyzing their interconnections. In other words, the focus is on determining which principal components are required and how they function together as a cohesive unit.

Figure 12.2 shows the Architecture Diagram representing storage server, customer, and admin operations with customer satisfaction as an output.

12.3.2 Unsupervised Learning Algorithms

Step 1: Required data extracted from the server. Here we extract customer transactions (orders) from the server.

Step 2: Data preprocessing is done, where the irrelevant data are removed and the required data are extracted for processing. In our project, irrelevant data means customer id, name, mobile, and so forth.

Step 3: Once data preprocessing is done, desired data are input to the efficient unsupervised learning algorithms such as Apriori algorithm and ECLAT algorithm for processing.

Step 4: The algorithms process the data and find the customers' area of interest, means identifying the desired customers for the recommendation of ads.

Step 5: Both the algorithms are tested and the results are compared to find the best algorithm.

Step 6: The efficiency of both algorithms is compared and the best algorithm is chosen.

Step 7: Using that best algorithm, ads will be recommend for the desired customers (target customers).

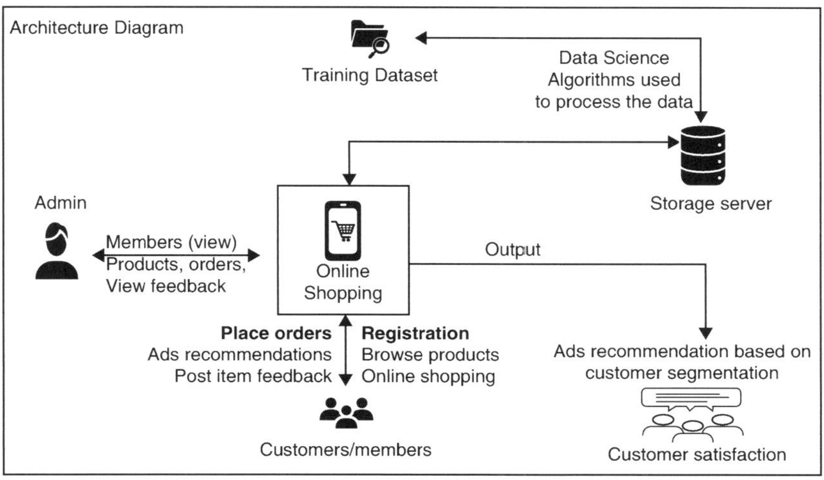

FIGURE 12.2 Architecture Diagram.

12.3.2.1 Apriori Algorithm

Apriori Algorithm Pseudo-code

```
Apriori (T, minSupport)
Cl = {candidate I-itemsets}; L1 = {c∈C1|c.count≥
minsup};
FOR (k=2; Lk-1□ĭ; k++) DO BEGIN
Ck=apriori-gen(Lk-1);
FOR all transactions t∈D DO BEGIN Ct=subset (Ck,t);
FOR all candidates c∈Ct DO c.count++;
END
Lk={c∈Ck |c.count • minsup}
END
Answer=* Lk;
```

Outcome: The result would be a frequent itemset found in the dataset with support greater than or equal to "minSupport". This represents patterns that occur in the data that can be potentially used for association rule mining.

Figure 12.3 shows the flow chart of the Apriori algorithm.

12.3.2.2 ECLAT Algorithm

12.3.2.2.1 ECLAT Algorithm Pseudo-Code

Scan the dataset and determine the support count(s) of each item. Add the transaction IDs instead of specifying the actual support.

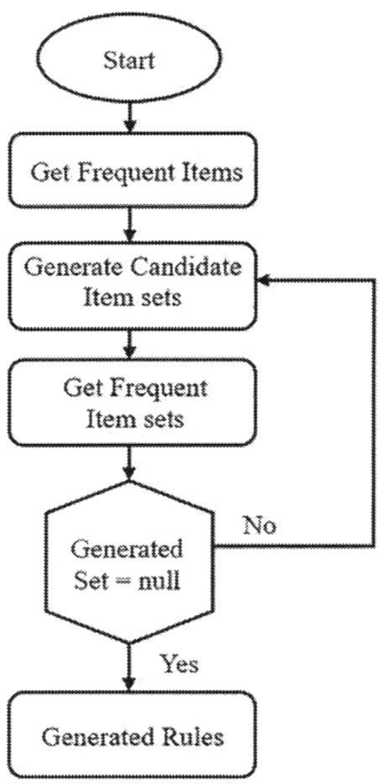

FIGURE 12.3 Flow of the Apriori Algorithm.

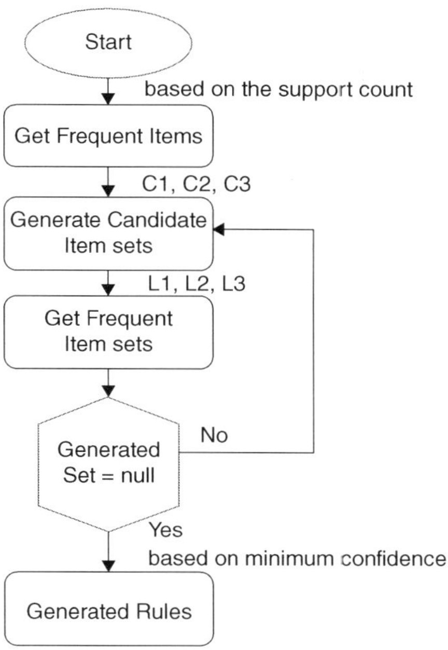

FIGURE 12.4 Flow of the ECLAT Algorithm.

Generate L1 (Frequent one item set) by comparing with minimum support count.

Use Lk-1, join Lk-1 to generate the set of candidate k item set. Scan the candidate k item set and generate the support of each candidate k item set. When we find support count of candidate items, we compare with the previous step. There is no need to again scan the data base and compare with the original dataset.

Add to frequent item set, until C=Null Set.

For each item in the frequent item set, generate all non-empty subsets.

For each non-empty subset, determine the confidence. If confidence is greater than or equal to this specified confidence, then add to Strong Association Rule.

Outcome: The process involves scanning the dataset to determine support counts for each item, generating frequent one-item sets (L1) based on minimum support, joining Lk-1 to generate candidate k item sets, and scanning candidate sets to calculate support without rescanning the entire database. Frequent item sets are iteratively added until no candidates remain. For each frequent item, non-empty subsets are generated and confidence is calculated to identify strong association rules meeting a specified threshold.

Figure 12.4 depicts the flow chart of the ECLAT Algorithm.

12.4 RESULTS AND DISCUSSION

The Apriori and ECLAT algorithms are both widely utilized in information mining for association rule mining, yet they exhibit different awesome characteristics.

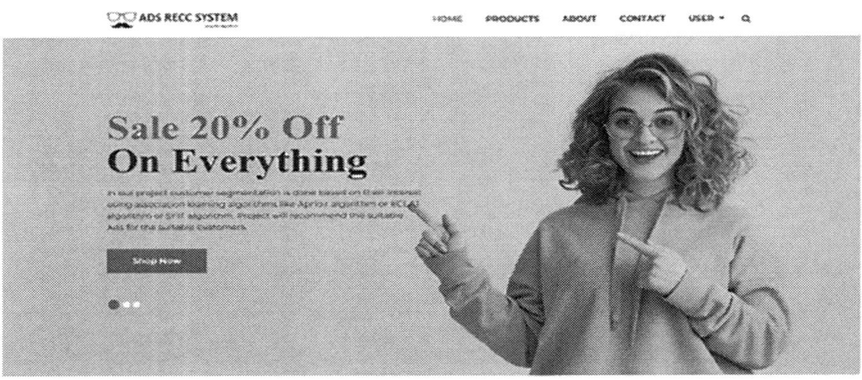

FIGURE 12.5 Home Page of the Website.

FIGURE 12.6 Browsing Page for Customers.

Apriori operates with the aid of iteratively generating candidate item set of increasing length based totally on the common item set found in the preceding generation. It prunes the hunt area by way of applying the Apriori assets, which states that if an item set is infrequent, all of its supersets can also be infrequent. This pruning technique enhances efficiency; however, it can also lead to higher computational overhead, specifically for massive datasets with numerous candidate item sets. In evaluation, ECLAT stands out for its vertical information layout technique, where transactions are represented as sets of objects and intersection operations are finished to become aware of frequent item sets. This method frequently results in quicker processing times and reduced memory requirements in comparison to the Apriori algorithm. ECLAT's efficiency stems from its avoidance of candidate technology and the use of vertical data systems, which facilitate direct computation of ad counts. But, ECLAT may battle with datasets containing long transactions or a big range of unique objects due to its reliance on vertical record structures. In the end, the choice between Apriori and ECLAT relies upon on factors such as dataset size, transaction duration, and computational resources available.

Figure 12.5 depicts the homepage, which displays the advertisements offered by the website.

Figure 12.6 shows customers' and visitors' browsing page for searching products.

12.5 CONCLUSION

This chapter has delved into the realm of purchaser segmentation and targeted marketing, leveraging affiliation rule learning algorithms like Apriori and ECLAT to recommend commercial enterprise strategies. Through the development of a primarily GUI-based e-trade application, the device attempts to revolutionize consumer interactions by means of providing personalized commercials based on individual hobbies. This technique is not only the most effective for improving consumer delight but also boosts enterprise profitability by means of aligning advertising and marketing efforts with client possibilities. The project's exploration of Apriori and ECLAT algorithms discovered distinct blessings and concerns for association rule mining. While Apriori's iterative approach and pruning techniques improve computational efficiency, ECLAT's use of a vertical data format and direct computation of support counts provides faster execution and reduced memory requirements. The selection between these algorithms depends on factors such as dataset length, transaction duration, and computational resources. Normally, the assignment's objectives of purchaser-centric services, predictive advertising and marketing, and real-time choice-making were met. Destiny upgrades could take cognizance of refining algorithmic implementations, integrating extra advanced machine learning techniques, and expanding the gadget's scalability and adaptability to evolving market dynamics. The variations in the results depend on the performance of the system on which the program is being executed. The computation of both algorithms relies upon the CPU and GPU of the gadget with factors like records handling by using the set of rules and also the assessment among customer's transaction facts. The end result of the venture depicts a commercial recommendations gadget via the use of Apriori and ECLAT with top-notch contrast of the computation ensuing in better overall performance by way of ECLAT, with much less computational time and greater accuracy.

REFERENCES

1. Saikat Raj, Santanu Roy, Surajit Jana, Soumyadip Roy, Takaaki Goto and Soumya Sen, "Customer Segmentation Using Credit Card Data Analysis," in *2023 IEEE/ACIS 21st International Conference on Software Engineering Research, Management and Applications (SERA)*. 2023. IEEE. 979-8-3503-4588-9/23/$31.00. https://doi.org/10.1109/SERA57763.2023.10197704.
2. L. Ying and W. Yuanyuan, "Application of Clustering on Credit Card Customer Segmentation Based on AHP," in *2010 International Conference on Logistics Systems and*

Intelligent Management (ICLSIM), Harbin, China, 2010, pp. 1869–1873. https://doi.org/10.1109/ICLSIM.2010.5461312.

3. W. Li, X. Wu, Y. Sun and Q. Zhang, "Credit Card Customer Segmentation and Target Marketing Based on Data Mining," in *2010 International Conference on Computational Intelligence and Security*, Nanning, China, 2010, pp. 73–76. https://doi.org/10.1109/CIS.2010.23.
4. Hemashree Kilari, Sailesh Edara, Guna Ratna Sai Yarra and Dileep Varma Gadhiraju, "Customer Segmentation Using K-Means Clustering," *International Journal of Engineering Research & Technology (IJERT)*, 11(3), March 2022.
5. M. Aryuni, E. Didik Madyatmadja and E. Miranda, "Customer Segmentation in XYZ Bank Using K-Means and K-Medoids Clustering," in *2018 International Conference on Information Management and Technology (ICIMTech)*, Jakarta, Indonesia, 2018, pp. 412–416. https://doi.org/10.1109/ICIMTech.2018.8528086.
6. V. Lakshman Narayana, S. Sirisha, G. Divya, N. Lakshmi Sri Pooja and S. Afraa Nouf, "Mall Customer Segmentation Using Machine Learning," in *International Conference on Electronics and Renewable Systems (ICEARS 2022) IEEE Xplore Part Number: CFP22AV8-ART.* ISBN: 978-1-6654-8425-1.
7. J. Tikmani, S. Tiwari, and S. Khedkar, "An Approach to Customer Classification using k-means," *International Journal of Innovative Research in Computer and Communication Engineering*, 3(11), 2015, pp. 10542–10549.
8. T. Kansal, S. Bahuguna, V. Singh, and T. Choudhury. "Customer segmentation using K-means clustering," in *2018 international conference on computational techniques, electronics and mechanical systems (CTEMS)*, IEEE, 2018, pp. 135–139.
9. T. Choudhury, V. Kumar, and D. Nigam. "Intelligent classification & clustering of lung & oral cancer through decision tree & genetic algorithm." *International Journal of Advanced Research in Computer Science and Software Engineering*, 5(12), 2015, pp. 501–510.
10. Siva Koteswararao Chinnam, S. Reshmi Khadherbhi, P. Sandhya Krishna and D. Anveshini, "Sentiment Analysis in Services Provided by Telecommunications," *International Journal of Advanced Science and Technology (IJAST)*, 29(3), 2020, pp. 9167–9176.
11. Heba Adnan Raheem and Tawfiq A. Al-Assadi, "Recommender Systems for E-Commerce in Online Video Advertising: Survey," in *2021 International Conference on Advanced Computer Applications, (ACA2021*). Maysan, Iraq: Imam ALkadhum College.
12. D. Das, L. Sahoo and S. Datta, "A Survey on Recommendation System," *International Journal of Computer Applications*, 160(7), February 2017. ISSN: 0975-8887.
13. S. Sidana, *Recommendation Systems for Online Advertising* (Computers and Society [cs.CY], Université Grenoble Alpes), 2018.
14. Y. Divya Bharathi, "Recommendation System for Video Streaming Websites Based on User Feedback," *International Journal of Engineering and Advanced Technology (IJEAT)*, 8(6), August 2019. ISSN: 2249-8958.
15. S. Sivapalan, "Alireza Sadeghian and Hossein Rahanam, Recommender Systems in E-Commerce," in *Conference: World Automation CongressAt: Proceedings*, Kona, Hawaii, 2014.
16. Nur Seher Ayyıldız, Ahmet Akçay, Berat Yalçuva, Alperen Sayar, Seyit Ertuğrul and Tuna Çakar, "Segmentation for Factoring Customers: Using Unsupervised Machine Learning Algorithms," in *2023 Innovations in Intelligent Systems and Applications Conference (ASYU)*. 2023. IEEE. 979-8-3503-0659-0/23/$31.00. https://doi.org/10.1109/ASYU58738.2023.10296639.
17. G. Livne, A. Simpson and E. Talmor, "Do Customer Acquisition Cost, Retention and Usage Matter to Firm Performance and Valuation?" *Journal of Business Finance & Accounting*, 2011, pp. 334–363.

18. F. F. Reichheld, *Loyalty Rules How Today's Leaaers Lasting Relationships.* Boston, MA: Harvard Business School Press, 2001.
19. J. R. Bult and T. Wansbeek, "Optimal Selection For Direct Mail," *Marketing Science*, 1995, pp. 378–394.
20. P. C. Balakrisnan, M. C. Cooper, V. S. Jacob and P. A. Lewis, "Comparative Performance of the FSCL Neural Net and K-Means Algorithm for Market Segmentation," *European Journal of Operational Research*, 1996, pp. 346–357.

Index

Made in the USA
Las Vegas, NV
19 September 2026

6ee4b6f7-6a64-4193-8209-69a85d3dba25R01